"More times than not, those who treat our physiological or even neurological needs are not in alignment with our belief construct. Who says that science and faith can't be collaborative in accomplishing wholeness? Dr. Leaf loves God and cares about people. Her new book, *The Perfect You*, is a blueprint for feeling better and living better. In it she provides scientific, philosophical, and theological guidance on how to step into your 'Perfect You.' If you've ever wanted or even needed to reimagine your life, this book may very well be the catalyst to that end. It's actually a guidance system that clears away the pollutants that have restrained you from expressing the greatest version of you the world has ever seen!"

Bishop T.D. Jakes and Serita Jakes

"Laurie and I highly recommend this life-changing book, which will help you discover who you are—your Perfect You—and give you a blueprint for pursuing your God-given identity."

Matt and Laurie Crouch, TBN

"Dr. Caroline Leaf achieved the near-impossible with her latest book. She delved deep into complex theories of theology, philosophy, and science, then deconstructed these highly abstract concepts and synthesized them into an innovative, creative, and enriching Christian-based book on self-discovery! Her Unique Qualitative Assessment tool and practical exercises will empower readers to find and celebrate their own unique and perfect selves in today's fast-changing world. My journey through the book left me in awe of her talent and excited to begin the voyage of discovering not only my own uniquely perfect self but also the perfect other in the individuals around me. Every reader will be strengthened by revisiting their perceptions using her guiding principles, developing a revised view of their unique selves, and staying true to their own perfect selves in their everyday lives. This latest addition to Dr. Leaf's growing list of books is also a testimony to the perfect uniqueness of Dr. Leaf herself."

Dr. Brenda Louw, professor and chair, Speech-Language Pathology and Audiology, East Tennessee State University

"Dr. Caroline Leaf's new book *The Perfect You: A Blueprint for Identity* could just as well have been subtitled "Blueprint for Success" or "Blueprint for Peace of Mind." I wholeheartedly recommend it!"

Kenneth Copeland, Kenneth Copeland Ministries

"*The Perfect You*, with its application tools, will be a daily recommendation in my integrative neuroscience practice. Its revelatory principles—the culmination of Dr. Leaf's thirty-plus years in the neurosciences—offer more hope for change and more help for true healthcare (not just disease management) than any other tool I've seen."

Robert P. Turner, MD, MSCR, neurologist and clinical associate professor of Pediatrics and Neurology, USC School of Medicine

"This masterpiece is a must-read for anyone who truly desires to be deeply educated on how our souls are wonderfully and fearfully made by the Creator of the universe. The application of the principles in this work facilitate functioning to our fullest potential, individually and collectively, for his good pleasure and purpose."

Avery M. Jackson, neurosurgeon, CEO, and founder of the Michigan Neurosurgical Institute PC

"Pioneers in any field propose ideas that are not accepted at the time. Those ideas are even thought to be ridiculous. However, eventually they are proven right. Dr. Caroline Leaf is such a pioneer in the field of the mind. She has God-given insight into the composition of our minds, what makes us unique, and how we can operate successfully in our uniqueness. This book fashions a profound mix of quantum physics, philosophy, and psychology into effective, practical applications to help every one of us excel in what we have been created by God to accomplish."

Dr. Peter Amua-Quarshie, MD, neuroscientist and assistant professor

"Dr. Leaf beautifully illuminates the brain, the mind, and how we make choices, then helps us make better ones. Both scientific and spiritual, this book has something for everyone."

David I. Levy, MD, clinical professor of neurosurgery and author of *Gray Matter*

"As an endocrinologist I find Dr. Caroline Leaf's books very detailed yet very easy to read. What makes you be who you really are? And how can you achieve *The Perfect You* as we all strive to maintain and restore health? I was so excited to read Dr. Leaf's skillful explanations of discoveries made in the medical, psychological, and quantum physics fields in the last thirty years in this new book. She fosters proactive steps you can take to change your health and your life. *The Perfect You* checklist is an amazing tool that will allow you to get to know yourself in a much deeper way and help you make changes in behavior using the chart and exercises. It will help you become the person you long to become, achieving your full potential in such a way that you can indeed feel 'fully alive' and accomplished in your professional life and your relationships but also in your 'inner self.' I encourage anyone to read this amazing book!"

Dr. Irene Stanciu, endocrinologist

"Dr. Leaf has released yet another brilliant piece of work. She masterfully details how our true identity is found when we abandon ourselves to Christ and immerse ourselves in His unrelenting love, thereby unlocking our natural gifts and talents. Christianity is not centered on rules and regulations; it is rather a journey of self-discovery that results in healthy, nontoxic actions and relationships. We often reference Dr. Leaf's work as it uses proven scientific arguments that apply the Word of God to our lives. We recommend this book to anyone looking to discover their purpose in life and ready to embark on a journey of true self-discovery."

Bishop Lawrence and Dr. Lillian Robertson,
Emmanuel Ministries, Bremerton, WA

"I love the title of the book, *The Perfect You*, because it is a bold declaration of who we are and an accurate vison of how God sees us and wants us to see ourselves and to help each other become the Perfect You. Its timing is perfect because we live in a season when the imperative for raising children and building strong families and communities is the highest priority on any parent or leader's mind. Dr. Leaf has given us an important tool that shows us in a step-by-step, loving, and caring way how we can live in victory and unspeakable joy. The book is carefully written with much wisdom and love of the Lord. As I read through the pages I could feel the healing power the words will bring to anyone who is blessed to get this precious book into their hands."

Tsitsi Masiyiwa, philanthropist and cochair
of Higher Life Foundation

"Once again, Dr. Caroline Leaf is using her expertise, experience, and conviction to bring a life-changing book to the table. We live in a world of increasing complexity when it comes to the foundational truths of life. I am confident *The Perfect You* will enable you to explore and find the freedom you were created for."

Bobbie Houston, founder and global senior pastor
of Hillsong Church

"A valid perspective on identity is the turning point for a healthy and successful existence. Like a skilled architect, Dr. Leaf has expertly crafted a blueprint to demolish erroneous thinking and rebuild lives with solid foundations that will remain. *The Perfect You* will provide truths that not only change your mind but, if applied, will transform the trajectory of your entire life. This woman is a gift and this book is a masterpiece."

Priscilla Shirer, speaker and Bible teacher

"In her new book, *The Perfect You*, Dr. Caroline Leaf reveals the science behind how your thoughts shape who you are. Using scientific knowledge and biblical revelation, she effectively ministers God's truth. We've been friends with Dr. Caroline Leaf for many years. She is a faithful member of our church and has delivered powerful messages in our weekend services and conferences."

Robert and Debbie Morris, senior pastors of Gateway Church

"The brilliant Dr. Caroline Leaf again challenges the 'why' of many things we automatically take on in our thought life. As a friend and one who has benefitted from her ministry, I know this book will be a great blessing to you."

Darlene Zschech, HopeUC

"Caroline's book, *The Perfect You*, is truly a great achievement, both brilliantly written and well documented. Caroline has a way of opening up readers to gather the courage to step into a new dimension of operating in their personality, traits, and God-given giftings and to explore who God really meant them to be on this earth. This book will definitely challenge you—but more importantly it will encourage and inspire you to believe that you are well able to take on the challenge, because you've been given the precise blueprint according to God's amazing design for becoming the Perfect You."

Rick and Denise Renner, senior pastors
of Moscow Good News Church

"Have you ever asked 'Who am I?' Well, answers to this question and more are in *The Perfect You*. Dr. Caroline Leaf beautifully explains how God created a unique blueprint for your identity.

This book will bring understanding to the way you think and will challenge you to become all you were created to be!"

John and Lisa Bevere, bestselling authors, ministers, and cofounders of Messenger International

"In her new book, Dr. Leaf shows you how you can unblock your Perfect You—who you are at your core—and live out your divine blueprint for identity, regardless of what you have been through, are going through, and will go through. I personally know what it is to have a distorted view of my uniqueness because of damage done to me, and I know that the principles in this book will help you discover your God-given purpose and potential regardless of your past."

Christine Caine, author of *Unashamed*

"This book is a treasury filled with great wisdom and insight that serve as brilliant tools to guide you in the discovery of the 'Perfect You.' Dr. Caroline Leaf brings thrilling new scientific discovery and theory to the truth of our God-ordained, individual identity as found in the unchanging truth of God's Word. In a culture that accepts only what science can articulate, Dr. Leaf's research and theories give strong credence to God's creation, purpose, and plan for each of our individual lives."

Dr. John and Helen Burns, lead pastors of Relate Church, Vancouver, Canada

"Dr. Leaf is one of the world's foremost experts of the study of the brain. She is a knowledgeable student of the Word of God as well, which brings a unique work in helping us all to understand and follow God's best for our lives. A must-read."

Bishop Keith Butler, Keith Butler Ministries

"Many scientists are uncomfortable with the reality that our human selves are not easily quantified. Caroline Leaf not only acknowledges this but also embraces the rare, the unique, and the ephemeral contained within us, understanding that it is these elements that define our humanity as well as our divinity."

Elizabeth Basden, attorney and principal of iCompany

"Dr. Caroline has an amazing ability to take complicated concepts and make them easily digestible. Her book *The Perfect You: A Blueprint for Identity* will realign you to a healthy and holistic life."

Esther and Joel Houston, Hillsong Church

"Wow, another masterpiece by Dr. Caroline Leaf! She weaves the scientific with the practical in an exceptional way. You'll discover how to grow in becoming the *you* God uniquely made you to be."

Dr. Robb and Pastor Linda Thompson, Family Harvest Church

"Reading *The Perfect You* is like connecting the dots between your potential, your passion, and your purpose! As a cheerleader of dreams, I applaud Dr. Leaf for this manual—a wake-up call to get honest with yourself, be intentional in your choices, and start making destiny decisions!"

Terri Savelle Foy, president of Terri Savelle Foy Ministries, host of *Live Your Dreams*, and author of *Pep Talk*

"Caroline has written a book full of good news for you! She will introduce you to the person you always wanted to be: the Perfect You! A person everybody loves, trusts, and wants to be friends with. In your hands is the blueprint for your best future."

Mylon and Christi Le Fevre, authors and Grammy Award–winning recording artists

"*The Perfect You* is a must-read for anyone who has ever second-guessed their identity, value, or worth as a person. Dr. Caroline Leaf so brilliantly and simply helps us see we can make good choices that will set us on our perfect destination of love and purpose that God has chosen for each of us. Dr. Caroline Leaf is a brilliant and beautiful person who has impacted our lives, church, and world for the better."

Mel and Desiree Ayres, senior pastors of In His Presence Church, Los Angeles

"The only way we can correctly comprehend our unique design is from the perspective of our Designer. In this latest book, Dr. Caroline offers both the information and inspiration to help you assess and actuate the Divine Blueprint of his purpose for you!"

Pastor Colleen Rouse, Victory World Church

"I am always challenged and encouraged by Dr. Caroline Leaf's life and teaching. She speaks with the authority of a scientist and the heart of a pastor. It's rare that a speaker can touch the heart of each generation in such a profound way. I know that lives, hearts, and futures will be greatly impacted through her new book, *The Perfect You*."

Pastor DawnChere Wilkerson, Vous Church

THE PERFECT
YOU

A BLUEPRINT FOR IDENTITY

Dr. Caroline Leaf

BakerBooks

a division of Baker Publishing Group
Grand Rapids, Michigan

© 2017 by Caroline Leaf

Published by Baker Books
a division of Baker Publishing Group
PO Box 6287, Grand Rapids, MI 49516-6287
www.bakerbooks.com

Printed in the United States of America

The Library of Congress Cataloging-in-Publication Data
Names: Leaf, Caroline, 1963– author.
Title: The perfect you : a blueprint for identity / Dr. Caroline Leaf.
Description: Grand Rapids : Baker Books, 2017. | Includes bibliographical references.
Identifiers: LCCN 2017001690| ISBN 9780801015694 (cloth) | ISBN 9780801075711 (pbk.)
Subjects: LCSH: Identity (Psychology)—Religious aspects—Christianity. | Self-actualization (Psychology)—Religious aspects—Christianity.
Classification: LCC BV4509.5 .L43 2017 | DDC 248.4—dc23
LC record available at https://lccn.loc.gov/2017001690

This publication is intended to provide helpful and informative material on the subjects addressed. Readers should consult their personal health professionals before adopting any of the suggestions in this book or drawing inferences from it. The author and publisher expressly disclaim responsibility for any adverse effects arising from the use or application of the information contained in this book.

In keeping with biblical principles of creation stewardship, Baker Publishing Group advocates the responsible use of our natural resources. As a member of the Green Press Initiative, our company uses recycled paper when possible. The text paper of this book is composed in part of post-consumer waste.

green
press
INITIATIVE

19   20   21   22   23   24   25   8   7   6   5   4   3   2

This book is dedicated
to those Perfect You moments with . . .

My precious husband, Mac
My precious children,
Jessica, Dominique, Jeffrey, and Alexandria

You have shown me how to experience life and God
in a totally new way.
In fact, you have helped me see and understand life and God
from a whole new perspective.
You inspired this book.
You are . . . Perfect You.
You are mine.
I love you.

Contents

11

PART **FOUR**

Foreword

by Dr. Robert P. Turner

It is with the utmost gratitude and excitement that I endorse this new, remarkable work by Dr. Caroline Leaf. Over the course of my thirty-year career in clinical, academic, and research neurosciences I have longed for a tool to hold in my hand and incorporate into my life and the lives of my patients that thoroughly, accurately, and passionately brings cutting-edge, evidence-based neuroscientific research to practical, life-saving use and also melds together the spiritual, psychological, and physiological realms to help us choose love-based thinking—and keep it at the forefront of everything we do.

As we in allopathic healthcare finally transition out of a pharmacology-only era—where we've been stuck for nearly eighty years—Dr. Leaf has provided such a tool for everyday application to effect positive, love motivated, life giving changes in our minds *and* brains. Every statement and principle explained in this text is supported by current, sound, evidence-based neuroscience, and each chapter builds skillfully on the foundation of the previous one and is valuable for reading, reflection, and diligent application.

Dr. Leaf's "Perfect You" philosophy builds on the wisdom of past generations of sound, experienced thinkers and boasts the utmost spiritual, scriptural, and scientific validation. Following her philosophy leads directly to discover our own unique styles of thinking, speaking, and acting that our father God designed for our Perfect You. Dr. Leaf captures this perfectly in chapter 4: "We are his masterpieces, designed to reflect his glory into the world. We were created to bring heaven to earth."

As a neuroscientist, I love chapter 5! Writing from thirty-plus years of study, research, and experience, Dr. Leaf helps us understand the anatomical and physiological underpinnings of our particular ways of thinking, feeling, and choosing. I appreciate how she weaves together three interrelated disciplines: neurospirituality, neuropsychology, and neurophysiology. The living and loving application of these disciplines truly allows us to begin to walk in the true freedom that God has lovingly in store for us.

The Unique Qualitative (UQ) Assessment Tool outlined in chapter 6 was an amazing exercise for me personally, and it has been skillfully designed to clearly characterize our uniqueness within the seven metacognitive modules. This is not a personality inventory or neuropsychological analysis; rather it is a noncondemning, nonjudgmental tool to help each of us understand who we are—good and bad—and how our Father God wants us to experience the daily joys of his love as we learn how to become our Perfect You.

In chapter 8 Dr. Leaf clearly and carefully explains the "discomfort zones," bringing to light an experience that perhaps all of us, as human beings, experience, and some of us struggle with more than others. God has designed us with warning systems or prompts, and when we are not flowing in his perfect will for our lives, discomfort results. If we do not recognize or if we choose to ignore the "discomfort" prompting, the result will be the progressive manifestation of dysfunction in us spiritually, psychologically, and physically. One begins to realize that at least 80 percent of current medical and psychiatric disorders are rooted in the spiritual realm. Understanding the discomfort zones and opening up to the loving promptings of the Holy Spirit will result in becoming the

Perfect You—experiencing "life on life's terms" with the grace and peace God lovingly and freely gives us every moment.

The Perfect You will be a daily recommendation in my integrative neuroscience practice. Its revelatory principles—the culmination of Dr. Leaf's thirty-plus years in the neurosciences—offer more hope for change and more help for true healthcare (not just disease management) than any other tool I've seen.

When *The Perfect You* program and its life-changing principles are faithfully applied on a daily basis, changes will take effect in our minds and our brains (our "mind-brain continuum"). Naturally resulting from these changes, our wholly interconnected body systems will gradually manifest healthy improvements—in our gastrointestinal, cardiovascular, immune, and other systems. Personally I have begun to experience these changes in my own life, and I am awed and privileged to begin to see these transformations in patients who implement these principles. As a neurologist and neuroscientist, I can easily demonstrate quantitative changes via analysis of patient EEGs. These analyses bear witness to the glorious changes God is effecting inside us!

I invite you to the reading and diligent application of *The Perfect You*. It promises to help you see the changes that so many of us long for on a daily basis.

Thank you, Dr. Leaf, for your painstaking and comprehensive research and study. You are helping us witness transformation throughout the *microcosm* of our brains and nervous systems as well as the *macrocosm* of the earth and all of her inhabitants, whom we are called to love and to serve.

Robert P. Turner, MD, MSCR
CEO and owner, Network Neurology LLC & Network
Neuroscience Research Institute
Clinical Associate Professor of Pediatrics & Neurology,
USC School of Medicine
Associate Researcher, MIND Research Institute

Prologue

Who am I? Does anyone out there understand me? Am I merely the product of blind evolutionary forces or what Richard Dawkins calls a "stroke of dumb luck" in a material world?[1] Or do I have purpose and meaning, a unique part in a divine plan? Does anyone understand who I am, or who I am meant to be? Do I even understand me? Can I accept the way God has allowed me to be? Do I really accept the blueprint for identity that God has given me?

God does understand *you*. He has placed significance in you—your "Perfect You"—your unique way of thinking. The blueprint of your identity is a brilliant design that unlocks something you alone can do. As neuroscience shows us, every thought you think matters because it changes your brain! You create your unique reality and shape your brain with your thoughts. In this book you will discover the science behind your Perfect You by learning what it is, filling in a profile called the Unique Qualitative (UQ) Profile to understand the structure of your thinking, and practice applying it to your life with a series of fun and enlightening exercises that will take you to a whole new level.

Understanding how the Perfect You is structured is just the beginning, but once you start the process, you launch out into a lifetime of lasting change! Development and growth is organic and ongoing. Your purpose is to live beyond yourself, but you can't share your Perfect You or shape your life according to someone else's Perfect You—because it's *your* blueprint for identity. Nor can you be your Perfect You if it's locked up. You can't find your value or your meaning or live in your purpose if you don't identify your blueprint and operate in your Perfect You.

God knew you before you were formed in your mother's womb (see Jer. 1:5). You are wired for love, because God is love (1 John 4:8). You are addicted to love because you are made in his image (Gen. 1:27). When he calls you, he calls you by name to a life of love (Matt. 4:18–22). Philosopher Keith Ward puts it this way:

> The real world is a world of finite spirits, beings of value-saturated experience and creative purpose, existing within one supreme spirit of unrestricted consciousness and value. Human life is not a pointless flicker of awareness in an indifferent and finally decaying machine. It is a developing awareness by finite spirits (but unfortunately not always developing) of the wider consciousness and purpose of the supreme spirit within which they exist, and with which it is their inherent goal to unite in that blissful state of completed desire that is termed love.[2]

Many people long for and seek this blissful state in earthly things, yet it cannot exist apart from God, who is love. We have to see his image reflected in us if we truly want to understand our unique blueprint for identity. Science and Scripture both show you are uniquely designed to reflect his love into creation. But how can you reflect his glory if you cannot see it in you? Abraham and Daniel resolved to be the people God made them—both of these men operated in their Perfect You (Gen. 12–15; Daniel 6). Can you make the same resolution? Can you grow into your God-ordained self by unblocking your Perfect You?

Although you may not think you do, you actually know who you are! Your identity flows out of how you think, speak, and act, no matter how much you try to suppress it. Research shows that as you think, you influence your genetic expression and build your distinctive interpretation into physical thoughts—thoughts that are different from everyone else's. You have been designed with a beautiful way of thinking, evident from infancy, that fits your remarkable and unequaled Perfect You. You have been given a divine piece of eternity (Eccles. 3:11). When you do try to suppress your identity, which happens when you react negatively to the circumstances of life, you step out of your Perfect You and create a toxic environment.

Yet you are not defined by where you are or where you have been but rather where *you will be*. Finding out who you are at your very core is a journey, and it can be an awe-inspiring one—depending on the attitude you adopt! The more you step into your Perfect You, the more wisdom you will develop, which will increase your capacity for accessing and living in God's love and reflecting that love to a world filled with pain and suffering. Stepping into your Perfect You makes you humble and not proud! As *New York Times* columnist David Brooks notes, humility is low self-preoccupation, not low self-esteem.[3] Whatever you think about the most will grow! If you, your talents, and your problems are all you think about, you become your own idol—this is not only toxic to your health but also a form of pride. The universe does not revolve around any one person. You are designed to serve and love others, like the Messiah. Indeed, one of the best ways of overcoming a problem is to go out and give to others!

The choice to unlock your Perfect You and live out your blueprint for identity is yours. The more you unlock your Perfect You:

The more miracles you will activate in your life and the lives of the people around you.

The more intelligent you will become, since your Perfect You is tied to your intellect.

The more your gifts, skills, and abilities will develop.

The more your relationships will improve.

The more your mental health will improve.

The more your physical health will improve.

The more you will find joy in life.

The more you will see others through the eyes of God.

The more humble you will become, because you will see God's magnificence in you.

The more you will understand yourself and others.

The more you will desire to understand and help your neighbor.

The more you will celebrate others instead of envying them.

When people pursue an identity apart from God, it leads to confusion. The more you step into your Perfect You, the more you will understand the blueprint of your identity, your purpose, and your part in his kingdom. Socrates once said that the unexamined life is not worth living. This book will give you the tools to examine your thoughts and unlock your brilliant Perfect You. It will enable you to answer when Jesus calls you, *by name*, to participate in the great task of kingdom building. It will allow you to use and multiply the talents he has given you (Matt. 25:14–30), reflecting his glory, bearing his image, and bringing *heaven to earth*.

This, truly, is a life worth living!

Acknowledgments

All my years of being in this field have given me the privilege of connecting directly and indirectly with so many people, and I acknowledge all of you, because you have shown me what the material of this book needed to express: the importance of your unique experiences and the importance of you. You have helped me understand the need for helping people find their Perfect You.

Jessica, my research assistant and daughter, you truly are a magnificent support and I acknowledge both our hours of discussions about this book as you listened to me working the concepts out aloud and your outstanding and honest editing. It is a privilege and pleasure working with you.

My precious family—Mac, Jessica, Dominique, Jeffrey, and Alexy—I acknowledge your endless love and support . . . there is nothing like it!

The Baker team: once again, I have been thrilled and blessed by your professional and loving support. You have become like family to me and play such a huge role in making my work accessible to so many in such an excellent way. Thank you, Chad, Mark, Lindsey, Patti, Erin, Dave, Karen, Colette, Eileen, and the rest of the team at Baker: you are truly amazing! I acknowledge you and thank you.

PART
ONE

1

The Big Picture

The inescapable nature of true man is that authenticity
thrives independently of externality.

Jeffrey Leaf, writer

In a discussion one windy morning with my son about how literature inspires him and how he observes life, he said, "Mom, when
I feel the wind beating against my face it makes me feel emotion
I would not otherwise feel, and words start pouring through my
mind; I literally move into another world. I am reminded of the
inescapable passage of time." However, he went on to say, quite
correctly, "Mom, when you feel the wind, you think of the quantum
action in the brain, of probabilities collapsing and metacognition
and the physical impact of toxic choices like leaves falling off a
tree. We are both wired so differently."

This short conversation provides a good summation of thirty
years of my research and the question that has baffled philosophers
for years. Indeed, it underscores a question that is considered to

be one of the hardest problems of science: What is subjective, conscious experience? Why do we, as individual human beings, perceive reality in such different ways? How do we all have the same "colors" of life, to use an artist's analogy, but paint such different pictures? My son and I each had what is known as a *quale* during that conversation—or a conscious subjective and personal experience in reaction to a sensory incoming stimulation (the wind).[1] Our individual, unique responses were inspired and driven by our individual, unique designer blueprint: our Perfect You.

What Experience Feels Like

Experience—what "it" feels like—is anything but abstract. What we mean when we say that feeling the wind elicits an "experience" is that it does something to *us* in particular. It is an experience exclusive to us. We might feel one or several emotions intertwined within our memories as we perceive something as simple and as beautiful as the wind—for my son, specifically, watching the rustling leaves made him feel calm and peaceful, and it was a transcendent experience. For me, however, it was an analogy of the scientific process of detoxing the mind and hence the brain.

If healthy conscious experience is what it feels like to be in the Perfect You, then "what it feels like" for you means the specific set of associations you have previously made through the filter of your Perfect You. These associations—the thoughts, feelings, and emotions you have built into your mind—have been automatized into long-term memories by your thinking about them repeatedly over time, and the current stimulus interacting with these long-term memories brings them to your conscious awareness. This is what it means when we say "This is how *I* think, how *I* feel, how *I* choose—this is *my* thinking—this is how *I* am wired." The memories activated by stimuli coming from life or your internal thoughts, or both, and the set of emotional states associated with each of these memories is completely original and exclusive to you—your blueprint for identity.

So your Perfect You is like a filter, and when the filter is locked up by low self-esteem or toxic thinking, you are not free to be you. We have all been there: when we feel like there is a battle inside of us, like who we have become is fighting who we know, deep down, we really are. When we step out of our Perfect You, we will be in conflict and this will make us frustrated and unhappy, and even temporarily reduce our intelligence and potentially lead to mental ill health.

Our Perfect You operates—that is, it is unlocked—in environments of love. Love changes the physical nature around all 75–100 trillion cells of our bodies and gives us the courage to face and deal with blocks and locks of our Perfect You. When we learn to focus on our God, who is love, and what he says about us, we learn how to embrace our unique identity and discover who we truly are in him (1 John 4:8). We have, after all, his love, power, and a sound mind (2 Tim. 1:7)!

A Model of How We Think, Feel, and Choose

I have spent the past thirty years researching, developing, and expanding my theoretical and conceptual model to explain our "sound minds," which I call the Geodesic Information Processing Model.[1] This model conceptualizes how we uniquely think, feel, and choose, through the filter of our Perfect You, and the causal effect this has on our brains and thus our behavior. More specifically, it traces the information-processing pathway from the input stage—which can be external through the five senses, or internal from memories, or both—to the output stage, a pathway that uses deliberate, *mindful* thinking. My theory underlies this book, so I have included in it my updated version of the model (see pp. 84–85), using the quantum physics theories expanded by Henry Stapp to account for the mind-brain connection.[3]

Geodesic means a global and comprehensive approach to thinking and learning, which has an all-encompassing quantum nature that still accounts for individuality. This model contrasts with traditional behavioristic and cognitive approaches that are more classical in nature and limited and cannot account for the uniqueness of the Perfect You and the pivotal role of the individual's thinking, feeling, and choosing. Hence I have proposed a structure for a metaphysical conception of the mind-brain connection, including the uniqueness of the Perfect You.

In this geodesic model, the mind is divided into the nonconscious and conscious levels. The structure of the Perfect You resides within the nonconscious level and is described through the UQ profile in chapter 6 of this book. The model as a whole reflects the processing of information through the mindful, intentional thinking of the individual, which causally affects the structure of the brain. So each individual, with their unique interpretation of life, plays a pivotal role in effecting behavioral and emotional change in their own life as well as leaving a footprint of this change in the brain. This way of approaching cognitive neuroscience is in accordance with quantum physics. Not only do we direct our behavioral, emotional, and intellectual changes but we also create structural change in our brains and bodies as a result of our individualistic and complex thinking processes.

I describe the role of the nonconscious and conscious levels of the mind using quantum physics to explain the mind-brain interaction, as opposed to merely correlating cognitive activity with brain behavior. As scientists Henry Stapp and Jeffrey Schwartz note, quantum physics provides a way of analyzing the complex higher cortical functioning that is occurring between the mind and the brain. It is an effective way to highlight the impact of the Perfect You (our individual thinking, feeling, and choosing) on physical and behavioral functioning, or what Stapp calls "psycho-physical functioning."[4]

Mind Controls Brain

It is important to remember that our thinking changes the structure of our brains because our minds are separate from our brains. Your mind controls your brain. Your brain does not control your mind. You change your brain; your brain cannot just change itself. When you think, feel, and choose you are updating your experience, and this is reflected in structural and functional changes in your brain: you are both literally and figuratively building memories. Your brain responds to what you do, so if there is communication and behavioral and intellectual change, then the brain has been changed by the mind and this change is expressed through words and actions.

This way of thinking about the brain is relatively new in science. In the mid-eighties, when I was embarking on my postgraduate work, I often asked myself if the mind could change the brain. I observed the incredible progress of both the brain-injured patients in my practice and the disadvantaged and learning disabled children in schools I worked in who, despite their physical disabilities, achieved extraordinary results through their positive determination and hard work.

I have worked with patients with all manner of voice, language, speech, and learning disabilities; traumatic brain injury (TBI); cognitive and aphasia symptoms, post stroke and heart attack; cerebral palsy, autism, emotional issues, and trauma.[5] My patients suffering from TBI significantly improved their cognitive, behavioral, academic, and intellectual performance after being exposed to the intentional mind techniques I had developed. Through using their minds, they were able to change the physical structure of their brains as evidenced in their behavioral changes. A consistent pattern of positive change began to arise among the patients and clients I was working with, even the most challenging cases. Statistically, this improvement ranged from 35 to 75 percent as they practiced mindful self-regulatory awareness and deep, intentional thinking, repeatedly, over long periods of time. In fact, I spent twenty-five years working hands-on in very impoverished areas of South Africa in addition to my practice, which allowed me to work with both ends of the economic spectrum. I consistently saw cognitive, emotional, and behavioral changes with those students and adults who *chose* to intentionally and deliberately use their minds in a very disciplined, consistent, and mindful way.

I will never forget the remarkable story of one of my patients, a sixteen-year-old girl who had a TBI as a result of a severe car accident. She had recently come out of a two-week coma and was operating around a fourth-grade level at school instead of a twelfth-grade level like her peers. Using the self-regulatory, mind-driven five-step learning process I had developed, I worked with this young lady on a one-on-one basis. She was determined to catch up with her peer group, and I believed she could achieve her previous levels of academic performance again. Within eight months the "miracle" happened: this young woman was able to graduate high school with her own class and went on to university. In fact, compared to before the accident, her IQ increased twenty points and her overall academic performance improved. (I have documented this case in my master's thesis.[6]) This was highly unusual, as research showed the opposite was normally the case in TBI; a negative trend was turned into a positive trend through intentional mind work. Yet that is not the end of the story. The young woman's emotional, self-evaluative, and self-monitoring skills also improved, even though they were indirectly treated during her clinical sessions, indicating that mind change includes intellectual and emotional changes. Indeed, as a Christian, I knew that she had control over her mind and could change the way she thought (see Rom. 12:2; 2 Cor. 10:3–5; Phil. 4:6–8). Even the Greek meaning of *repentance* means "to change one's *mind*"!

Your Brain Really Can Change

At that time back in the '80s, however, many scientists believed that a damaged brain could not change. Healthcare and therapy professionals like myself were taught to help their patients compensate for brain disabilities and mental ill health; total recovery was, for the most part, out of the question. Yet new brain imaging techniques such as PET and later MRI and fMRI scans started transforming the way we understood memory and cognition. These technological advances, which can observe a basic level of the brain live in action, have taught us—and are still teaching us—how different areas of the brain become metabolically active during various tasks and have enabled us to improve diagnosis and surgery and to prevent unnecessary surgery in the area of brain and body health. Some of my closest friends are neurosurgeons, and watching them in action is both humbling and inspiring.

In fact, one of the key breakthroughs to come from the development of brain imaging technology has been the discovery of *neuroplasticity*, which is the brain's ability to regrow in response to mind stimulation. Neuroplasticity, alongside *neurogenesis* (the birth of new neurons) and quantum physics, has given us a way to explain how the brain can change in response to mind-action, helping me to understand the results of my own research more deeply and certainly providing a great gift to science!

The Problem with Overemphasizing Scans

There is a danger, however, in seeing these scans as a reliable and detailed road map to human consciousness. As Schwartz points out,

> Not even the most detailed fMRI gives us more than the physical basis of perception or awareness; it doesn't come close to explaining what it feels like *from the inside*. It doesn't explain the first person

feeling of red. How do we know that it is the same for different people? And why would studying brain mechanisms, even down to the molecular level, ever provide an answer to those questions? It is when you think about it a little peculiar to believe that when you have traced a clear causal chain between molecular events inside our skull and mental events, that you have explained them sufficiently, let alone explained the mind in its entirety. If nothing else, there is serious danger of falling into category error here ascribing to clusters of neurons properties that they do not possess—in this case, consciousness.[7]

We are not merely the "firing of our neurons on a colorful scan." As in the discussion of the wind I mentioned at the beginning of this chapter, we each perceive reality in a way that is wonderfully unique to us. We may have the same kinds of neural structures and cells, the same set of brushes and colors, but we each have our own painting to create.

We need to be wary of what the Dana Foundation calls *neuro-reductionism*. Neuroreductionism is a symptom of the pervasive materialism that dominates our society today, which I will discuss in more detail in chapter 4. Essentially, materialists reduce explanations to physical material, like atoms of the firing neurons on a brain scan. In a recent research paper the Dana Foundation noted how many scientists succumb to this materialist reasoning and have

rushed to adopt new technologies for examining the physiological or anatomical correlates of behavior and thought. The most important contributions of MRI will be studies of the structure of the brain, not today's conceptually flawed attempts to localize cognitive functions and consciousness. The key conceptual problem faced by those who would correlate cognitive processes with brain activity is their implicit assumption that the mind comprises separate modular parts that can be isolated and examined independently of each other. This premise assumes that the hypothetical cognitive processes produced by the brain interact linearly (one can simply add or subtract one from another, as opposed to their being complex multiplicative functions of each other) and that they maintain their same properties when used in different tasks. For example, it assumes that a component of a reaction-time process (such as the time it takes to select a response) remains the same regardless of how many stimuli are simultaneously presented. This latter criterion is one of the most fragile of the assumptions underlying the current stampede of work seeking the locations in the brain of what I believe are more likely to be the result of highly interconnected neural mechanisms, none of which operate in complete isolation from other cerebral regions.[8]

These kinds of scientific explanations operate in isolation, while the universe is inherently interconnected—from the macro level to the subatomic level to the level of quantum waves of energy; this is evident throughout the natural world. Indeed, we see this interconnectedness in Scripture. In Ephesians 4:16, for instance, Paul notes how God "makes the whole body fit together perfectly. As each part does its own special work, it helps the other parts grow, so the whole body is healthy and growing and full of love" (NLT). We need each other!

Although functional magnetic resonance imaging (fMRI) has become an increasingly popular form of research in neuroscience, psychiatry, and psychology over the past twenty-five years, an eye-opening report from Johns Hopkins University calls the entire field into question. According to researchers:

> More than 40,000 studies have been published using fMRI but the methods used in fMRI research can create the illusion of brain activity where there is none up to 70% of the time. Eklund, along with his colleagues in Sweden and the UK, Thomas Nichols, and Hans Knutsson, investigated the software programs commonly used to analyze fMRI data, and they found that the assumptions made by these programs lead to a high degree of false positives, up to 70% compared to the expected 5%. False positives are significant as

they can make it seem that a particular area of the brain is "lighting up" in response to stimuli, when in fact, nothing of the sort is occurring.[9]

These "false positives" can and have led to a number of erroneous claims that actually detract from the uniqueness of human thinking and responsibility. It essentially becomes a sad and confusing tale of "my brain made me do it." The individual and unique experience is reduced to the firing of neurons or, to use the painting analogy, the painting is reduced to its individual colors and their chemical makeup.

There is no question that mental activity will have associated complex neural activity in the brain. The brain is, after all, the substrate through which the mind works. And the brain should be complex—we are made in the image of a complex God! However, there are limits on what can be learned, even with these wonderful new imaging devices, especially if experiments are based on the simplistic and reductionist hypothesis that cognitive modules can be isolated to specific regions of the brain with the assumption that those regions are producing that specific thinking behavior.

In fact, the Hopkins study was not the first to warn against uninhibited use of fMRIs in neuroscience. In 2009, researchers at Dartmouth University warned of the dangers of the false-positive effect. During an experiment they placed a dead Atlantic salmon into the fMRI and "showed it a series of photographs depicting human individuals in social situations." The data produced by the imaging technology made it appear as though "a dead salmon perceiving humans can tell their emotional state."[10] If an fMRI can show a dead salmon as able to read human emotions, we most certainly need to question this technology as the "proof" that free will and consciousness are nice but sad illusions. It is more likely that mind activity represents an indivisible, entangled entity that cannot be broken up into its physical parts.

Consequently, I have chosen to move away from neuroreduction-ism to a more integrated cognitive and metacognitive behavioral approach. I evaluate the language, intellectual, behavioral, academic, and emotional changes before and after deliberate and mindful thought intervention using techniques I developed during my thirty years of research and practice.

The Power of Choice

The most important facet of all my research and practice, however, is individual *choice*. The moment people recognize the power of their minds—the individuality of their thinking and how they have control over their lives—they are truly able to transform their world. When people see themselves the way God sees them, as his wonderful works and particular reflections of his image, then they see what is inside of them and perceive the universe in a different way (Ps. 139:14). Each of us is meant to bear his glory in our own unique way—we all have a beautiful way of stewarding eternity (Eccles. 3:11; Gen. 1–2). True self-awareness comes from recognizing the Perfect You—*the true you*. It changes you from the inside out. You are unlocked. This is so much more than "finding your purpose." It is about finding yourself.

We all want to know who God is. We reflect his image. The world will lose out if you do not operate in your Perfect You: you are a specific part of his reflection, the missing piece that brings a unique perspective and hope to the world. There is no one like you, which means there is something you can do that no one else can do. Because of your Perfect You, your experience of life will enhance mine. When you are not you, we all miss out on knowing God better, because you reflect his image in a unique and beautiful way!

Only you can be you with your special type of "youness." You are an observer with your own unique Perfect You making your own unique choices. I, in turn, have my unique Perfect You and make my own choices. We enrich each other's experience; that is, we enrich each other's Perfect You by walking alongside each other and *celebrating* our differences.

And operating in your Perfect You is also a way for you to celebrate who *you are*. In a world where we are often told that we are not worthy or do not live up to a particular standard, this celebration is critical. We cannot truly live for God or transform our societies if we hate what we see in the mirror. Your Perfect You is so deeply and intrinsically wired into the fabric of who you are that when you recognize it, you develop an intimate awareness of and desire for the need to be yourself. You recognize that who you are is fundamentally good (Gen. 1:31).

Furthermore, your own Perfect You is *more* than enough. Once you begin to understand your Perfect You and its structure—because truly getting to fully understand your Perfect You is a lifelong journey—you can walk in anticipation and freedom through life, rejoicing *despite* the circumstances. Your Perfect You sets you free to be who you are and to do what you love. Operating in your Perfect You brings satisfaction and contentment. It reveals your innermost qualities, which are bound in love, joy, peace, patience, kindness, gentleness, faithfulness, and self-control (Gal. 5:22–23). It is hopeful—it never gives up, enduring through every circumstance.

Your Perfect You is dynamic and ever-changing. It is the key to understanding life experiences and the lessons you've learned, updating your mindset and giving you the opportunity to walk into the future with unlimited potential to grow into your own success. You, as the observer, keep updating your experiences as new data comes to light, shaping the way you approach the world.

Operating in your Perfect You is the way you choose to see your world filled with love instead of fear. It is what we all crave, so that impatience and unkindness, irritability, pride and boastfulness, bitterness, unforgiveness, wrong choices, and trauma—all of which disrupt this fulfillment—cause us to seek to recapture this Perfect You "feeling" in an attempt to restore order in our minds and bodies. The Perfect You also removes you from the mindsets of shame and guilt, the "did-I, should-have, could-have, would-have." You can enter into a mindset of hope, of the endless possibilities and attitudes you can choose as new opportunities come to light.

The Perfect You will take you from missing the mark of being made in God's image to stepping into who you truly are. In this way, you will move from trauma to freedom, from pain to peace, from indecision to action, from confusion to clarity, from envy to celebration, from frustration to anticipation, from being overwhelmed to being set free, from fear to courage, from suppressing issues to having the courage to face them, from numbing thoughts to capturing them, from passivity to passion, and from hopelessness to hope. It will help you understand what you are stewarding and how to remain a good steward of your life no matter what comes your way. If you understand your Perfect You, you will understand how you think, feel, and choose and therefore how to renew your mind, enabling you to face life's challenges (Rom. 12:2).

Of course we all think, feel, and choose, but your Perfect You will help you understand how *you specifically* think, feel, and choose. It is our identity, our way of being authentic to ourselves. Identity is intrinsic to our nature, so we are always seeking after the Perfect You. It is the core of who we are, and it will need to be satisfied in some way or another.

Finding a Stable Identity

In our current postmodern society, it can become very confusing to find any stable identity, so it is critical that we begin to understand what it means to be made in God's image. Each of us needs to find our image, because if we don't the world will brand us. We will become whatever we focus on the most. The Israelites exchanged their glories (their Perfect You as image bearers of God) for the image of the golden calf, and we too can lose ourselves trying to be what we are not called to be (Exod. 32:4; Rom. 1:18–25). We become what we love, so we must learn to love our God by seeing his incredible piece of eternity inside of us. Focusing on God will increase the authenticity of our Perfect You; nothing else will satisfy us.

When you read about someone's accomplishments and adopt their road map, their blueprint for identity, as your own, you will limit where your Perfect You can take you. You can only be *you*. Who you are at the core will leak out, no matter how much you try to suppress it or change it. The Perfect You enables you to love, to reach beyond yourself, but you cannot grow into the fullest expression of God's design and plan if you live in doubt or unrest, or if you constantly undermine your gift by trying to copy other people's Perfect You.

In order to sustain a consistent outlook and pattern in your life, your spirit, thoughts, feelings, choices, words, and actions must line up. So when you say something that your brain doesn't "believe," if your statement isn't part of your Perfect You, it is unsustainable and can become toxic. You can try as hard as you can to be something or someone other than how God has designed you, but this will create conflict in your mind and body, because at your core you will always try to return to your natural inclination—your Perfect You.

The Perfect You Defined

But what exactly is your Perfect You? It is **how you uniquely and specifically think, how you uniquely and specifically feel, and how you uniquely and specifically choose.** These are functions of the *mind in action*: the intellect, emotions, and will. The *mind in action* builds thoughts. Thoughts are the roots of your unique words and behaviors, which, in turn, are the visible manifestations of your Perfect You. It is the manifestation of your particular worldview.

Why is it so important to understand your Perfect You? It is the reflection of God—out of it springs your identity and your purpose as a steward of his creation and glory.[11] The Perfect You empowers you to communicate and act according to how you uniquely think, feel, and choose, enabling you to reflect this image like a light on a hill (Matt. 5:14–16).

If we operate in accordance with our godly wired-for-love design, we will act and speak the Word in season, and peace and productivity will reign in our relationships and lives (Isa. 50:4). And as we strive to selflessly understand other people's "images," we will understand God better because we each reflect an aspect of our multifaceted God. In our Perfect You we have everything we need to achieve our unique and marvelous purpose: God has planted eternity in us, a divine sense of purpose (Eccles. 3:11).

Maybe you have been told over and over that you are "special" but have not really been able to believe it. Maybe you have discovered your particular Perfect You but haven't been living or growing in it. Maybe you have never truly been operating in your Perfect You, chasing success by imitating the lives of others. It is time for you to recognize and activate your divinely pre-wired Perfect You!

You can discover what your Perfect You is by learning its structure and how to begin living in it: this is what this book is all about. Once you start this process of discovery, you launch out into a lifetime of lasting change. Your purpose is to live beyond yourself through reflecting God's glory to a broken world order, but you can't share your Perfect You, your identity, if it is hidden. "No one lights a lamp and then puts it under a basket" (Matt. 5:15 NLT). You cannot grow into your God-ordained self if your Perfect You is blocked.

● ● ●

The structure of this book is as follows. In part 1, you will begin the process of understanding what the Perfect You is in terms of your unique thinking, feeling, and choosing, and how important it is to stay in the Perfect You. In part 2 you will learn about the philosophy and science undergirding the Perfect You. In part 3, you will begin to unlock your Perfect You by filling in the Unique Qualitative (UQ) Assessment Tool through a three-hundred-plus question journey that will help you gain a better understanding of how you uniquely think, feel, and choose. And this is not a one-time thing, either—you can periodically, over your lifespan, fill this profile in as many times as you want as you grow as a person. You will also learn about the Perfect You checklist, a simple, easy-to-use way in which you can monitor whether you are functioning in your Perfect You. In part 4, you will learn about the discomfort zones and how to use these to recognize and regulate when you are in and out of your Perfect You, freeing you from comparison, envy, and jealousy, which affect both your mental and physical health. You will learn to be mindfully aware of what is going on in your body and mind, and to lean in to your own experience rather than trying to forcefully change it. You will also find a summary chart that ties all the concepts of the Perfect You together in an easily accessible format. Lastly, part 4 will also give you a series of great, simple exercises to help you develop and grow your Perfect You.

You will learn throughout this book how to redefine what success means to you. Released from the suffocating box of expectations, you will embrace your true blueprint for identity and develop a clear sense of divine purpose in your life.

True Success

We must remember that success, in terms of shalom or biblical prosperity, is not defined by a collection of assets, an accumulation of power, or cash in the bank. If that were the formula, there would be no cares for those in the highest tax brackets. Rather, success is living out God's purpose for our lives, using the Perfect You he has given us, to transform our community, and in doing so, bringing heaven to earth (Matt. 6:9–13). Every single one of us will express shalom differently, because every single one of us can do something that someone else cannot.

I challenge you to dig deeply into the truths of this book as an opportunity to find the blueprint of your identity, your Perfect You. Find it in yourself. Find it in your children. Find it in your spouse. Find it in your colleagues at work. Find it, because in your Perfect You, you will also find the truth of God's living promises. You were not built to struggle. You were built to learn how to flourish in the midst of life's challenges. You really are a conqueror of your world (Rom. 8:37). There are a lot of personality tests out there that are designed to label you and put you in a particular box. But there is so much more to you than a personality profile can capture. You embody a blueprint that cannot be categorized: you have an infinite, irreducible truth-value. You are *enough*!

2

The Perfect You

Thinking, Feeling, Choosing

The task is . . . not so much to see what no one has
yet seen; but to think what nobody has yet thought,
about that which everybody sees.

Erwin Schrödinger, physicist

The Perfect You is a way of describing how we process and exhibit
our uniqueness, or blueprint for identity, through our ability to
think, feel, and choose. It has two key components: the brain and
the body. The brain is where we wire in and store the thoughts
we choose to build with our minds—the mind controls the brain.
Hence these thoughts are the physical product of thinking, feeling,
and choosing. The body, on the other hand, uses these thoughts
to express the Perfect You. This process is different for each of us.

Essentially, the Perfect You is a filter that designates how we
as individuals process information. It is at the core of our being,

the particular essence of who we are, laid down in our spirit. It expresses itself through the active mind, or through how we think, feel, and choose. It expresses itself through what we say and do. Because of our Perfect You, there is something each of us can do that no one else can do! It is the inimitable way we reflect the image of God.

Using science, we can attempt to understand and unlock the structure of the Perfect You. We have to intentionally consider how we think, feel, and choose and how each individual brain is organized to reflect a particular way of thinking, feeling, and choosing.

The Mind Changes the Brain

In science, we can consider how the mind impacts and changes the brain. If the brain is the physical substrate through which the Perfect You works, where our thoughts are stored and from which we speak and act, then each human brain is uniquely attuned to each person. From the macro level of the structure of each part of the brain, to the micro level of the neurons, to the subatomic level, to the quantum level of vibrations, we are all different. Even our proteins vibrate in different ways![1] The mind is intimately correlated with the brain's structure: the unique mind is expressed through the unique brain.

In effect, your unique responses to certain stimuli such as movies, foods, celebrities, and words may seem trivial, but they say a lot about you. Researchers from Binghamton University have found they can identify different people from their brain wave responses.[2] Likewise, we even each have our own unique sense of smell, called an olfactory fingerprint.[3] Our views of the world are reflected in the architecture of our brains.[4]

When we think, feel, and choose, our minds process the incoming knowledge and change the wiring of our brains. So if we mindfully tune in to our ability to think, feel, and choose by paying attention to our thoughts, we can understand our Perfect You, the very core of who we are—our blueprint for identity! To find out who you are and what you are made for, you have to understand how your mind and brain interact, and you can do this by understanding your thinking, feeling, and choosing.

But what are these thoughts? Essentially, the matter or substance of the brain is really an appearance of what your mind—your thinking, feeling, and choosing—looks like, much like a painting reflects the artist's perceptions. A painting is not merely a set of colors on a piece of canvas; it is an outpouring of the artist's Perfect You.

In other words, your thinking, feeling, and choosing actually create matter. Your physical memories are made of proteins that are expressed by your genes, which are switched on or off by your thinking. These thoughts produce fruit: the words and actions that are exclusive to you are a construct of *your* mind. Thus your mind is not only unique but powerful as well, since it has the power to create realities (physical thoughts made of proteins) out of probabilities of perception (thinking signals).

It is therefore not a surprise that 2 Timothy 1:7 tells us we have love, power, and a sound mind. Through our minds we each have our own eternal reality planted deep within us (Eccles. 3:11). We are created in the image of God, whose mind, his *logos*, created the universe: in the beginning was the Word (John 1:1). We have the mind of Christ (1 Cor. 2:16)!

Free Will and the Perfect You

As Albert Einstein reputedly said, "I want to know God's thoughts; the rest are details." The mind of God becomes integral to understanding the Perfect You because "in Him we live and move and have our being" (Acts 17:28). God has designed each of us to see matter and create matter in our particular way. The nature of our consciousness, our Perfect You, is *separate* from the consciousness of God but is also *from* the consciousness of God.

Yet there is uncertainty within this nature of the Perfect You that underscores the uniqueness of how we think differently as individuals. Your Perfect You is exclusively *yours*; only you know what you are truly thinking, feeling, or choosing at any given moment. If someone knows you well, they can hazard a guess of what you are thinking based on how you have acted in the past, but they will never be entirely certain until you say or do something. Indeed, not only can you not tell what a person is thinking but you also cannot tell what is going to happen next.

So thinking, feeling, and choosing—your Perfect You—is a place in space-time where you decide to do what is right or what is wrong. Nothing determines your choices except *you*.

That is not to say we always define the circumstances we find ourselves in, of course. A lot of things can influence our choices, since none of us live in a vacuum. Yet nothing determines your choices, or how you react to the circumstances of life, except you. You alone are responsible and can be held accountable for how you react to what happens in your life: your future is open, filled with an eternity of possible situations and choices.

As we see in quantum physics, God has created a probabilistic, open-ended universe. There is an infinite set of possibilities of perception. Although this may sound complicated, it is essentially another way of describing free will and the power of Deuteronomy 30:19. We can choose life or death, blessings or curses. Quantum physics, in other words, is a mathematically based description of the open-mindedness of choice. God uses science to reveal his majesty and the gift of freedom he has given us.

Einstein also once said that God does not play dice with the universe. He was a classical physicist and believed in a rational universe with specific laws that determined everything that would happen. Einstein did not like the concept of an open universe and free will, which he called an illusion. However, according to quantum physics, it looks very much as though God does play dice, but in a loving and generous sense. He does not force us to love and serve him. He designed us as intelligent, unique reflections of his glorious image, free to choose how we want to live our lives. He took a risk giving us free will, but love inherently involves risks. As philosopher Keith Ward notes: "If God wanted humans to be free, not determined, able to make their own choices, then God would have to play dice with the universe in order to allow freedom to exist."[5] Giving us the freedom to choose is a profound demonstration of his love and desire to have an intimate relationship with us.

The creative freedom we have within our Perfect You is a powerful reality, not an illusion. With our Perfect You we build thoughts that become realities. These realities are tremendously important because everything is connected, first in God and then in each other. Every thought we think affects everyone else, and vice versa. Because everything was created in and through God, creation is entangled. And, as image bearers, we have a particular effect on the world and each other. We were created to reflect the glory of God into the world and reflect the praises of creation back to God.

The Perfect You in an Entangled World

Quantum physics helps us understand how entangled our world is. If a photon comes into existence a billion light-years from here, it affects us, even if we don't notice it affecting us. John Bell, famous for Bell's Theorem, formulated at CERN in Geneva in 1964, said there is an inseparable quantum connectedness of every part with every other. No matter how far apart in distance and time, all particles in a relationship affect each other: these relationships exist beyond space and time.[6]

Relationships, of course, would not be relationships if we were all the same. Our differences shape and enhance our relationships. Although we could never understand the impact of our thoughts on everyone around us, since we cannot know everything, we can get a sense of our interconnectedness when a loved one is sad and our hearts ache, or if we watch the news and feel compassion for people going through incredibly difficult circumstances. We all have a piece of God's eternity in us, and collectively we represent his eternal creation. He is the whole system and we are the parts in him. Like cells in the human body, we originate from one source but have different functions depending on who and where we are within a larger community.

Yet the Perfect You is not just relational. It defines the multiple roles you will have as you go through life: as a daughter or son, mother or father, friend, lover, or work colleague. It is about fulfilling a career and contributing to society. It is about finding out who you are and why you are alive.

Within this context, it is worth taking a look at how the World Health Organization defines mental health, which is really just another way of saying someone is in their Perfect You: "Mental health is defined as a state of well-being in which every individual realizes his or her own potential, can cope with the normal stresses of life, can work productively and fruitfully, and is able to make a contribution to his or her community."[7] We can find this notion of mental well-being in 3 John 2: "Dear friend, I pray that you may enjoy good health [physically] and that all may go well with you, even as your soul is getting along well [spiritually]" (NIV).

Mental ill health is the opposite of the above, since we are operating out of our Perfect You, or who we truly are. We lose our sense of identity and purpose, which affects our ability to live our lives. In effect, each time we step out of our Perfect You, we fall short of God's glory. We become broken mirrors reflecting the image of a broken world—we no longer reflect the image of a loving and merciful God.

3

Discovering the Potential
of Our Blueprint for Identity

He has made everything beautiful and appropriate
in its time. He has also planted eternity [a sense of
divine purpose] in the human heart [a mysterious longing which nothing under the sun can satisfy, except
God]—yet man cannot find out (comprehend, grasp)
what God has done (His overall plan) from the beginning to the end.

Ecclesiastes 3:11 AMP

Each person who understands him- or herself in this
way, as a spark of the divine, with some small part of
the divine power, integrally interwoven into the process of the creation of the psycho-physical universe,
will be encouraged to participate in the process of
plumbing the potentialities of, and shaping the form

of, the unfolding quantum reality that it is his or her birthright to help create.

Henry Stapp, quantum physicist
and mathematician

When we recognize the unique power that is in our minds, "plumbing the depths of our divine nature" will become a revelation of our sense of worth as human beings. It will enable us to love ourselves and, in turn, love others as we acknowledge the divine spark that is in them as well (Mark 12:31). Fundamentally, it will allow us to love our God as we learn to appreciate the marvelous image of our Creator (vv. 30–31). As the psalmist declares, human beings worship their Creator by being fully human (Ps. 148).[1] When we find out how we are human by understanding our uniqueness, we worship our glorious Creator!

Love or Fear

This divine nature is revealed through our Perfect You. Our powerful minds operate through free will and are made out of love (Deut. 30:19; 1 Cor. 2:16; 13:13; 1 John 4:8). The default ingredients of our humanity are joy, peace, patience, kindness, gentleness, faithfulness, self-control, compassion, calmness, inspiration, excitement, hope, anticipation, satisfaction, and so on (Gal. 5:22–23). When we are in our "love zone," as I like to call it, we operate *in* our Perfect You and move into positive stress, which is good for us as it makes us alert and focused; toxic stress has the opposite reaction, which you will learn more about in chapter 8. It enables us to face the circumstances of life with true hope and joy, to keep running our races no matter what comes our way (Phil. 2:16; 3:14).

Yet when we operate *outside* of our Perfect You we go into the "fear zone" and experience toxic stress. Out of this fear flows hate, anger, bitterness, rage, irritation, unforgiveness, unkindness, worry, self-pity, envy, jealousy, obsession, and cynicism. Since whatever we think about the most will grow, we become what we meditate on, which in the fear zone can have dangerous health consequences (Luke 6:45).[2]

Research showing that love mindsets are the norm and fear mindsets are learned is revolutionary for scientists, but not new if you look at Scripture.[3] In 1 John 4:18 the author declares that "there is no fear in love. But perfect love drives out fear" (NIV). Over the past several decades, scientists have researched the anatomy and physiology of love and fear right down to a molecular, genetic, and epigenetic level that can be described in detail. These are two different systems, and at any one conscious moment we will be operating in one or the other for each cluster of thoughts we think.

An attitude is a cluster of thoughts with emotional flavor, and every type of emotion has one of only two roots: love or fear. How do these attitudes get a love or fear flavor? Through our thinking, feeling, and choosing—our Perfect You.

Science is, in fact, showing us there is a massive "unlearning" of negative toxic thoughts when we operate in love. We can unlearn negative fear—it is not a part of our innate natural functioning—our Perfect You. Recent neuroscientific research demonstrates that some of the chemicals the brain releases when we are operating in our Perfect You include oxytocin, which literally melts away the negative toxic thought clusters so that rewiring of new nontoxic circuits can happen. This chemical also flows when we trust, bond, and reach out to others. So choosing to operate in the default nature of love literally can wipe out fear![4]

Another amazing chemical called dopamine also works with oxytocin. It flows as we expect and anticipate something. It also puts us on heightened alert to facilitate the building of new memories as we imagine helping someone do well in a test or restore a relationship, or as we suddenly understand something we have been battling with, for example. It gives us a thrilling surge of energy, excitement, confidence, and motivation to carry on, as well as influencing the actual building of long-term memory.[5]

Research also shows that when we do good things and reach out in love, endorphins and serotonin are also released that make us feel great, which detoxes our brains and increases our motivation and wisdom, helping us negotiate life more successfully when we operate in love. Once again we have the situation of mind affecting matter. Anticipation causes a series of chemical responses to occur in the brain.[6]

On the other hand, scientists have shown that when we are in a toxic fear mode we will get caught in a toxic cycle of chemical and neurological responses that influence the choices we make and the reactions we set in motion.[7] Unless we consciously choose to veto and override these reactions, we will voluntarily be at the mercy of the environment, the reactions of our bodies, and the toxic memories of the past. Our Perfect You will be blocked and our true self will vanish for a time.

I say *voluntarily* because our power to choose always overrides biology. As I discussed at the beginning of this book, *mind controls matter*. In the depths of our nonconscious mind, where about 10^{27} actions per second are being performed, we have billions of existing thought clusters with attached emotions giving their specific attitude "flavor," and each of us has our own unique flavor.

The Dangers of Toxic Thinking

This is so important to understand, because these thought clusters are referenced, and some made conscious, every time a new thought starts to form, helping our brains make sense of new information. So when we are exposed to or think about something toxic, and there are thought clusters involved with attached toxic emotions, they will set in motion a chemical cascade, launching our minds and bodies into toxic stress mode.

In toxic stress mode not only are we out of our Perfect You but we are also endangering our physical health. Our blood vessels will constrict, reducing blood flow and oxygen to the brain and potentially putting ourselves at risk for cardiovascular issues. In addition, fourteen hundred different electrical/chemical and infinite quantum responses will go haywire in our brains and bodies because we are stepping out of the Perfect You.

We see the profound consequence of choosing between love and fear in Scripture. Deuteronomy 30:19 declares, "This day I call the heavens and the earth as witnesses against you that I have set before you life and death, blessings and curses. Now choose life, so that you and your children may live" (NIV). In Ecclesiastes 7:29 the author reminds his readers that "God created people to be virtuous, but they have each turned to follow their own downward path" (NLT). We have incredible minds that are truly worth celebrating. We must also remember, however, that with this incredible power in our minds comes responsibility for how we use it: we cannot escape the consequences of our choices.

Thinking, feeling, and choosing in our Perfect You are paramount and fundamental factors that shape our realities.

Wired for Love

Back in the 1920s a shift in scientific thought began concerning human beings and our psyches. This discussion kindled a revolutionary change in the philosophical and scientific view of humanness that is still going on today. The discussion took place in Copenhagen, Denmark, primarily between Werner Heisenberg, Neils Bohr, and Wolfgang Pauli—all Nobel Prize laureates who came from monotheistic backgrounds. These men, among others, began to challenge the classical model of Newtonian physics, which had dominated science for over three centuries. Of course, Isaac Newton was also a theist and said God could overrule the laws of motion anytime he desired. Yet his work was viewed over the years through a mechanistic and deterministic filter that portrayed humanity and nature as merely a physical reality. With the introduction of quantum physics theories in the 1920s, however, scientists began to realize that our intentional thinking, feeling, and choosing could make a difference in how the matter in our bodies behaves.

Normally incoming information goes through a certain route as it enters the brain, passing through structures as it is being processed and creatively adding to our knowledge base. Neuroscientific research has been able to identify some of the important structures involved in this route, including the *thalamus*, which acts like a transmitter station, the *amygdala*, which is like a library holding emotional perceptions, and the *cingulate cortex*, which is in the conscious evaluative part of the brain. This route is activated when incoming information is received, appraised, and evaluated, and the mind decides on the appropriate and healthiest response from the body.

Essentially, our thinking, feeling, and choosing in response to life is a quantum signal that physically moves through the substrate of the brain, using it to store and express what we think via what we say and do. For example, we also have an area in the brain called the *corpus striatum* that seems to be involved in positive reinforcement. This wired-for-love system is designed to respond to calmness, peacefulness, and feeling good, filled with self-confidence and esteem. These positive love-sensations of feeling safe and confident activate the striatum. When we do not feel safe, it does not get activated.

Interestingly enough, the corpus striatum is also the area falsely activated by cocaine and other addictive drugs—including the modern American diet, which can be more addictive than heroin, cocaine, alcohol, psychotropics, and cigarettes![8] These addictive substances make a person temporarily feel good and entice the person to use the drug or addictive substance more often. Yet this enticement is the desire to hide pain; it is not merely because the substance has "hijacked" the brain. This means the *choice* to overcome an addiction is the most powerful and effective factor to overcome addictive behavior.[9]

Indeed, we are wired to be addicted to and consumed by God (Ps. 42:2; 63:1; 73:25; 119:20; Isa. 26:9; John 4:13–14; 6:35; Rev. 21:6). God created us for relationship with him. Nothing else will satisfy this need to pray continuously and set up a constant internal dialogue with the Holy Spirit, so that we stay addicted to him, offering up our minds and bodies as a living sacrifice every day (Rom. 12:2). Despite the allure of powerful chemicals released by our bodies, we must never forget that "He who is in you is greater than he who is in the world" (1 John 4:4). God has given us the ability to break free from any toxic pattern, and this happens when we are in the Perfect You (Rom. 8:37–39).

Stuck in Fear

We have all experienced the power of stepping out of our Perfect You—hence out of love and smack-bang into fear. It affects us deeply, and we handle it in several ways, based on the choices we have made and will make. We can control the fear through conscious cognitive evaluation, really believing that "God has not given us a spirit of fear, but of power and of love and of a sound mind" (2 Tim. 1:7), or we can become dominated by the unconscious toxic thoughts that have actualized into habits over time, which throw the brain and body into toxic stress. Instead of controlling fear, we make it worse and increase the toxic stress response in our brains and bodies.

Illustration 3.1
Love Tree

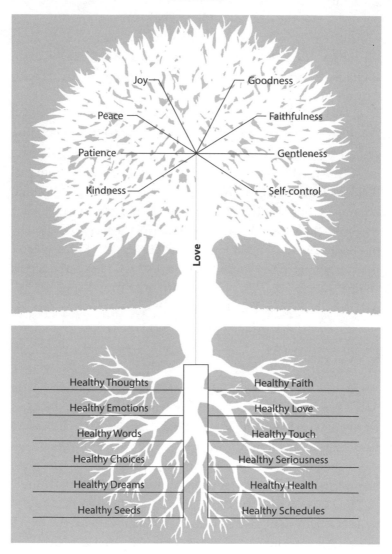

Illustration 3.2

Fear Tree

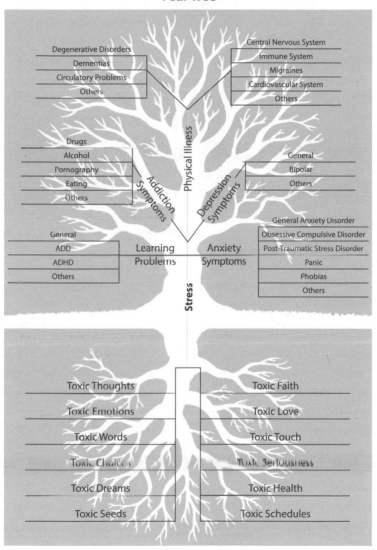

55

The latter situation, concentrating and ruminating on the fear, can bring about a fearful state even in the absence of an actual fear stimulus. For example, this is typically what happens in post-traumatic stress disorder (PTSD), where the memory of a trauma can invoke a response in people that is as real as when it happened, even if the trauma occurred decades ago. The attitudes—clusters of thoughts with emotions attached—produce the chemicals for anxiety and worry even though the person is no longer in threatening circumstances.

Every thought changes the brain chemistry, which impacts all 75–100 trillion cells of the body at quantum speeds.[10] The impact is instantaneous, literally beyond space and time. Hence, an experience of toxic stress can progress into mental ill health if it is constantly ruminated on and not dealt with. Remember, whatever we think about the most will grow!

Stepping Out of the Perfect You and into Mental Ill Health

Mental ill health is not just a disease. It is trauma and habituated incorrect thought reactions that have not been dealt with, where we have stepped out of our Perfect You in response to the events and circumstances of our lives.[11] This creates neurological chaos that can manifest as disorders of the mind, with concomitant symptoms erroneously termed biological diseases.[12]

Thoughts about a toxic occurrence—not necessarily the actual toxic occurrence—can set off a negative stress response. Thoughts are real things made of proteins that occupy mental real estate. If we worry every day about what might happen or what has happened, we repeatedly re-create the signal that stimulates genetic expression to build and strengthen that thought into a long-term memory, which leads to a feeling of uneasiness resulting in a toxic stress response—unless we *choose* to control our thinking.

Illustration 3.3
Descent to Disorder

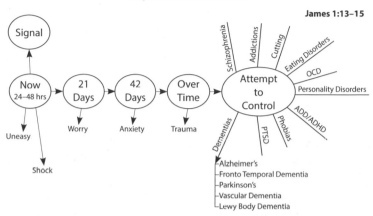

Over a period of about three weeks, or twenty-one days, this un-controlled uneasiness turns into worry. As we continue to worry—daily ruminating on the toxic thought—it will progress into anxiety over the next twenty-one days and will eventually become a trauma after about six weeks. Throughout this progression from worry to anxiety to trauma, there will be an increasing feeling of being out of control in thinking, feeling, and choosing. This is an indication of stepping out of the Perfect You and will result in symptoms of the labels seen in Illustration 3.3—schizophrenia, depression, and so on. These are symptoms of underlying issues, not diseases. Never allow yourself to be labeled with one of these symptoms. They are merely descriptions of your experiences. Take a look at the schematic of my disorder model above to see this more clearly. The more energy we give this toxic thought, the more it grows, and the more we feel consumed and trapped by it. This stress response will produce toxic fruit (see the love and fear trees on pages 54 and 55). Thus, this toxic fear is a distorted love circuit, which I mentioned at the beginning of this chapter. We were created for love and all that goes with it, but we have *learned* to fear.

Stepping Back into the Perfect You

What would the correct reaction look like? The neurological love pathway consciously evaluates the toxic thought cluster and, choosing to hand the situation to God, does not submit to the fear. And this is the stronger of the two pathways![13] We are wired for love, which means that love is our normal default mode; it is designed to dominate.

Regardless of the way we have chosen to react in the past, painful toxic thoughts can be reconstructed, even toxic feelings you have been nursing for so long and are so familiar with you think they are normal. You can analyze them and rewire them because of the brain's neuroplasticity.

For instance, you may have been scared of math for years, and as soon as you walk into a math class, emotions of anxiety and fear well up in you, resulting in a negative attitude. This will block your ability to take in any information during the lesson. Don't react to it; think first and, if possible, put the negative attitude back on the shelf and tell yourself something positive such as, *I don't like math because I think I am not so good at it, but I am going to conquer this fear, face it, and ask questions till I do understand.* And if it doesn't work the first time (which it won't, since true change takes time!), do it again and again and again. This is renewing the mind in action (Rom. 12:2).

Science shows us we need to practice using something or studying something at least seven times in repeated intervals over time before we are going to be able to use the information or perform the skill.[14] Getting our attitude under control normally takes about sixty-three days. The first four are the hardest, so don't give up! Like everything in life, true change is a process, and the results are well worth the effort. Eventually you will be able to use this amazing love circuit of the brain to balance your reason and emotions. When you do that, you have taken a giant leap in the direction of bringing all your thoughts into captivity (2 Cor. 10:5) and renewing your mind (Rom. 12:2).

Learning to Choose Your Emotions

As I noted earlier, there are only two types of emotion—love and fear—and all other emotions stem from these, each derivative forming its own chemical "signature." That is, each thought has its own chemical signature. The result is that your thinking quite literally becomes feeling with a resultant chemical reaction in your brain and body. The problem of stepping out of love and your Perfect You begins when your thoughts and emotions become unbalanced and toxic. If feelings dominate, a neurochemical rush can start to distort them in the direction of fear, which can result in stress. Emotions out of control will completely block your ability to think things through. Submitting to them causes chemical chaos in the brain and makes your mind foggy. You lose concentration and will find it difficult to listen to anything anyone is trying to say to you. And this goes for all emotions.

It may sound daunting to try to capture all of your thoughts and control your emotions. Yet when you understand how you can scientifically choose what becomes part of who you truly are (your Perfect You), you will also understand you have an amazing ability to change. We all have the opportunity to choose to walk in the Perfect You God has given us, despite our circumstances.

Take a moment to think of a time when you let your emotions get out of control and try to remember how you felt when it happened. Fear fuels those distorted emotions and wipes out any decent control from the brain's frontal lobe—unless you make the choice to stop and bring balance back again. Going through life on an emotional roller coaster is a Perfect You disaster, but one you are not forced to ride. You can choose!

The Genome and the Perfect You

Research on the regulatory aspect of the human genome, the 97 percent, along with epigenetic research hints at the power of the thought life to cause changes in our brains and bodies.[15] The emerging science of epigenetics is beginning to shine a light on how mental and physical health are within our reach. This science contradicts the dominant, mechanistic belief that humans are biological machines.[16] Epigenetics highlights our ability to respond to our environment, which includes everything from what we think to what we generally understand by environmental exposure.[17] Thoughts and emotions—alongside exposure to sunlight, exercise, food, and everything we choose to put onto and into our bodies—directly affect DNA expression.[18] A growing body of research is highlighting how these methylation and acetylation patterns change in response to *thinking and lifestyle choices*.[19] Thinking toxic thoughts can change gene expression, just as certain diets or exposure to chemicals and pollutants can also result in changes that affect our genes.

More than 97 percent of our genome is fulfilling vital functions in a regulatory manner. It specifically controls the switching on and off of genes. It is a language, operating like a genetic switch that controls the other 3 percent. So our DNA is designed to react to the language of our thoughts and resultant words as well as the biological signals.[20] We are made in the image of a powerful God who brought the earth into existence with his words (Gen. 1:3, 6, 9; 1 John 1:1), and we have this power of words and language invested in us (Eccles. 7:29; 2 Tim. 1:7). In John 1:1, *Word* in Greek is *logos*, or intelligibility/reason/intelligence, so when we operate in our image-bearing nature—our Perfect You—we activate this "Word" power with our thinking, feeling, and choosing and we impact the regulatory language of our DNA. In turn, our Perfect You activates our DNA and structural change occurs in the brain: this is intelligence and wisdom.

Logically, the converse is also true. Stepping out of our Perfect You still activates the regulatory language of our DNA, but because the signal of the words is toxic, going against our image-bearing nature, this affects how proteins actually fold. A toxic thought, which is the opposite of wisdom, is born. This has a disruptive and damaging effect in the brain. As leading quantum physicist Henry Stapp says:

> The free choices made by the human players can be seen as miniature versions of the choices that appear to be needed at the creation of the universe. Quantum theory opens the doors to, and indeed demands, the making of these latter free choices. This situation is concordant with the idea of a powerful God that creates the universe and its laws to get things started, but then bequeaths part of this power to beings created in his own image, at least with regard to their power to make physically efficacious decisions on the basis of reasons and evaluations.[21]

Our conscious efforts will, therefore, have the capacity to affect the actions of our brains and bodies because of the divinely invested power in our design. Our free will, these choices of our Perfect You, is rooted and grounded in feelings of worth and value—we matter and what we think matters. And what we think, feel, and choose changes matter. We have a role to play as *part* of God's creation that *impacts* God's creation. This is what biblical stewardship means, and it is a responsibility we need to take very seriously.[22]

The Mind-Brain Connection

Jesus's call for us to be the "light of the world" is particularly notable (Matt. 5:14). Light is a nonphysical wave made up of packets of energy called *quanta*, also known as *photons*. This is the energy, God's energy, in our DNA[23] that was made into reality for us at the beginning of creation and at the work of the cross—it is "the evidence of things not seen" (Heb. 11:1). Since God created space and time, he is beyond space and time, so everything we need as humans has been and is and will be provided for us. We, through the power of our God-given intellect, access what God has provided for us through the choices we make as we use our Perfect You.

In both science and life, God inspires and we laboriously investigate and explore the correct mix of the "ingredients" to reflect his glorious ideas. For example, God through the Holy Spirit will release a divine inspiration, a spiritual prompt, in someone to begin a process of exploration, using his or her intellect, of the Perfect You. This leads to the discovery of how the things of nature and man—God's creation—work. God's creation is a literal "global informational structure" that represents tendencies for real wired-for-love events to occur, and in which the choice of which potentiality will be actualized in various places in the hands of human agents. This is called a "quantum state of the universe."[24]

When we operate in love, our brains respond in the way they are designed to respond. Based on the information we get from brain technology (which, we need to bear in mind, is limited), we can see that areas of the corpus striatum will be activated more than other areas, neurotransmitters and peptides and hormones will be secreted, and we will feel good and be able to rejoice despite the circumstances and, as James says, "Consider it wholly joyful, my brethren, whenever you are enveloped in or encounter trials of any sort or fall into various temptations" (James 1:2 AMP-CE). The substrate of the brain physically responds to the action of the mind, which incorporates the intellect, will, and emotions. Mind is changing matter through the free will of the Perfect You.

Another example of this mind-brain connection is the chemical signature of emotions intertwined into thoughts. Every time we think, we release chemicals in response that produce feelings and reactions in the body. Clusters of electromagnetic and quantum energy embossed in proteins form thoughts with attached chemical messengers, which form the substrate of our memories. In turn, these collectively form attitudes. We express our attitudes—love or fear—through our Perfect You via what we say and do. So when we add either love or fear emotions to a thought cluster and give it a unique flavor, then it becomes an attitude. A bad attitude is proof we are not operating in our Perfect You. A good attitude is proof we are operating in our Perfect You. These attitude filters either distort or enhance the thinking process, blocking or unblocking the effective operation of the Perfect You.

If you have a toxic fear thought while you are processing information in your own unique way, you have to push that information through the toxic thoughts (toxic attitude) in your brain. Toxic thoughts and their tangible bad attitude block the Perfect You. In turn, operating outside of the Perfect You, which essentially means operating outside of love, inhibits your ability to think and operate in wisdom and inhibits your overall health in mind and body.

Attitudes reflect the core of how you are spending your time thinking, feeling, and choosing. They reflect your spiritual development and what you are doing with your power, love, and sound mind in a causal way. Because attitudes cannot be hidden over a sustained period of time, overcoming blocks to your Perfect You is imperative to walking in your image-bearing design of the Perfect You.

Love Is Stronger Than Fear

Fear may be powerful if we give it energy through our thinking, feeling, and choosing, but it is important to remember that *love is much more powerful* and our brains were made to operate in love. Each of us has our own electrical chemical balance where we feel at peace. It's almost like a perfect idling rate that runs on the love attitude—this is the Perfect You. We need to constantly seek after this peace by remembering that we cannot control our circumstances (life and people), but we can choose to control our reaction (attitude) to those circumstances.

A love attitude is disrupted each time we create a new toxic thought or activate an existing toxic thought (a fear attitude, which is stepping out of the Perfect You). Any disruption in the body and mind's regular and consistent quantum and electrical chemical balance—love attitude—will result in discomfort and we will consciously and unconsciously try to restore the balance. It is important that we learn to identify this discomfort zone, which I will discuss more in chapter 8, since it is a conscious and nonconscious mental activation of an attitude.

If you continue to focus on fear, you will continue to block your Perfect You and will never truly feel like "you." Your brain and body will respond to your choices and distort the love circuit into the fear circuit. However, even though fear is powerful, operating in love is even more powerful. You can choose. Even though you may not be able to determine your circumstances, you have the choice to operate in love or fear within those circumstances.

Philippians 2:5 tells us to "have the same attitude that Christ Jesus had" (NLT). Since God is love, this is our wired-for-love design (1 John 4:8). This might seem impossible to do when we are operating in fear; it is impossible because we cannot operate in both love and fear at the same time (Matt. 6:24; Luke 16:13). Yet when we seek love above all things, as Paul tells us, we can keep an eye on all our thoughts and choose to renew our minds with the help of the Holy Spirit (Rom. 12:2; 1 Cor. 13:4–13; 2 Cor. 10:5). When we begin to recognize how powerful our unique choices are, not only for us but also for the world around us, we truly begin to understand the responsibility we have to act in our wired-for-love state.

There is something you can do that no one else can do, and the world needs you to do it! This interconnectedness highlights our humanness; it underscores our responsibility and sense of belonging and reduces feelings of powerlessness, shame, and isolation. You, with your wonderful Perfect You, *matter* and *change matter*.

PART
TWO

4

The Philosophy of the Perfect You

The essential feature of dualist-interactionism is that the mind and brain are independent entities . . . and that they interact by quantum physics.

John Eccles, Nobel laureate

Dualism helps preserve free will. We determine our actions in the light of reasons and desires, we intuit and nothing any neuroscientist has produced shows it is any different. Quantum probabilities show things cannot be predetermined. Indeterminism is compatible with the uniqueness of man.

Richard Swinburne, philosopher

Before discussing the science behind the Perfect You, I will briefly explain my philosophical position on the mind-brain connection, which underpins the way I have approached the unique style in which we all think, speak, and act.

Mind Comes First

Since the advent of quantum physics and the search for the origins of the natural world of space and time in the late nineteenth century, the face of science has changed. *Matter* has become a tricky word, illusive and difficult to define. Werner Heisenberg, one of the leading pioneers in the original formulation of quantum theory in the early twentieth century, said that elementary particles like atoms form a world of pure possibilities; they are not "things" per se. Physicist John Wheeler, a Nobel Prize laureate, said no elementary phenomenon (that is, atoms, electrons, and all other particles we learned about back in school) is real unless it is observed.[1] As English philosopher Keith Ward notes, they are merely "possibilities of perception."[2]

Mind or consciousness, therefore, comes first: this is one of the key features of an *idealist* approach to the universe. The whole of reality, said Nobel Prize laureate Eugene Wigner, is a construct of the *mind*. The mind did not evolve out of the physical matter of the brain. In the beginning was the Word, or *logos* (John 1:1–5). Logos is consciousness; it is defined by intelligibility, rationality, and *thought*. God, as consciousness, was before the universe. His mind, his words, created everything and sustains everything (Gen. 1–2; John 1; Acts 17:28). The conscious world dominates over, yet is intrinsic to, the physical world. This is the meeting of heaven and earth (Matt. 6:9–13).

Philosophical idealism is key to understanding how the Perfect You functions as a distinctive way of thinking, feeling, and choosing. The real world is a pure world, or a mathematical world only known by the mind of each individual. Matter comes from mind, not mind from matter. Your reality is constructed by your mind, the collection of thoughts and memories that are entirely yours as an individual, which is a reflection of the source of all reality: the mind of God (1 Cor. 2:16).

So what is real? The contents of consciousness, or mind. "God is always looking" said Anglican bishop George Berkeley. Essentially, "if there wasn't a God there wouldn't be anything."[3] God is the source of all consciousness; he is truth (John 14:6); he is the supreme consciousness. As John exclaims at the beginning of his Gospel, "God created everything through him. . . . The Word gave life to everything that was created, and his life brought light to everyone. The light shines in the darkness, and the darkness can never extinguish it" (1:3–5 NLT). We are made in his image (Gen. 1:27). The image-bearing creative power of God is in us: "we have the mind of Christ" (1 Cor. 2:16). We need to develop the same mindset as Christ so that we create realities that are in alignment with God's plan to bring heaven to earth.

Application of Idealism

As we uniquely perceive, so we create unique realities. As we use the sound mind God has given us (2 Tim. 1:7), we think, we choose, and we create. This means the way you perceive, think, and feel about what someone has just said to you is going to create your unique response. Perhaps you smile, perhaps you agree, or perhaps you misunderstand what they are saying and get irritated.

Essentially, you respond uniquely by selecting from a number of possibilities, and your response creates a reality: the smile, the agreement, the argument, or however you choose to respond. As Lao Tzu purportedly said, "Watch your thoughts; they become words. Watch your words; they become actions. Watch your actions; they become habits. Watch your habits; they become character. Watch your character; it becomes your destiny." We create destinies with our choices!

Our minds are creative forces to be reckoned with and are to be used in the best ways possible, which is why we have to constantly watch our thoughts and make sure we use our image-bearing power in positive ways. We need to reflect the image of a loving God, not a hurting world order. When we step into our Perfect You, this is exactly what we do. When we step out of our Perfect You, however, we will not be using the creative force of our minds for God's kingdom, and both our health and the health of those around us will suffer.

Materialism

Philosophical idealism stands in contrast to materialism. Materialism dominates the sciences, including neuroscience, today. In essence, a materialist worldview claims that the mind comes from matter: the physical or material aspect of thinking is all that counts. As J. C. Eccles notes:

> The physical world comprises the whole cosmos of matter and energy, all of biology including human brains, and all artifacts that man has made for coding information, as for example, the paper and ink of books or the material base of works of art—this is the total world of the materialists. They recognize nothing else. All else is fantasy.[4]

So, according to materialism, you are fundamentally what your brain does. The overarching construct of materialism is that matter is the first cause, and matter alone is sufficient to generate what we call the mind or the mental activity of thinking, feeling, and choosing. One of the leading materialistic theories of the mind, known as "identity theory," argues that mental states are identical with electrochemical states of the brain, and "all else is fantasy." The brain is a super-complex computer in which material processes in the cerebral cortex *somehow* generate thoughts and feelings. Materialist monism is also deterministic (that is, it places a lot of emphasis on cause and effect), mechanistic (for example, the physical world acts like billiard balls bumping into each other), and reductionist (the whole context is reduced to its parts).

In an entirely materialistic universe, everything that makes us human is simply an artifact of neurons firing and chemical reactions. Physical reductionism thus explains the complexities of humanity—how we uniquely think, feel, and choose—in terms of the physical components of the brain. This way of approaching mental activity can be dangerous: when we make bad choices, are we simply victims of our biology, with no responsibility for our thoughts, emotions, choices, or actions? And what kind of challenge does this way of thinking pose for the biblical worldview, with its emphasis on choices that lead to life or death (Deut. 30:19)?

Added to materialist thinking are the behaviorist theories of the nineteenth century, a form of classical deterministic materialism, which proposed that behavior could be examined on the basis that free will was illusory and human beings could be conditioned like animals. This way of thinking climaxed in the mid-1990s with the advent of brain technology—such as MRI, fMRI, PET, and SPECT that allowed many neuroscientists to "more accurately" map the mind and the experience of consciousness on the brain. This was the "evidence" many materialists used, and still use, to argue that the brain produces mind—in so many words, that the physical produces thinking, feeling, and choosing. We have all seen those newspaper articles titled "This is your brain on . . ." followed by colorful scans claiming that "the brain made me do it."[5] As mentioned above, this pattern of thinking can have serious repercussions. Do murderers kill people because of a misfiring of neurons? Can we even call them murderers? Where does human choice fit in?

In many ways, this is a "chicken or the egg" question. We cannot use traditional scientific methods to prove the brain produces the mind, since we cannot measure the mind like we can measure a physical object in a lab. Who is to say that the mind did not produce the activity we see on a scan? Likewise, many studies indicate that thoughts and feelings can impact physical realities. Perceiving events negatively has been linked to a 43 percent decrease in health over the following twelve months, for example, while chronic stress enhances the spread of cancer through the lymphatic system.[6] What we think and how we choose to react matters and can impact our reality.

More Than Neurons

As image-bearers of God, with a responsibility to steward creation, we are so much more than the firing of our neurons. As Oxford professor and philosopher Richard Swinburne notes:

> Our mental lives cannot be captured in purely physical terms. Neuroscience adds further bits of information, for example the mechanism that the lack of food causes a desire to eat, but neuroscience never showed nor will show the choice of the person to act on the desires, to choose whether to do good or evil.[7]

Certainly, what we choose is reflected in the activity of our brains. But what we choose cannot be reduced to the activity of our brains. The Bible, from Adam and Eve in Genesis to John's book of Revelation, constantly emphasizes the fact that our choices are powerful and can lead to life or death. Being human means accepting this responsibility.

When we approach science with a mindset that reduces the whole context of life to material objects like atoms and neurons, there will be consequences. God created us as triune beings with a mind, spirit, and body (1 Thess. 5:23). The whole created order stems from the Word (*logos*)—consciousness or the mind of God—not a material atom or particle (John 1:1–5). When we separate out these elements and focus only on the physical brain or body, we go against the natural fabric of the universe and this can have negative repercussions.

It is perhaps not surprising that, regardless of the many amazing scientific and medical advances that have come about in the modern era, federal data from 2016 shows that the death rate in the United States rose in 2015 for the first time in decades. According to Robert Anderson, the chief of mortality statistics at the National Center for Health Statistics, "It's an uptick in mortality that doesn't normally happen, so it is significant. What does it mean? We need more data to know but if we start looking at 2016, and we see another rise, we'll be a lot more concerned."[8] The human body is more than its material parts, and we need to take this into consideration when we think of "health" and "wellness."

This is particularly necessary in the field of mental healthcare. Today, it is common to "medicalize misery."[9] Rather than focusing on the context of an individual's life, such a poverty, unemployment, or lack of purpose, many psychiatrists focus on a biological cause, like the purported "chemical balance." By emphasizing that the problem lies within an individual's biology, we are less inclined to look at their experiences and the social context of why they are feeling the way they feel. We look at the biological parts instead of economic exploitation, violence, or inept political structures. Children in foster care are told they have malfunctioning brains and given mind-altering substances. The child who moves a lot in class is forced to take mind-altering medication that is as addictive as cocaine in the long run, and we do not question whether the school systems we have in place are adequate for the diverse expression of humanity.

We have to start asking hard questions. Is being told you are a faulty machine, a broken biological automaton, going to help bring peace, freedom, and healing? Are you extraneous to the equation because your brain is producing all your behaviors? Are you not able to have a decent relationship because a scan shows you have an ADHD brain or an fMRI shows you have schizophrenia? Are you doomed to taking mind-altering, brain-damaging meds for the rest of your life, often with disturbing side effects?

Materialists often see brain scans as full descriptions of the mind. Yet materialistic theories as to how gray matter generates consciousness are challenged when a fully conscious man is found to be missing most of his brain! "Any theory of consciousness has to be able to explain why a person like that, who's missing 90% of his neurons, still exhibits normal behavior," says Axel Cleeremans.[10] A theory of consciousness or the mind that depends on "specific neuroanatomical features" (i.e., the physical makeup of the brain) would have trouble explaining such cases. Where does the mind come from? Nor can materialism and brain technology explain the distinctive nature of our thoughts, feelings, and choices.

Interactive-Dualism

Materialism, however, is not the only way to approach science/neuroscience or the question of consciousness. The belief that the mind and brain are separate yet influence each other is called *dualism*, which was first proposed by René Descartes in the seventeenth century. Essentially, dualism argues that there is a mental world in addition to the physical world, and the two interact.

Over the course of several decades, partly in collaboration with Sir Karl Popper, Noble laureate Sir John Eccles used dualism as a basis to develop his alternative theory of the mind, known as dualist-interactionism or interactive-dualism. According to Eccles:

> The human mystery is incredibly demeaned by scientific reductionism, with its claim in promissory materialism to account eventually for all of the spiritual world in terms of patterns of neuronal

activity. This belief must be classed as a superstition . . . we have to recognize that we are spiritual beings with souls existing in a spiritual world as well as material beings with bodies and brains existing in a material world.[11]

Yet interactive-dualism has become unfashionable with many people who prefer monism and identity theory, which go hand in hand with materialism. Materialism's total emphasis on the physical is perhaps not surprising, since the enigma of mind-brain interaction has challenging implications for the role of the human consciousness—our ability to think, feel, and choose. As Keith Ward notes, dualism provokes a real exploration of the deepest things of science, which point back to God and to taking responsibility for what we think, feel, and choose—not necessarily something materialists or atheists like very much.[12]

Materialism has unfortunately dominated scientific and philosophical thinking for many years. Even today it still has the power to generate explosive discussions among scientists, philosophers, and laypeople with particular viewpoints and agendas. As Keith Ward notes, the "new" atheists such as Richard Dawkins, Sam Harris, and Daniel Dennett espouse this materialistic view to try to prove that we are biological robots and that God does not exist. "The new atheists," says Ward, "have a peculiar interpretation of science that is already absolute. Most philosophers that claim that science is atheistic are not physicists or mathematicians, but they are zoologists and biologists and don't deal with the ultimate state of matter, which physicists do."[13] Indeed, Ward goes on to point out,

Science, far from having a commitment to materialism, actually undermines materialism comprehensively. Darwin said he wasn't an atheist in his autobiography, he was more of a theist or agnostic but people like Dawkins say a Darwinian view eliminates God because things happen by chance and laws of nature and it is all random. The Newtonian view of laws of nature—even though Newton was a devout believer—gave rise to a world view that the world is mechanistic and God just got it going, but this is not what Newton himself thought. So the sciences have given rise to a new sort of materialistic thought, but fortunately materialism is destroyed by Quantum Physics.[14]

Each of us, think, feel, and choose with our minds. Neuroscience and classical physics *only* describe the *physical response of the brain to the mind-in-action*, the mind being the first cause. The brain is the substrate through which the mind works—it reflects the action of the mind. The mind controls the brain; the brain does not control the mind.

Quantum physics, with its examination of science beyond the traditional paradigms of space and time, points directly to the belief that the universe has a creative mind behind it (consciousness), and therefore a creative purpose.[15]

That is, the free choices made by the human players can be seen as miniature versions of the choices that appear to be needed at the creation of the universe. Quantum theory opens the door to, and indeed demands, the making of these later free choices. This situation is concordant with the idea of a powerful God that creates the universe and its laws to get things started, but then bequeaths part of this power to beings created in his own image, at least with regard to their power to make physically efficacious decisions on the basis of reasons and evaluations. I see no way for contemporary science to disprove, or even render highly unlikely, this religious interpretation of quantum theory, or to provide strong evidence in support of an alternative picture of the nature of these "free choices." These choices seem to be rooted in reasons that are rooted in feelings pertaining to value or worth.[16]

This understanding of consciousness supports the unique dignity of human personality found in the Bible: we are infinite minds made in the image of an infinite God (Gen. 1:27). We each have eternity planted deep within us (Eccles. 3:11).

I have been blessed to observe, and still observe, the unique creative power of the human mind. My research and experience working clinically with those with language and learning disabilities or emotional issues as well as TBI, autism, stroke, and CVD victims, partnered with the many studies pouring out of the scientific world and, most importantly of all, what the Scriptures say, all tell me we are most certainly not biological robots or accidents of random, unguided scientific processes. I have seen individuals with injured brains go on to get multiple degrees and make advances in their fields of study. I have seen individuals recover from the worst kinds of trauma and go on to transform their communities. We are not, as Richard Dawkins would have us believe, merely dancing to the tune of our DNA.[17] The mind is imbued with a unique and powerful design that originates in the mind of God, what I call the Perfect You. We are his masterpieces, designed to reflect his glory into the world. We were created to bring heaven to earth.

5

The Science of the Perfect You

> In quantum theory, experience is the essential reality,
> and matter is viewed as a representation of the primary
> reality, which is experience.
>
> Henry Stapp

You are special. Although this may sound like a silly, overused cliché, it is nevertheless true. You are unique. You have a particular way of thinking, feeling, and choosing that acts like a filter through which you experience reality. This is your individual stream of consciousness. It shapes the worldview you build into your mind, which in turn shapes your future thoughts, feelings, words, and behavior.

If this filter is broken, your perception of reality can become distorted. If you are bitter or have low self-esteem, for example, your worldview can become clouded by toxic thinking, which in turn shapes your mindset and actions. Likewise, if you try to make a different filter fit the way you are designed—that is, if you try to be like someone else—your worldview becomes distorted, which impacts your mental and physical health.

It is essential to know and understand your unique design. It empowers you to make the right choices, moment by moment and day by day. Your choices shape your brain and thus shape your reality. You can use your unique way of filtering to unlock and develop your Perfect You, shaping your brain and reality to align with your "type you." This is your natural, default thinking style, which enables you to cope with the circumstances of life.

Perfect You, "type you" thinking results in increased clarity of thought, clearness of vision, intellectual processing, and emotional balance. It produces a mindset that is able to examine all factors and perspectives related to thinking, feeling, and choosing. It is the key to understanding your psyche, your personhood, and the uniqueness of your actions and reactions. It activates your consciousness of things you desire to achieve, which is your divine sense of purpose—and thereby the wherewithal and courage to achieve them.

Neurologically, it activates the reward thinking/learning circuit in the brain. Operating in your Perfect You essentially allows you to face the challenges of life and rejoice despite the circumstances (James 1:2–4). In contrast, if you don't consider your Perfect You as you go through your day, your unique way of thinking can be dampened, diminishing the capabilities you have to deal with "stuff" ranging from normal day-to-day pressures to extreme situations of trauma. Subsequently, your perceptions and management of particular situations can become distorted, potentially leading to the suppression of the ensuing pain through incorrect means such as drugs, food, sex, and so on.

If your Perfect You is repeatedly distorted or suppressed, habituation occurs and patterns of toxic reactions are set up. These toxic thinking patterns create disorder in the mind and neurological and neurodegenerative chaos in the brain. The mind and brain fail to communicate correctly, which results in reduced cognitive and coping strategies. Toxic thinking is essentially a roadblock in the Perfect You. If these negative thought patterns are not controlled, they can even lead to psychiatric symptoms including depression, anxiety, suicidal ideation, OCD, eating disorders, and psychotic breaks.[1]

The Perfect You is the driving force behind our natural, wired-for-love design. It is a particular reflection of God in this world, our unique way of worshiping him by thinking, feeling, and choosing well. It is a byproduct of living according to our truth value: the Perfect You has been designed by God to reflect his glory to the world. Our thinking is designed to reflect his image, since we have the mind of Christ. When people ask me why they should know about their Perfect You, my answer is simple: knowing your Perfect You will unlock you and set you free to be *you*, a particular reflection of the Creator, which fulfills your sense of purpose, increasing your intelligence and your joy in the process.

This book is designed to help you discover *you*. I want you to literally plumb the depths of who you are and get to understand the value God vested in you as the pinnacle of his creation, a human being who is able to think, feel, and choose. This is serious business and requires serious consideration; hence, this is quite a serious book.

Trauma and sin can interrupt this design: people seek love in other directions in an attempt to recapture the feeling of being truly themselves by bringing some level of order in their minds and bodies. Yet there is always hope. The Perfect You is still stronger than negative thought patterns, since the mind controls the brain, and the brain is neuroplastic, so it is always amenable to change.[2] We can, as the apostle Paul tells us, renew our minds (Rom. 12:2).

Of course, scientific endeavors never fully explain reality. Science takes us down a pathway of attempting to understand reality. Hence, the science of the Perfect You has developed vastly since I first began to research this concept thirty years ago, and we still have so much more to learn and discover. Below is a complex explanation of some of the scientific concepts that undergird the Perfect You concept. I have made them as simple as I can, but you don't have to read or fully understand all the science to be able to benefit from the next few chapters. I would, however, strongly recommend reading this chapter—the information is worth the investment! There is also a positive side effect of trying to understand complicated information: you increase your intelligence! And this particularly "sciency" section is followed by a simple application chapter and chart to help pull all the pieces of the puzzle together.

The Perfect You Design

The Perfect You has a structure that can be explained using the Geodesic Information Processing Model I developed nearly thirty years ago.[3] The UQ profile in part 3 was developed out of this structure. In the rest of this chapter I will explain this structure to help you understand how the UQ profile works.

The Perfect You has several different components. There are seven *metacognitive modules*: interpersonal, intrapersonal, linguistic, logical/mathematical, kinesthetic, musical, and visual/spatial. Each metacognitive module has four *processing systems*: speaking, reading, writing, and listening. Each processing system is broken down into three *metacognitive domains*: the declarative (the "what" of the information of the memory), the procedural (the "how" of the information of the memory), and the conditional (the "when/why," or the purpose and emotional component of the memory). These metacognitive domains provide the structure of *descriptive systems* (memories). The exclusivity of your memories is housed within these three elements.

The activity happening in these components is controlled by mind-in-action regulation—your thinking, feeling, and choosing. On a nonconscious level, where approximately 90 percent of learning takes place, this is called *dynamic self-regulation*. On a conscious level, where only approximately 10 percent of learning takes place, this regulation is called *active self-regulation*.

Finally, *metacognitive action* is the term for the deep thinking that causes the what, how, and when/why elements of your memory to start interacting through deliberate, intentional thinking. The more intentional and deliberate the active self-regulation, the more likely it is to interact with dynamic self-regulation (nonconscious level). The memories with the most energy—the memories, which are thoughts, that have had repeated effortful attention paid to them and are therefore embedded in an accessible format—will move into the conscious mind. Whatever moves into conscious awareness is thus what we have spent the most time thinking about.

The Seven Metacognitive Modules

All seven metacognitive modules work together in an entangled fashion. More specifically, these modules work in unique ways for each of us. The seven metacognitive modules of the Perfect You structure/design are housed within the complex, quantum nonconscious mind, which works 24/7 at vast speeds of 10^{27}.

These seven modules are not exhaustive but rather representative of the range of human knowledge and intellectual potentials—a range as unlimited as our God. All individuals possess the full spectrum of the seven metacognitive modules, but in varying amounts and combined in different ways, thus revealing specific cognitive features—hence the Perfect "You."

A point to note here is that the seven metacognitive modules of my geodesic model differ from the seven intelligences of Howard

Gardner's "multiple intelligences" theory.[4] My seven modules incorporate all three types of knowledge within the metacognitive domain: declarative, procedural, and conditional knowledge. Gardner's intelligences only incorporate procedural knowledge and are therefore incomplete in terms of the range of human knowledge.

We cannot approach the way we think, feel, and choose in a reductionist manner. Even though these modules function as independent units, each with their own cognitive characteristics, they are designed to interact as you process information (thinking, feeling, and choosing). When these modules interact, higher-order thinking is produced, because the net result of interaction *between* the modules is improved quality *within* the modules.

It is important to understand that the seven metacognitive modules work in *harmony*. You can't observe or listen to a person and notice all seven. What you will see is the end product of all seven modules working together in a way that is unique to that person. It is the collective whole that is expressed through someone's words and actions: the Perfect You is in how each of us has our own "harmony."

The Processing Systems

As I mentioned above, the metacognitive modules are divided into four processing systems: *read, speak, listen,* and *write*. Each of these processing systems in turn has a *function*, such as reading for concepts, reading a novel for pleasure, reading a complex technical manual, writing an email, writing a story, giving a speech, having a conversation with your best friend, and so on.

A *processing system* is a result of a whole arrangement of processes. For example, the processing system of reading a book, which would be part of the linguistic metacognitive module, is made up of various processes such as the visual tracking of letters,

Illustration 5.1

THE GEODESIC INFORMATION PROCESSING MODEL

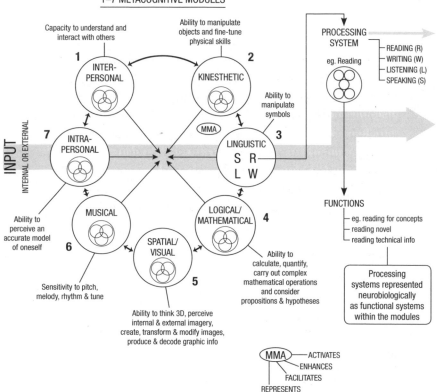

NON-CONSCIOUS

METACOGNITIVE LEVEL

90% of Learning

MMA

Root of thinking process and then structure of the non-conscious

Automatized complex higher cortical functions

1–7 METACOGNITIVE MODULES

Capacity to understand and interact with others

Ability to manipulate objects and fine-tune physical skills

1 INTER-PERSONAL

2 KINESTHETIC

PROCESSING SYSTEM

eg. Reading

READING (R)
WRITING (W)
LISTENING (L)
SPEAKING (S)

Ability to manipulate symbols

7 INTRA-PERSONAL

MMA

3 LINGUISTIC
S R
L W

INPUT — INTERNAL OR EXTERNAL

Ability to perceive an accurate model of oneself

6 MUSICAL

5 SPATIAL/VISUAL

LOGICAL/MATHEMATICAL **4**

FUNCTIONS

eg. reading for concepts
reading novel
reading technical info

Ability to calculate, quantify, carry out complex mathematical operations and consider propositions & hypotheses

Sensitivity to pitch, melody, rhythm & tune

Ability to think 3D, perceive internal & external imagery, create, transform & modify images, produce & decode graphic info

Processing systems represented neurobiologically as functional systems within the modules

MMA — ACTIVATES
ENHANCES
FACILITATES
REPRESENTS

NEUROPSYCHOLOGICAL LEVEL

BIOLOGICAL REPRESENTATION

1–7 represented biologically as modular colums of neuronal cells ascending from the cortex to the subcortex to the limbic system across the left and right hemispheres

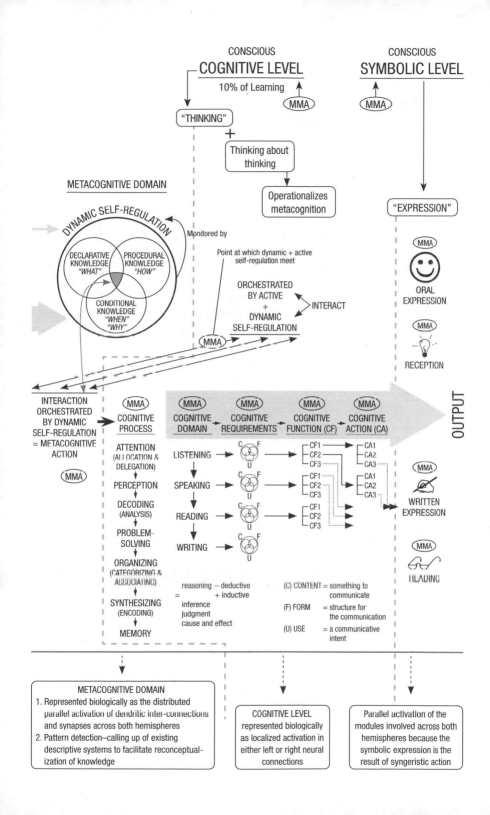

the visual discrimination of letters, and the combining of these letters into units of meaning. The processing system of reading also has various functions, such as reading for factual knowledge or reading to learn what happens to characters in a novel. We each have our own interpretation/filter (the Perfect You) as we are doing this.

A processing system is represented neurologically as a functional structure composed of interrelations of different parts of the brain. Processing systems will eventually be expressed on the symbolic level by cognitive action—what you say and what you do. (See the schematic of my theory, the Geodesic Information Processing Model, on pages 84–85.) A processing system is viewed on my model as the channel through which the intellectual abilities specific to a particular domain are expressed.

Functioning in the Perfect You will maximize the selection and integration of functions into the most efficient processing systems to operationalize the cognitive acts, resulting in optimal performance. This means you will say and do the best for that situation.

Dynamic Self-Regulation

In order to be able to read that novel or give that speech, you need to activate or operationalize the processing system. This is called *dynamic self-regulation*, a very powerful driving force of your nonconscious mind-in-action and one very specific to your Perfect You.

As mentioned above, your nonconscious mind is always in action, 24/7, so dynamic self-regulation is always going on. Your nonconscious mind does not stop analyzing, cleaning up, reading, and integrating all the memories you have, which are changing and growing in response to the experiences of your daily life.

Ultimately, the activity of the nonconscious mind accounts for the high-level decision-making action that is going on even when we get distracted with other tasks on a conscious level. Dynamic self-regulation controls up to 90 percent of thinking and learning and is responsible for activating and energizing long-term memories and belief systems (worldviews) to move into our conscious awareness and, as such, has an enormous influence on our conscious thinking, feeling, and choosing. Dynamic self-regulation also maintains awareness and alertness in the seven metacognitive modules as internal reconstruction (redesigning, growing, and changing of memories) is taking place.

Active Self-Regulation

Conscious cognitive thinking is called *active self-regulation*. The deeper we think, the more active self-regulation interacts with dynamic self-regulation. Active self-regulation is intentional and controlled by your *choice* to pay attention to something. Its effectiveness is determined by how mindful and deliberate you are in any given moment.

It is important to remember that thoughts (also known as descriptive systems or memories) are automatized (made into a habit) through deliberate, repeated, and conscious cognitive thinking. This type of thinking has to occur for a minimum of three cycles of twenty-one days in order for true understanding to take place.

The Metacognitive Domain and Descriptive Systems

Each of the seven metacognitive modules uses its own operating system, known as the *metacognitive domain*. These domains use declarative (what), procedural (how), and conditional (when/why) *types of knowledge* to build pattern-nature memories (*descriptive systems*). These memories, in turn, grow into belief systems or worldviews, which are reflected in our attitudes (*expanded and strengthened descriptive systems*).

Every moment of every day we are merging with our environment. Through thinking, feeling, and choosing, we are learning and planting thoughts, which are real physical things, into the brain. This sophisticated and complex process is essentially the expansion and solidification of descriptive systems through the addition of the three types of knowledge (thinking, feeling, and choosing) to the metacognitive domain. It happens in our minds 24/7, even when we are asleep! We truly are superbly intellectual beings, even when we are not aware of what is going on in our minds.

Yet what occurs on the metacognitive level is unique for each of us. The particular way you build and store memory is based on your specific perceptions and interpretations, which are exclusive to you. The various mechanisms in the nervous system are, in fact, activated to carry out specific operations on the information, and structural change occurs in the brain—and this is unique for each person. The repeated use of, elaboration of, and interaction among the computational devices will lead to forms of knowledge that are useful, intelligent, and *exclusive* to you. Thus the metacognitive domains in the geodesic model reflect the idea that human beings are so constituted as to be sensitive to certain information in their own unique way. When a particular form of information is presented, *your* mind goes into action and works through the substrate of *your* brain. Your self-regulation will be completely different from mine; the person thinking and using his or her Perfect You drives all these processes.

In the Geodesic Information Processing Model, memory is essentially seen as part of the cognitive process, where the new descriptive systems are reconceptualized or redesigned. Once a new descriptive system is reconceptualized, it is stored in the appropriate metacognitive domains of the specified metacognitive modules in the form of declarative, procedural, and conditional knowledge. The reconceptualization of new knowledge is actualized and enhanced on the cognitive level, then stored on the metacognitive level, where it will be used in the future reconceptualization of new knowledge.

Metacognitive Action

Mindful, intentional, and deliberate active self-regulation will activate interaction between active and dynamic self-regulation, the result of which is thinking deeply. This deep thinking is called *metacognitive action*, which is when the *what*, *how*, and *when/why* elements of your memory start interacting through deliberate thinking until they generate enough energy to move into your conscious mind. If conscious thinking is not deliberate (that is, with the aim to develop understanding, which is when active and dynamic self-regulation interact), over a period of approximately sixty-three days, then what you are thinking about will not become an influential part of your nonconscious mind.[5]

Intentional, deep thinking shapes your worldview. These thoughts become deeply rooted in the nonconscious mind and, even though they are not available to conscious introspection, they still influence the cognitive end-products of our thinking, feeling, and choosing. They become available to conscious introspection only when we think deeply, using our Perfect You, which literally gives them the energy to move into conscious awareness.

So *metacognitive action* is your deep thinking, feeling, and choosing, expressed as the fundamental elements of the Perfect You and shaped through the Perfect You. As the memory bubbles up into the conscious part of your mind, you become aware of it, and the memory influences or doesn't influence—you can consciously choose—your current processing of whatever it is you are focusing on.

And, as the relevant memories move from the nonconscious to the conscious mind, experience is enlarged and increased with new knowledge added to the memories. Better integration among memories will occur the deeper we think, also contributing to the reconceptualization of knowledge. Essentially, we don't just add facts to our memories; we literally *redesign* them with each new piece of information we uniquely perceive and understand. If a person is not a deep thinker—thinking, feeling, and choosing in a repeated, intentional, deliberate way and taking responsibility for his or her learning—the input will not be strong enough to induce cognitive, emotional, behavioral, and academic change.

Research, in fact, shows that when we think deeply in our unique way (our Perfect You), we induce *neuroplasticity*: our brains change.[6] Our minds read or interpret the activities and patterns of the neurons and dendrites of our brains. Dendrites store the memories made by the signals of the mind. The more we think and generate metacognitive action, the more we influence and change this configuration of the physical memory, which is then ready to be read again (remembered) at a later time through metacognitive action. This all requires the brain to function properly.

An example of this process could be a discussion with your spouse that activates memories that may be healthy or toxic—or both—of similar discussions, reactions, and outcomes you had in the past. These memories become conscious through the process described above and filter through your Perfect You, assembling into your unique thinking, feeling, and choosing. Your choosing, in turn, generates and projects your words and actions, with their unique attitudes and flavoring, into the conversation. Configurations and interpretations can go wrong (toxic) when we step out of our Perfect You and make toxic choices or if the brain gets damaged in some way.

The Readiness Potential

Scientists see traces of this nonconscious dynamic self-regulation activity in what is called the "readiness potential." This potential involves the interaction between dynamic and active self-regulation, which is activated through deliberate, deep thinking. Once this interaction occurs, the cognitive process is activated. Cognition is regulated by metacognition and carries the metacognitive action of the processing system through to the symbolic expressive level—what we say and do.

Benjamin Libet, a pioneer in the field of human consciousness, performed one of the first studies on cognition and metacognition.[7] His research began in the early 1980s (when I was doing my first level of graduate research) and has shaped the way many scientists approach the question of consciousness. Libet connected people to a machine that measured brain activity while they were asked to randomly decide to press a button. The subjects were then asked to consciously note when they decided to press the button. He found that just prior to the conscious decision to press the button—approximately 200 milliseconds—there was a conscious buildup of activity in the brain, which he called the "readiness potential." And at approximately 350 milliseconds the subjects showed unconscious activity before reporting any degree of conscious awareness. Later studies saw this buildup ten seconds prior to a conscious decision.[8]

Some adherents of materialism interpreted Libet's findings in a way that negated the power of choice. They concluded that the studies showed that the brain is the cause of conscious activity, since the buildup of "readiness potential" occurred prior to a conscious decision.[9] Subsequently, they used this interpretation to deny the existence of free will. More research showed, however, that the "readiness potential" was still there, even when subjects did not make specific, conscious decisions. In one study subjects had to push a button when they saw a cube among many other shapes. Measured brain activity during the task showed that the "readiness potential" was there even before the stimuli appeared. As one of the researchers noted:

> Our results show that neural activity, which is present prior to motor responses, emerges well before the presentation of a stimulus. At that time the participants were not capable of knowing whether to press the left- or right-hand button before a stimulus appeared. In addition, the activation preceding the stimulation did not differ significantly between the two response alternatives. Thus the observed activity cannot be regarded as a specific preparation to press one of the buttons rather than the other one.[10]

In essence, we cannot tell that the "brain decided" to press one button. "Readiness potential" exists whether or not there is a button to press (or some other stimulus); something else is responsible for the specific decisions we make at any given moment. We cannot look at a brain and decide why a human being makes the choices he or she makes because the brain with its neural correlates does not tell us about a person's experience and free will.

Libet, in fact, did not deny free will.[11] He noted that the mind has the ability to veto an action while neural activity continues. He called this the "conscious veto," which supports the idea of free will that pervades the Bible. The brain will run on autopilot and carry out tasks, yet the mind or self (the Perfect You) has the ability to interfere by preventing activity from being carried out. Our choices matter.

These studies do not merely demonstrate that the brain runs on autopilot. Free will is not just an illusion, as several prominent materialists would have us believe.[12] Rather, the brain, as a physical substrate, appears to be responding to (or is being "used" by) the nonconscious mind, which is orchestrated by dynamic self-regulation and the process of selecting the appropriate descriptive systems (memories) that need to move to the conscious mind. Once the memories have moved into the conscious mind and we filter the information through our Perfect You, we think, feel, and make a choice about whether to comply with or override an action.

So, using the earlier example of being in a conversation with a spouse, you can choose to override how your spouse responded in the past and give him or her the benefit of the doubt, or you can do the opposite and get into an argument. If you are fully operating in our Perfect You, you will do the former, since you will not be reacting from a toxic mindset but one based on love.

The Holy Spirit's Role

To ensure that we stay in our Perfect You and correctly respond to the circumstances of everyday life, we need to train ourselves to consult with the Holy Spirit on a daily basis.[13] We can ask the Holy Spirit to help us renew our mindsets and teach us how to react and behave (John 14:15–17, 26; 16:12–15; Acts 2:38; Rom. 15:13; Gal. 5:22–23). The Holy Spirit will guide us, if we *choose* to listen to him, and show us the correct way to "consciously veto" our thinking, feeling, and choosing. In this way, we fulfill the requirements of Scripture to constantly pray (1 Thess. 5:17).

The process of developing a mindful awareness, which includes constant dialogue with the Holy Spirit, is integral to our mental and physical health. Mindfulness increases our chances of staying in the Perfect You, thereby improving our insight and self-regulation and helping us access the nonconscious stores of our minds. It also promotes the desire to seek more knowledge and learn about the effects of toxic nonconscious thoughts. Once a toxic attitude is changed, for instance, it is easier to learn new, healthy thinking habits.

So when you are in the Perfect You, it activates your desire to obtain true knowledge and to think deeply to understand and apply this knowledge. Deep thinking and application lead to wisdom. Wisdom, in turn, recognizes the need for more knowledge, and so the cycle carries on. I call this "the wisdom model," which is one of the key benefits of operating in your Perfect You. The potential to become aware of the operation of our seven metacognitive modules is, in fact, a special feature of our humanness. The more the seven metacognitive modules interact, the more your deep thinking kicks in and the wiser we become.

Wisdom is the net result of the interaction between the seven metacognitive modules. As we deliberately and intentionally improve the quality of interaction within the seven metacognitive modules—the quality of our thinking, feeling, and choosing—the fundamentals of our Perfect You improve.

The Difference between Your Perfect You and Mine

The difference between your Perfect You and mine involves differences in the components of the seven metacognitive modules, their metacognitive domains, and their processing systems. In fact, the metacognitive action of both dynamic and active self-regulation is also exclusive to the individual. How you drive your mind is unique: your type-you or Perfect You is captured and reflected in the "what, how, when/why" plus how you manage these through dynamic and active self-regulation. As you work through the UQ profile in the next section, this exclusivity is what you are unlocking. The net result is a mindful awareness of your identity: it is a particular insight into your Perfect You, so you can enhance and improve your ability to think, feel, and choose. This is *intelligent mindfulness*, which is the overall purpose of understanding and using the discomfort zones and the exercises in part 4 of this book.

All seven metacognitive modules work together in a simultaneous, entangled fashion, and in unique ways for each of us. This uniqueness represents individualistic thinking, feeling, and choosing. We all have the ability to think, feel, and choose, but each person's Perfect You is different and exclusively our own, just like our fingerprints.

Strength in the sum of the parts is the fundamental principle of this modular perspective. The quality of higher cortical functions is influenced by the harmonious interaction of the seven metacognitive modules, which is facilitated by doing exercises that tap into the abilities of all the modules. When we move out of our Perfect You, we don't tap into the modules correctly and instead only tap into a selection of them.

For this reason, the profile in the next chapter is a process of mindful exploration to increase your awareness and insight into how your seven metacognitive modules interact to produce the unique way you think, feel, and choose. The UQ profile teaches you to think about your thinking and understand who you are. It results in pattern detection, which is the calling up of existing descriptive systems in your mind, so it is a way of getting insight into your unique mental framework. It essentially shows *your unique* complex interplay between metacognition, cognition, and the brain's biological structure.

The exercises that follow in part 4 will help you stay mindful and self-regulate your thoughts, feelings, and choices, which are the fundamental elements of your Perfect You. You will learn about the discomfort zones so that you become aware of when you are stepping out of your Perfect You. Most importantly, you will learn how to stay in your Perfect You as much as possible and reflect God's glory more and more every day!

Knowing and understanding your identity empowers your choices, which impact not only your own life but the lives of those around you. Unlocking your Perfect You is not optional; it is essential to the good life.

Learning

When you operate in your Perfect You, you are learning well. All thinking, feeling, and choosing leads to learning, so you learn even when you are not thinking correctly (in other words, operating out of your Perfect You). You should be very aware of what you are focusing on: you could be learning things that will have a negative impact.

Learning is the creative reconceptualization of knowledge. It is controlled by active and dynamic self-regulation. It has the quality of personal involvement, it is pervasive, and its essence is *meaning*. What we learn determines the meaning of our lives, since it shapes our worldview—or the mindset filter through which we see everything.

When we operate in our Perfect You we are learning in a healthy way and building healthy memories. However, when we operate outside of our Perfect You we learn in a distorted way and build toxic memories that damage the brain and body.

We all have to ask ourselves what we want in the memory storages of our minds. Whatever we focus on the most will grow and influence our perspectives and belief systems (or worldviews). As the saying goes, we become what we love. This can be both a positive and negative experience. Operating in the Perfect You keeps you in alignment with your godly, image-bearing design. It enables you to reflect God's glory, since you are focusing on him and learning to become more like him.

The Perfect You is reflected in Paul's letter to the Philippians. The apostle exhorts followers of Christ to "Fix your thoughts on what is true, and honorable, and right, and pure, and lovely, and admirable. Think about things that are excellent and worthy of praise" (Phil. 4:8 NLT).

When we think on God's things, we become more like him. The "implanted word," not Google or gossip, will save your soul

(James 1:21). It is critical to remember that Perfect You thinking will produce an end product: your words and actions. We are what we think—or as it says in Proverbs, "as he thinks in his heart, so is he" (23:7).

The Quantum Angle of the Perfect You and the Geodesic Model

As discussed above, we each have our different form of knowing that is expressed through the Perfect You. This way of knowing results in changes in the brain—the brain responds to the mind. Quantum theory shows the interaction between the mind and the brain and uses mathematics to describe this relationship.[14]

The human brain, as the substrate through which the mind works, cannot be explained by classical physics alone. As quantum physicist and mathematician Henry Stapp explains:

> The most radical departure from classical physics instituted by the founders of quantum mechanics was the introduction of human consciousness into the dynamical and computational machinery. This change constitutes a revolutionary break with the classical approach, because the success of that earlier approach was deemed due in large measure precisely to the fact that it kept consciousness out. However, the need for a rationally coherent and practically useful theory forced the creators of quantum mechanics to bring into the theory not merely a passive observer, superposed ad hoc onto classical mechanics, together with the knowledge that flows passively into his or her consciousness, but, surprisingly, an active consciousness that works in the opposite direction, and injects conscious intentions efficaciously into the physically described world.
>
> It is, of course, obvious that we human beings do in practice inject our conscious intentions into nature whenever we act in an intentional way. But in classical physics it was assumed that any such human action was merely a complex consequence of the

purely physical machinery. However, the quantum generalization of the classical mechanical laws proposed by Heisenberg and his colleagues do not generate by themselves a dynamically complete deterministic physical theory. They have a causal gap. Something else is needed to complete the dynamics.[15]

The more we examine and understand human consciousness and the power of choice, the more we see that humans are not just complicated biological machines of cause and effect. As Stapp himself asks, "How do the motions of the miniature planet-like objects of classical physics give rise to individualistic feelings and understanding and knowing? Classical physics says one day these connections will be known, but how can they be understood in terms of a theory . . . that eliminates the agent of the 'connection'[?]"[16]

Classical physics is not about your experiences but rather a predetermined physical world with no mention of your physical thoughts. But you are a player in a game, a co-creator of your evolving physical reality. Many materialists tend to deny the intangible power of consciousness and choice, citing that we will understand how this comes about "one day," while explanations that challenge their reductionist paradigms are disregarded. This is not good science; indeed it is not science at all.

Werner Heisenberg, who received the Nobel Prize in 1932 for the creation of quantum physics, proposed a quantum generalization of classical laws, yet there was still a causal gap in his work.[17] What causes change in the brain? Laws cannot generate by themselves; they need someone or something to generate them. John von Neumann's form of quantum mechanics solved this by *introducing the individual with his or her free choices* in order to fill the causal gap—the Perfect You.[18]

The individual observer was incorporated into the core of quantum mechanics by Heisenberg's replacement of numbers by actions. The number represents "internal properties of a physical system," whereas the action that replaces the number represents *the person with their free will* observing or probing the system.[19] Actions replacing numbers challenges the materialism of classical physics, for, as was discussed in the section on interactive-dualist philosophy, the mind (the individual observer) freely changes the brain (the physical realm). In essence, the freely chosen, conscious intentions and perceptions of the individual (Perfect You) are injected into a physical system (brain), changing it structurally. This, in turn, results in words and actions, and more physical change occurs in our brains and thus in our world. Choices have the power of life and death (Deut. 30:19).

This mind-brain quantum theory is called the Von Neumann Orthodox Formulation of Quantum Mechanics. It is built around the effect of a person's psychologically described, intentional actions on physically described properties (the person's brain). It specifies the causal connections between the realm of the mind and the realm of the brain with the basic laws of physics. This formulation overcomes the main objection to Cartesian dualism, which was the lack of an understanding of how the mind can affect the brain. Notably, it shows that human consciousness cannot be "an inert witness to the mindless dance of atoms."[20] We are not merely dancing to the tune of our atoms or our DNA.

The brain has a quantum nature, shown by quantum physics calculations and quantum neurobiology, that cannot be adequately explained by classical physics. Ionic processes occurring in nerves, which are at the atomic level and cannot be accounted for by classical physics alone because they are too small, control brains. The process of exocytosis, for example, which deals with the dumping of neurotransmitter molecules into the synapse, requires the more fine-tuned explanations of quantum mechanics.[21]

It is no surprise that quantum physicist Christopher Fuchs declares that "quantum mechanics is a law of thought."[22] Quantum theory evinces the importance of the mind-in-action, the mind-brain connection, and the power of our intellect, will, and emotions, which can cause physical changes in the brain. As a result, quantum theory is a very powerful way of explaining thinking and the Perfect You, alongside neuroscience and neuropsychology.

Philosopher and theologian Keith Ward calls quantum theory "the most accurate model ever developed to understand the deepest things."[23] Two of the "deepest things," two of the biggest questions we all face at one time or another, is how we uniquely think as human beings and what our purpose on this earth is. Why do we have the minds we do? What is our part in eternity and divine sense of purpose (Eccles. 3:11)? Quantum physics gives us a way of describing, scientifically, this divine sense of purpose by showing us how powerful our minds are. It provides a scientific theory that explains the power of an individual's ability to choose, and thus to change his or her brain, body, and the world. It thus highlights the importance of thinking and how we are all uniquely, fearfully, and wonderfully made (Ps. 139:14).

God is using science to show the power of thinking and free will in a practical way. We see, through quantum theory and neuroscience, that we can observe our thoughts are real—and they matter. What we think not only impacts us (spirit, mind, and body) but also those we are in a relationship with and even future generations. Quantum physics thus provides validation of something we all sense intuitively: our conscious thoughts have the power to affect our actions. It describes the ways in which our conscious thinking, feeling, and choosing enter into the physical realm and give us a way of describing the structural changes seen in the brain as a result of human thought.

Uncertainty and Choice

Moment by moment, every day, we are thinking, feeling, and choosing. We either do so by using our Perfect You in its default way or, on the other hand, through incorrect choices that cause us to step out of our Perfect You and hence out of wisdom.

As the stimuli of the events of life enter into your brain through your five senses, your unique structurally and spiritually designed Perfect You filters the information, and this specific activity fires up your brain. No one knows what you are going to choose except you. There is an infinite number of probabilities you can choose from—good and bad, which in quantum theory is spoken of in terms of Erwin Schrödinger's probability wave. Schrödinger's equation predicts probability—but it is just a prediction, so there is always a degree of uncertainty as to the outcome.

However, even though we don't know the details, we do know God's plans for us are good and that he wants to give us a hope and a future (Jer. 29:11). Anything we choose that is in the love zone, which I discussed at the beginning of this book, is going to have a positive outcome and be part of God's plan. On the other hand, there are a range of probabilities in the fear zone that can have a toxic impact on our lives. So as we choose, in quantum terms we collapse a probability wave (or, in neuroscience terms, our choice generates a signal that causes genetic expression). According to Fuchs, the wave function of all the probable possibilities does not objectively describe the world; rather it *subjectively* describes the person and his or her unique choices, so each of us has our own wave function, our own reality, and our own set of probabilities (or beliefs, attitudes, and choices).[24] Hence God has a *specific* plan for our lives, and we participate in that plan as *individuals* with the ability to freely choose.

Prior to the collapse of the wave, which is our choice, the wave function incorporated a number of probabilities. These probabilities are not actual waves but rather waves of probability in a conceptual space termed *Hilbert space*.[25] Hilbert space is a mathematical concept named after David Hilbert, one of the most influential mathematicians of the nineteenth and twentieth centuries. So the collapse of the wave is the updated knowledge of the observer (you) as you go through the process of thinking, feeling, and choosing for the range of probabilities in Hilbert space.

As you are thinking and feeling, you are in *superposition*. On an atomic level this means two particles are in a 1 and 0 at the same time (called a *quibit*) and are being held together by quantum entanglement before they collapse into either a 1 or 0 as the result of a choice. This means the brain, as a quantum computer, can calculate different computations simultaneously while the process of decision making is taking place. Simply put, we can hold two perspectives in mind at the same time. This *mind action* has a physical reaction on multiple levels, from the waves of energy to the atomic level and right up to the level of our choosing to believe one reality over another.

So what does this look like on a quantum level and in the brain? Information (choosing a holiday destination, a medical diagnosis, a situation at work, an opportunity, an argument with a spouse— anything) enters your brain through your five senses and activates electrochemical and quantum action in your neurons.

If we go inside the neurons, we find microtubules, around ten million per neuron (they are really minuscule). These microtubules are made up of proteins called *tubulin*, which in turn are made up of amino acids called *tryptophan*, which on a molecular level are made up of six carbon atoms in the form of a ring (which is called an *aromatic ring*). Quantum action is taking place at the level of the vibrating electrons oscillating from side to side in this ring. These electrons, because of Heisenberg's uncertainty principle (which, on a mind level, is you not having yet made your decision, so you don't know yet if it'll be Hawaii or Paris) don't have fixed positions. The electrons spread out like a literal wave of probabilities (or options/possibilities/tendencies) and the aromatic rings cross over and share electron clouds, going into superpositions of 1 and 0 (the quantum bit or quibit—you are essentially thinking Hawaii and Paris at the same time). There is not just one pathway of these but several, so they are called *topological quibits*, and because there are a lot of them working together it is called *coherence*. The more we talk to the Holy Spirit, the more coherence we will have and the more we will have access to his infinite wisdom, which will positively change our coherence and enable us to make a positive choice.

As we choose, we select a probability from Hilbert space and collapse the wave, which means we have turned a probability into an actuality or a reality. We have turned a nothing into a something. This collapse of the wave function is also called *decoherence* in quantum theory. Subsequently, we start building this reality into a physical effect in our brains through genetic expression. In this way we update our nonconscious mind with new information and increased levels of expertise and wisdom—if we choose correctly. If we choose incorrectly, the updated knowledge is toxic.

In turn, this leads us into the Quantum Zeno Effect (QZE), which is a type of decoherence effect.[26] QZE describes how, when we repeatedly pay attention to something and think, feel, and make choices (collapsing a wave function), we are creating a long-term memory that will become part of our belief systems and influence our choices in the future. In simple terms, it is the repeated effort that allows learning to take place; it is the "whatever we think about the most will grow" effect discussed above. Information becomes implanted, and if the information is good, it will "save" your mind (James 1:21). Operating outside of your Perfect You may even be viewed as repeated and therefore learned memories (QZE) that are incorrect and disrupt the reward/thinking/learning circuit in the brain.

In effect, people who operate in their Perfect You are the good soil in the parable of the sower in Matthew 13:1–23. They persist and push through even when they no longer "feel like it." They hold on to God's Word even when life is no longer carefree and

103

happy, or when that great church conference is over and they are back in the throes of everyday life. Yet the parable also includes people who ruminate endlessly on the worries and illusions of life: instead of building healthy thoughts from repeated effort, they build negative mindsets and worldviews that influence their choices on a daily basis. This is called the *plastic paradox* and highlights the fact that our brains simply follow the direction of where our minds take us—positive or negative. We can choose.

Our uniqueness pervades these choices. Since we act from what we have built in our minds, our choices literally describe us since they reflect our attitudes and deeply rooted belief systems. Finding the neural substrates of free will have long intrigued philosophers and scientists, and the power and reality of choosing being reflected in the brain—the brain being the substrate through which the mind works—has recently been confirmed by Johns Hopkins University researchers.[27] Science is catching up with the Word of God!

Entanglement

Quantum mechanics, with its emphasis on the entangled nature of consciousness and the physical world, is about *us in the world*, not the world or us. "Us in the world" becomes key to the release of the Perfect You. This is because in the humbling recognition that you can do something no one else can do as you operate in your Perfect You, the role you play in others' lives is magnified. In one study, people who served others who were going through something experienced a 68 percent increase in healing compared to those who only got treatment for themselves.[28] The research showed that helping others predicted reduced mortality specifically by changing toxic stress to healthy stress. Many studies indicate that helping behavior can buffer the effects of stress on mental and physical health, specifically when people reach out in love with a positive attitude to other people.[29] Furthermore, studies show that isolation has a negative impact on mental and physical health.[30] We are made to interact with each other and help each other even when we are going through hard times. In essence, the principle of entanglement shows how the Perfect You is not all about ourselves but rather how we can get to know God better and to serve others.

Indeed, life is an entangled thing—we see this principle clearly laid out in Scripture in Ephesians 4:16: "He makes the whole body fit together perfectly. As each part does its own special work, it helps the other parts grow, so that the whole body is healthy and growing and full of love" (NLT). We all need each other; it is through Christian fellowship that we come to know God better. We are the stewards of the world, and all of creation cries out for us to reflect God's glory (Rom. 8:19–21). We cannot escape the intertwined nature of our world.

Entanglement is in fact a primary law of quantum physics. God created us to have relationship with him, each other, and the earth we are required to steward. Quantum physics helps us understand just how entangled our world is. If a photon comes into existence a billion light-years from here, it affects you, even if you do not notice it affecting you. John Bell, famous for Bell's Theorem (formulated at CERN in Geneva in 1964),[31] observed that there is an inseparable quantum connectedness of every part with every other in our universe. No matter how far apart in distance and time, all particles in a relationship affect each other: these relationships exist beyond space and time.

Entanglement demonstrates the profound impact our thinking, feeling, and choosing has, not just on ourselves (spirit, mind, and body) but also on each other and the world around us. Forgiveness is a primary example of entanglement in action. By not forgiving, we are staying entangled in someone's life, and everything they say or do is as real as though they were still in our lives hurting us. By forgiving, we disentangle ourselves from the toxic situation we have experienced, protect our spirits, and re-create a healthy entanglement where we are no longer affected by that person's bad choices.

We cannot control the events and circumstances of life, since everyone is free to make their own choices, even if they negatively impact us. We can, however, control our reactions to the events and circumstances of life through the choices we make. When we understand how we react—when we understand how we think, feel, and choose (our Perfect You)—we realize we can choose to control those reactions and ensure they are true to our wired-for-love, image-bearing design. In turn, we shape our world, bearing witness to the love of God: we truly begin to reflect, like a light on a hill, his magnificent image!

Illustration 5.2
Perfect You Processing: Think/Feel/Choose

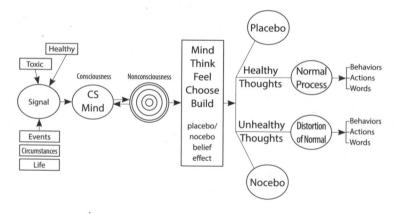

PART
THREE

6

Profiling the Perfect You

The Unique Qualitative (UQ) Assessment Tool

> Insist on yourself; never imitate.
> Ralph Waldo Emerson,
> essayist and poet

> Differences are not intended to separate, to alienate.
> We are different precisely in order to realize our need
> of one another.
> Archbishop Desmond Tutu

In the previous chapters I described what the Perfect You is, how it works, and how important it is to unlock it. In this chapter, you will be filling in the tool of the Perfect You, the Unique Qualitative (UQ) Assessment, which is a developmental profile that will begin to unlock you Perfect You and give you a feel for your "youness." I say *begin* because understanding your Perfect You is an ongoing, organic process that covers your lifespan.

But before you start, let us briefly look at what this UQ profile is *not* and why. The UQ profile is not an IQ test, since a numerical score based on answers to a limited number of questions is not an indication of your potential—it is merely a snapshot in time, while in actual fact you are constantly changing. The UQ profile is also not a personality test. You are not a category. You are not part of a group; you are your own category and group. Nor is the UQ profile a popular EQ (emotional quotient) or SQ (social quotient) questionnaire, because emotions and social interactions are complex, unlimited, and varying. They are part of a complex whole and, as such, cannot be reduced—they can only find their true expression in this "wholeness."

IQ, EQ, SQ, and similar personality profiles are derivatives of the aforementioned classical materialistic approach, which is reductionist and deterministic. These approaches exclude humanity's causal power of free will and the fact that we are made in God's unlimited image. Those types of profiles reiterate the belief that the state of matter at this point in time is complete, whole, and a prediction of how it will be in the future. They essentially tell you that your IQ today is your IQ forever. This kind of thinking almost disables you in that you can go through life blaming a label or category that has locked you in and doesn't actually distinguish you as the stand-alone "designer babe" you truly are, who is brilliant and takes responsibility for this brilliance *and* the mistakes.

The UQ profile goes beyond IQ, EQ, SQ, and personality profiles. It focuses on type-you with all your beautiful and limitless potential, tendencies, and unpredictability. The Greek philosopher Aristotle explained it this way: we have *potentia*, which are "objective tendencies" (to use Heisenberg's quantum physics description) that enable us to express ourselves and are the result of our choices.[1] No one knows what you are going to choose or what your "actuality" is going to be (to use another Aristotelian concept). These potentia are unlimited and immeasurable; only you and God know them, until you choose to make a potential into an actual choice that impacts you and your world. The UQ profile recognizes and honors the Aristotelian potentia in you.

As discussed under the science of the Perfect You, a metacognitive module is a cluster of intellectual abilities that form the raw material of thought and make up the structure of the nonconscious mind. These are sets of intellectual potentials or raw computational capacities. These modules influence the thinking process: each module produces a specific type of thought based on its nature. There are seven types and, hence, seven sections to the UQ profile. Processing of information (thinking, feeling, and choosing) is the result of how these modules interact and are used. You have your own unique thought processing pattern, which is comprised of how you use the content of each module and how your modules interact. The questions below are designed to help you unlock and understand how *you* use these modules. We all do everything you see in the questions below, just differently.

In fact, these modules are all essential processing skills that make up your UQ profile, so do not make the mistake of focusing on one and thinking you are, for example, just a visual/spatial learner or a logical/mathematical learner. This is a reductionist mistake that comes from years of doing IQ, EQ, SQ, and other kinds of personality tests. It is imperative to grasp that these elements of your Perfect You are the raw computational capacities that combine together to reflect you. *The accurate reflection of your "youness" is in the sum of the parts—not the parts alone!*

As you move through this UQ profile, you will become consciously aware of how you *specifically* use these raw computational capacities. These are probing questions that are designed to help you understand you, so dig and think deeply before answering each one. The more seriously you answer them, the more you will understand yourself.

111

There is no one correct answer. Every answer is correct, regardless of whether you answer yes or no as part of your answer. But a yes or no alone is not enough—you must write as much as you can, in as fully descriptive sentences as possible. Treat this as the process of asking, answering, and discussing as you work through the questions in a deliberate, intentional, and self-regulatory way.

You are profiling how you uniquely and qualitatively process thoughts through your Perfect You; hence the profile is called the *Unique* Qualitative Assessment Tool. You are looking at the "know-how, know-what, know-when, know-why" knowledge that makes up your metacognitive modules, how they interact and how you are self-regulating them. You are essentially getting a glimpse into your nonconscious mind! The answers should make you feel satisfied, as though you have *begun and accomplished* something necessary that just feels right. So take your time! Be as descriptive as possible: if you answer yes, describe the "why, how, when, where, and what" *you* do. If you answer no, describe the "why, how, when, where, and what" of what *you* do instead. If you rush through the questions you will not get the full benefit of using your Perfect You to unlock and understand your Perfect You.

And, most importantly, be honest! No one is going to see your answers—unless you want to show them.

The first few questions of the UQ are more detailed to get you into the flow. Thereafter it is up to you to work out the specifics of your uniqueness, which is not a prepackaged prescription, as I have stressed throughout this book. Your UQ profile is like an exploratory expedition into uncharted yet vaguely familiar territory—you are unlocking something that is already there but needs development to flourish.

Most importantly, let the Holy Spirit guide you "into all truth" (John 16:13).

How the UQ Profile Works

Each set of questions begins with a *brief description of the meta-cognitive module*. This is followed by a *set of probing questions* for each metacognitive module focusing on the what, how, and when/why (the metacognitive domain) of the way you create and store knowledge to reflect your unique perspective and interpretation of life, so you will see these words in each question. At the end of each set of questions there is an opportunity for you to reflect back on your answers by writing a *summary* of all your answers. This is a challenging but enlightening process, and a very necessary part of unlocking your Perfect You. It will force you to self-regulate at a very high intellectual level and take you deeper than you have already gone.

There is no time limit nor expiration date on your potential, so take as long as you want filling in the UQ profile. Redo it at least once a year to watch the eternity in you unfold, so I suggest you keep a regular diary so you can track the organic growth of your Perfect You over time, using the UQ profile.

The UQ profile is followed, in the next chapter, by the Perfect You checklist. I need to stress that this checklist only works when you have worked through the book and profile in the way laid out in the book, which is based on years of research, clinical application and expertise, science, and Scripture. There are no shortcuts, no instantaneous Twitter feed solutions here! There is only commitment, time, depth, and definite growth when you take *yourself* seriously. And you will keep getting better and better as you pick up this challenge!

• • •

Module 1: Intrapersonal Metacognitive Module—Thinking, Feeling, Choosing

The first metacognitive module is the Intrapersonal Metacognitive Module of thinking, feeling, and choosing. The brain tissue in this modular area is designed to handle information that deals with the raw computational capacities of deep thinking, decision making, organizing, focusing, analyzing, and free will; being aware of your range of emotions, controlling and working with your thoughts and emotions, and finding ways of expressing your thoughts; being motivated to identify and pursue goals; working independently; being curious about the meaning of life; self-managing ongoing personal learning and growth; attempting to understand inner experiences; empowering and encouraging others; enjoying thinking strategies, journal writing, and relaxing and self-assessment strategies; understanding your limitations; and assessing and evaluating situations.

Intrapersonal thinking enables you to stand outside of yourself and analyze your own thinking. While you analyze incoming and existing information, you are going to make decisions about what to think, say, and do: this is free will in action!

This metacognitive module is fundamental to introspection, self-knowledge, and the ability to understand your own feelings, thoughts, and intuitions. Subsequently, you are able to better guide your behavior, understand your strengths and weaknesses, imagine concepts, plan activities, and solve problems. This mode of thought also incorporates self-discipline through the process of introspection and decision making.

1. How do you find yourself introspecting and self-analyzing? Perhaps you have been called "introverted" and are even prone to ruminate on certain issues. Look at these words to help you understand what the essential skill of introspection looks and feels like: wistful, meditative, contemplative, thoughtful, deliberative, subjective, lost in thought, pensive, self-examining, speculative, tending to ruminate, brooding, cogitative, absorbed, pondering, preoccupied, engrossed, reflective, buried in thought. Now, please describe as fully as you can what this

looks like in your life on a day-to-day basis, including how often you think like this. Rate yourself in your description. For example, "I tend to ruminate a lot on things, probably more than half of each day or 75 percent of the day. I find something I have read or heard leads to my thinking through all kinds of scenarios in my mind and I get very pensive. I am often lost in thought." Or maybe you will say something like, "I only get speculative when I have to complete a task and have to work out how to do it, but I don't spend a lot of time getting self-analytical, maybe only an hour or less a day." The more descriptive you are, the better.

_____

_____

_____

_____

2. Our minds (remember, the mind is separate from the brain) are designed in such a way that we are able to stand outside ourselves and observe our range of emotions as we deal with the events and circumstances of the day. How aware are you of your feelings as the day unfolds? Do you have a sense of watching yourself go from happy to sad, irritated, frustrated, or plain angry, or happy, then ecstatic with excitement, then bored and depressed, and so on in response to the events and circumstances of the day? Please describe below, as fully as you can, what this looks like in your life on a day-to-day basis, including how often you think like this. For example, "I am only aware of my emotions when I get worked up or excited about something, so only when it is an extreme situation and often only when someone points it out." Or, "I am aware of how I feel most of the time and can control

my emotions quite well." The more descriptive you are the better.

_____

_____

_____

_____

_____

3. As human beings we are designed to stand outside ourselves and observe our own thinking. This means you are able to watch yourself as if you were watching a reality show on TV, reading a book, or having a conversation. If you intentionally focus on this process, you can see your thoughts formulating; you can analyze them in a distant, objective manner; you feel like you are catching those thoughts and "holding them in your hands" to inspect them. Think about this and describe how you do this, in as much detail as possible.

_____

_____

_____

_____

_____

4. How do you control your emotions? Do you let them run rampant or suppress them? Do you analyze your emotional state? Be as honest as you can.

_____

_____

_____

_____

_____

5. How do you control your thoughts? Do you let them run rampant or suppress them? Do you deliberately analyze your thoughts throughout the day?

_____

_____

_____

_____

_____

_____

6. What do you do when you feel deeply about something? Do you bottle it up? Ruminate about it? Write about it? Talk about it and how it makes you feel? Describe in as much detail as possible.

_____

_____

_____

_____

_____

_____

7. Are you motivated to identify goals for yourself and pursue them? If yes, describe the what, how, when, and why. If no, describe the what, how, when, and why.

_____

_____

_____

_____

_____

_____

8. Do you work or study well on your own? If yes, describe the what, how, when, and why. If no, describe the what, how, when, and why.

_____

_____

_____

_____

_____

9. Are you curious about the meaning of life? About the philosophies behind your beliefs and the beliefs of others? Are you curious about your own and others' cultural mindsets? If yes, describe the what, how, when, and why. If no, describe the what, how, when, and why.

_____

_____

_____

_____

_____

10. Are you interested in working on your intellectual growth and development? If yes, describe the what, how, when, and why. If no, describe the what, how, when, and why.

_____

_____

_____

_____

_____

11. Do you attempt to understand your inner experiences? Do you often spend time thinking about your thinking? If yes, describe the what, how, when, and why. If no, describe the what, how, when, and why.

_____

_____

_____

_____

_____

12. Do you like to empower others? If yes, describe the what, how, when, and why. If no, describe the what, how, when, and why.

_____

_____

_____

_____

13. Do you like to encourage others? If someone seems "under the weather," do you reach out to them? If yes, describe the what, how, when, and why. If no, describe the what, how, when, and why.

_____

_____

_____

_____

_____

14. Do you enjoy alone time? Do you enjoy being alone more than social activities? If yes, describe the what, how, when, and why. If no, describe the what, how, when, and why.

_____

_____

_____

_____

_____

_____

15. Do you enjoy spending time deliberately thinking things through? Do you enjoy the process of working issues out in your mind? Or, to put it another way, do you enjoy switching off the external world and focusing on the internal thoughts of your mind? If yes, describe the what, how, when, and why. If no, describe the what, how, when, and why.

_____

_____

_____

_____

_____

_____

16. Are you able to express how you feel in detail? If yes, describe the what, how, when, and why. If no, describe the what, how, when, and why.

_____

_____

_____

_____

_____

17. Do you believe you are well balanced in terms of spirit, mind, and body health? If yes, describe the what, how, when, and why. If no, describe the what, how, when, and why.

_____

_____

_____

_____

_____

_____

18. Do you like to work independently? If yes, describe the what, how, when, and why. If no, describe the what, how, when, and why.

_____

_____

_____

_____

_____

_____

19. Are you organized? Do you like to arrange your work according to a particular system? If yes, describe the what, how, when, and why. If no, describe the what, how, when, and why.

_____

_____

_____

_____

_____

_____

20. Do you enjoy your own company? If yes, describe the what, how, when, and why. If no, describe the what, how, when, and why.

_____

_____

_____

_____

_____

_____

21. Do you often find yourself contemplating the meaning of life and life's deepest issues? If yes, describe the what, how, when, and why. If no, describe the what, how, when, and why.

_____

_____

_____

_____

_____

_____

22. Do you like to philosophize? How so? If yes, describe the what, how, when, and why. If no, describe the what, how, when, and why. Are you sure?

_____

_____

_____

_____

_____

23. Do you often find yourself contemplating the purpose of life? The purpose of your life? Do you feel hope or hopelessness

the majority of the time? If yes, describe the what, how, when, and why. If no, describe the what, how, when, and why.

_____

_____

_____

_____

_____

24. Is it very important for you to think about and understand your inner experiences? Does it disturb you if you don't? If yes, describe the what, how, when, and why. If no, describe the what, how, when, and why.

_____

_____

_____

_____

_____

25. Do you often find yourself thinking about the nature of humanity, of different people and cultures, and the rights of humankind? If yes, describe the what, how, when, and why. If no, describe the what, how, when, and why. What do you feel passionately about?

_____

_____

_____

_____

_____

26. Are you determined to make a difference in life? What kind of difference? If yes, describe the what, how, when, and why.

If no, describe the what, how, when, and why. Once again, are you sure? Dig deep to answer this.

_____

_____

_____

_____

_____

_____

_____

27. Do you only offer advice if asked? If yes, describe the what, how, when, and why. If no, describe the what, how, when, and why. When do you usually offer advice?

_____

_____

_____

_____

_____

_____

_____

28. Do you find it very easy to listen to another person's issue and advise them? If yes, describe the what, how, when, and why. If no, describe the what, how, when, and why.

_____

_____

_____

_____

_____

_____

_____

29. Do you feel that it is inappropriate to discuss your opinions with other people? If yes, describe the what, how, when, and why. If no, describe the what, how, when, and why.

_____

_____

_____

_____

_____

_____

30. Do you try to gain insight into current social, cultural, political, and economic issues? Do you keep up with current affairs? Do they interest you? How much time do you spend doing this? If yes, describe the what, how, when, and why. If no, describe the what, how, when, and why.

_____

_____

_____

_____

_____

31. Do you enjoy receiving feedback on your efforts? If yes, describe the what, how, when, and why. If no, describe the what, how, when, and why.

_____

_____

_____

_____

_____

32. Do you often have opinions that set you apart from more popular modes of thought? If yes, describe the what, how, when, and why. If no, describe the what, how, when, and why.

_____

_____

_____

_____

_____

33. Do you prefer self-directed learning, such as distance learning? If yes, describe the kind of learning environment you prefer—the what, how, when, and why. If no, describe the what, how, when, and why. What do you prefer?

_____

_____

_____

_____

_____

34. Do you consider yourself to have good self-esteem? Do you value yourself? What does this actually mean to you? If yes, describe the what, how, when, and why of how you value yourself. If no, describe the what, how, when, and why. What needs to change?

_____

_____

_____

_____

_____

Now take all your answers and in the space below write a summary of how you seem to be using the Intrapersonal Module. You might find that in this process you want to change or add to your answers—go ahead, this is a normal and good self-regulatory process. Once you have done the summary, look it over to see if you agree with what you have written and if you can add more. Edit the summary, asking yourself the following questions: *Is this me? Do I really think this way? Is this a people-pleasing statement or am I being true to me?* Don't be too hard on yourself. Add a few lines on how you can use the Intrapersonal Module to improve how you communicate and connect with people and to improve how you function in general. After all, you are you—but you get better at being you all the time.

_____

_____

_____

_____

_____

_____

_____

_____

_____

_____

Module 2: Interpersonal Metacognitive Module—Thinking, Feeling, Choosing

The next module is interpersonal mode of thought. This appears to be directly behind the Intrapersonal Metacognitive Module in terms of our current understanding of brain organization. The Interpersonal Metacognitive Module incorporates the computational capacities of communication; talking, social interaction, listening, and sharing; building relationships; and giving and receiving love, bonding, and influencing. Interpersonal thinking gives us the ability to understand and work with people and sensitivity to and empathy to others, particularly for their moods, desires, motivations, feelings, and experiences. It enables us to respond appropriately to others by reading their moods and putting ourselves in their shoes or warns us when people are untrustworthy through inconsistencies in their words or actions. It also refers to good managerial and mediating skills and the ability to motivate, lead, guide, and counsel others.

1. Are you particularly sensitive to the needs of others? Can you read others? Do you enjoy doing this? If yes, describe the what, how, when, and why in detail. If no, describe the what, how, when, and why.

_____

_____

_____

_____

_____

_____

2. Do you find yourself watching people and their reactions? Does this interest you? If yes, describe the what, how, when, and why. If no, describe the what, how, when, and why. What does grab your interest about people?

_____

_____

_____

_____

_____

_____

3. Do you consider yourself to be an empathetic person? Do you find it easy to tune in to others? If yes, describe the what,

how, when, and why. If no, how would you describe your version of empathy? Describe the what, how, when, and why.

_____

_____

_____

_____

_____

4. Do you find it easy to put yourself in another person's shoes—that is, feel and experience what another person is experiencing? Does it come naturally? Or can you do it but is it effortful? If yes, describe the what, how, when, and why. If no, describe the what, how, when, and why.

_____

_____

_____

_____

_____

5. Do you feel you respond appropriately to others? If yes, describe the what, how, when, and why. If no, describe the what, how, when, and why. Do you feel this is a problem? Or are you comfortable with it?

_____

_____

_____

_____

_____

6. Do you find it easy to encourage and motivate other people? If yes, describe the what, how, when, and why. If no, describe the what, how, when, and why.

_____

_____

_____

_____

_____

_____

7. Do you often find yourself in a situation where you are counseling and giving advice to other people? Do you find people open up to you easily? If yes, describe the what, how, when, and why. If no, describe the what, how, when, and why.

_____

_____

_____

_____

_____

_____

8. Are you good at networking (professionally or socially)? If yes, describe the what, how, when, and why. If no, describe the what, how, when, and why.

_____

_____

_____

_____

_____

_____

9. Do you like people around you all the time? Or most of the time? If yes, describe the what, how, when, and why. If no, describe the what, how, when, and why.

_____

_____

_____

_____

_____

_____

_____

10. Do you need to ask a lot of questions as you learn new information? If yes, describe the what, how, when, and why. If no, describe the what, how, when, and why.

_____

_____

_____

_____

_____

_____

11. For the most part, do you remember what people say? If yes, describe the what, how, when, and why. If no, describe the what, how, when, and why.

_____

_____

_____

_____

_____

12. Do you often quote other people? If yes, describe the what, how, when, and why. If no, describe the what, how, when, and why.

_____

_____

_____

_____

_____

_____

13. Do you negotiate with other people in business or social settings? If yes, describe the what, how, when, and why. If no, describe the what, how, when, and why.

_____

_____

_____

_____

_____

14. Do you often find yourself in situations where you are the peacemaker? If yes, describe the what, how, when, and why. If no, describe the what, how, when, and why.

_____

_____

_____

_____

_____

15. Can you teach and explain things to other people in a way that makes information easy to understand? If yes, describe

the what, how, when, and why. If no, describe the what, how, when, and why.

_____

_____

_____

_____

_____

_____

16. Do you notice if people understand and receive the new information you are discussing? Can you self-regulate to help people understand you? If yes, describe the what, how, when, and why. If no, describe the what, how, when, and why.

_____

_____

_____

_____

_____

_____

17. Do you revise what you are teaching and saying so others will understand you? Do you do this specifically if you realize they are not understanding you? Or do you carry on talking, oblivious to their reactions? If yes, describe the what, how, when, and why. If no, describe the what, how, when, and why.

_____

_____

_____

_____

_____

_____

18. Are you generally patient with people? If yes, describe the what, how, when, and why. If no, describe the what, how, when, and why.

_____

_____

_____

_____

_____

_____

19. Do you enjoy bouncing ideas off other people? If yes, describe the what, how, when, and why. If no, describe the what, how, when, and why.

_____

_____

_____

_____

_____

_____

20. Do you find that you need to talk out loud to other people as you are working out something in your mind? If yes, describe the what, how, when, and why. If no, describe the what, how, when, and why.

_____

_____

_____

_____

_____

_____

21. Do you form friendships easily? If yes, describe the what, how, when, and why. If no, describe the what, how, when, and why.

_____

_____

_____

_____

_____

_____

22. Do you keep good friendships for many years? If yes, describe the what, how, when, and why. If no, describe the what, how, when, and why.

_____

_____

_____

_____

_____

_____

23. Do you recognize that there are many different ways of communicating with other people? If yes, describe the what, how, when, and why. If no, describe the what, how, when, and why.

_____

_____

_____

_____

_____

_____

24. Do you make use of these different ways of communicating? If yes, describe the what, how, when, and why. If no, describe the what, how, when, and why.

_____

_____

_____

_____

_____

_____

25. Do you find it easy to tune in to and meet the needs of others by giving advice or whatever it is that they need? If yes, describe the what, how, when, and why. If no, describe the what, how, when, and why.

_____

_____

_____

_____

_____

_____

26. Are you able to perceive the thoughts and feelings of others? If yes, describe the what, how, when, and why. If no, describe the what, how, when, and why.

_____

_____

_____

_____

_____

27. Do you find it easy to counsel and guide people? If yes, describe the what, how, when, and why. If no, describe the what, how, when, and why.

_____

_____

_____

_____

_____

_____

_____

28. Do people tend to come to you for counsel and advice? If yes, describe the what, how, when, and why. If no, describe the what, how, when, and why.

_____

_____

_____

_____

_____

_____

29. Do you like to influence the opinions and/or actions of others? If yes, describe the what, how, when, and why. If no, describe the what, how, when, and why.

_____

_____

_____

_____

_____

30. Do you enjoy participating in collaborative efforts, such as group projects? If yes, describe the what, how, when, and why. If no, describe the what, how, when, and why.

_____

_____

_____

_____

_____

_____

31. Are you able to assume various roles in a group, from the follower to the leader? If yes, describe the what, how, when, and why. If no, describe the what, how, when, and why.

_____

_____

_____

_____

_____

_____

32. Do you prefer to lead rather than follow in a group? If yes, describe the what, how, when, and why. If no, describe the what, how, when, and why.

_____

_____

_____

_____

_____

_____

33. Are you quick to understand the verbal and nonverbal communication of a group or of a person? If yes, describe the

what, how, when, and why. If no, describe the what, how, when, and why.

_____

_____

_____

_____

_____

_____

34. Do you tend to get on well with your parents, siblings, extended family, and friends? If yes, describe the what, how, when, and why. If no, describe the what, how, when, and why.

_____

_____

_____

_____

_____

_____

35. Do you communicate effectively, both on a nonverbal and verbal level? If yes, describe the what, how, when, and why. If no, describe the what, how, when, and why.

_____

_____

_____

_____

_____

_____

36. Can you easily adapt your behavior and conversation to different groups and environments? If yes, describe the what,

how, when, and why. If no, describe the what, how, when, and why.

_____

_____

_____

_____

_____

_____

_____

37. Can you easily adapt your opinions, communication, or behavior based on the feedback of other people? If yes, describe the what, how, when, and why. If no, describe the what, how, when, and why.

_____

_____

_____

_____

_____

_____

_____

38. Are you good at mediating? If yes, describe the what, how, when, and why. If no, describe the what, how, when, and why.

_____

_____

_____

_____

_____

_____

_____

39. Do you enjoy mentoring and/or coaching people? If yes, describe the what, how, when, and why. If no, describe the what, how, when, and why.

_____

_____

_____

_____

_____

_____

40. Are you good at organizing others into a group, such as organizing and completing a group project? If yes, describe the what, how, when, and why. If no, describe the what, how, when, and why.

_____

_____

_____

_____

_____

41. Do you find it easy to work with people from diverse age groups and backgrounds? If yes, describe the what, how, when, and why. If no, describe the what, how, when, and why.

_____

_____

_____

_____

_____

42. Are you a good leader and visionary? If yes, describe the what, how, when, and why. If no, describe the what, how, when, and why.

_____

_____

_____

_____

_____

_____

43. Are you good at managing people, specifically in terms of action planning and getting things done? If yes, describe the what, how, when, and why. If no, describe the what, how, when, and why.

_____

_____

_____

_____

_____

_____

44. Are you good at arguing a point? If yes, describe the what, how, when, and why. If no, describe the what, how, when, and why.

_____

_____

_____

_____

_____

_____

45. Do you thrive on attention? If yes, describe the what, how, when, and why. If no, describe the what, how, when, and why.

_____

_____

_____

_____

_____

_____

_____

_____

46. Do you like to be needed? If yes, describe the what, how, when, and why. If no, describe the what, how, when, and why.

_____

_____

_____

_____

_____

47. Are you good at managing conflict? If yes, describe the what, how, when, and why. If no, describe the what, how, when, and why.

_____

_____

_____

_____

_____

_____

_____

48. Are you a good solution-finder? If yes, describe the what, how, when, and why. If no, describe the what, how, when, and why.

_____

_____

_____

_____

_____

49. Do you like to discuss many perspectives on a variety of topics? If yes, describe the what, how, when, and why. If no, describe the what, how, when, and why.

_____

_____

_____

_____

_____

50. Do you enjoy listening to many perspectives on specific topics? If yes, describe the what, how, when, and why. If no, describe the what, how, when, and why.

_____

_____

_____

_____

_____

Now take all your answers and in the space below write a summary of how you seem to be using the Interpersonal Module. You might find that in this process you want to change or add to your answers. Go ahead, this is a normal self-regulatory process. Once you have done the summary, look it over to see if you agree with what you have written and if you can add more. Edit the summary, asking yourself the following questions: *Is this me? Do I really think this way? Is this a people-pleasing statement or am I being true to me?* Don't be too hard on yourself. Add a few lines on how you can use the Interpersonal Module to improve how you communicate and connect with people and to improve how you function in general. After all, you are you—but you get better at being you all the time.

———————————————————————————

———————————————————————————

———————————————————————————

———————————————————————————

———————————————————————————

———————————————————————————

———————————————————————————

———————————————————————————

———————————————————————————

Module 3: Linguistic Metacognitive Module—Thinking, Feeling, Choosing

The Linguistic Metacognitive Module deals with the raw computational capacities of language—written, expressed, and comprehended language. This module appears to be in the middle of the brain. It also deals with sensitivity to the meanings of words, sounds, rhythms, and different uses of language. This sensitivity is expressed in different ways, such as being articulate or having the ability to think in words and use words effectively when you speak and/or write, which involves arguing, persuading, love of reading, and books. Thus the linguistic mode of thought responds to words—spoken, written, expressed, or read.

The domains that make up language, its structure and uses, include:

Semantics: the meanings or connotations of words.

Phonology: the sounds of words and their interactions with each other.

Syntax: the rules governing the order in which words are used to create understandable sentences. One example is that a sentence must always have a verb.

Pragmatics: how language can be used to communicate effectively.

These are all present in the Linguistic Metacognitive Module.

1. Do you love words and their meanings? If yes, describe the what, how, when, and why. If no, describe the what, how, when, and why.

_____

_____

_____

_____

_____

2. Do you often find yourself looking up information online or in a book? If yes, describe the what, how, when, and why. If no, describe the what, how, when, and why.

_____

_____

_____

_____

_____

3. Do you prefer to email or text rather than speak on the phone? If yes, describe the what, how, when, and why. If no, describe the what, how, when, and why.

_____

_____

_____

_____

_____

_____

4. Do you know how to use a variety of language to communicate effectively? That is, are you eloquent? If yes, describe the what, how, when, and why. If no, describe the what, how, when, and why.

_____

_____

_____

_____

_____

_____

5. Do you often find that you need to express yourself through speaking? If yes, describe the what, how, when, and why. If no, describe the what, how, when, and why.

_____

_____

_____

_____

_____

_____

6. Do you often find that you need to express yourself through writing? If yes, describe the what, how, when, and why. If no, describe the what, how, when, and why.

_____

_____

_____

_____

_____

_____

_____

7. Do you often find that you need to express yourself through both speaking and writing? If yes, describe the what, how, when, and why. If no, describe the what, how, when, and why.

_____

_____

_____

_____

_____

_____

_____

8. Do you enjoy debating? If yes, describe the what, how, when, and why. If no, describe the what, how, when, and why.

_____

_____

_____

_____

_____

9. Do you like to persuade people—that is, change their opinions? If yes, describe the what, how, when, and why. If no, describe the what, how, when, and why.

_____

_____

_____

_____

_____

_____

10. Do you like to instruct people? If yes, describe the what, how, when, and why. If no, describe the what, how, when, and why.

_____

_____

_____

_____

_____

_____

11. Do you like to entertain people with words, such as puns and jokes? If yes, describe the what, how, when, and why. If no, describe the what, how, when, and why.

_____

_____

_____

_____

_____

_____

12. Do you like reading? If yes, describe the what, how, when, and why. If no, describe the what, how, when, and why.

_____

_____

_____

_____

_____

13. Do you read a lot? If yes, describe the what, how, when, and why. If no, describe the what, how, when, and why.

_____

_____

_____

_____

_____

14. Do you read a lot of different types of literature? What types? If yes, describe the what, how, when, and why. If no, describe the what, how, when, and why.

_____

_____

_____

_____

_____

15. Do you like writing? If yes, describe the what, how, when, and why. If no, describe the what, how, when, and why.

_____

_____

_____

_____

_____

16. Do you like telling stories? If yes, describe the what, how, when, and why. If no, describe the what, how, when, and why.

_____

_____

_____

_____

_____

_____

17. Do you like writing stories? If yes, describe the what, how, when, and why. If no, describe the what, how, when, and why.

_____

_____

_____

_____

_____

_____

18. Do you have a good general knowledge? If yes, describe the what, how, when, and why. If no, describe the what, how, when, and why.

_____

_____

_____

_____

_____

_____

_____

19. Do you ask a lot of questions? Why? If yes, describe the what, how, when, and why. If no, describe the what, how, when, and why.

_____

_____

_____

_____

_____

_____

20. Do you ask and answer your own questions? If yes, describe the what, how, when, and why. If no, describe the what, how, when, and why.

_____

_____

_____

_____

_____

_____

21. Do you like using stories to help you explain something? If yes, describe the what, how, when, and why. If no, describe the what, how, when, and why.

_____

_____

_____

_____

_____

_____

22. Do you like debating during discussions? That is, do you often find yourself starting a debate during a discussion? If

yes, describe the what, how, when, and why. If no, describe the what, how, when, and why.

_____

_____

_____

_____

_____

_____

23. Do you enjoy writing poems, stories, legends, papers, and/or articles? Are there specific kinds of writing you particularly enjoy? If yes, describe the what, how, when, and why. If no, describe the what, how, when, and why.

_____

_____

_____

_____

_____

_____

24. Would you like to write a play or poem? If yes, describe the what, how, when, and why. If no, describe the what, how, when, and why.

_____

_____

_____

_____

_____

25. Do you enjoy describing events in detail? If yes, describe the what, how, when, and why. If no, describe the what, how, when, and why.

_____

_____

_____

_____

_____

26. Do you enjoy giving presentations? If yes, describe the what, how, when, and why. If no, describe the what, how, when, and why.

_____

_____

_____

_____

_____

27. Do you enjoy leading or guiding discussions? If yes, describe the what, how, when, and why. If no, describe the what, how, when, and why.

_____

_____

_____

_____

_____

28. Do you enjoy writing and/or typing journal entries? Or keeping notes on things that interest you or that you are thinking

about? If yes, describe the what, how, when, and why. If no, describe the what, how, when, and why.

_____

_____

_____

_____

_____

_____

29. Would you like to create a talk show program for radio, a podcast, or TV? If yes, describe the what, how, when, and why. If no, describe the what, how, when, and why.

_____

_____

_____

_____

30. Do you enjoy writing newsletters and/or blogs? If yes, describe the what, how, when, and why. If no, describe the what, how, when, and why.

_____

_____

_____

_____

_____

31. Do you love using tools such as encyclopedias, concordances, and thesauruses to expand your linguistic knowledge? If yes,

describe the what, how, when, and why. If no, describe the what, how, when, and why.

_____

_____

_____

_____

_____

_____

32. Do you like inventing slogans or sayings? Do you play with words and sayings? If yes, describe the what, how, when, and why. If no, describe the what, how, when, and why.

_____

_____

_____

_____

_____

_____

33. Do you like or would you enjoy conducting an interview? If yes, describe the what, how, when, and why. If no, describe the what, how, when, and why.

_____

_____

_____

_____

_____

_____

34. Do you use email and text a lot? Or do you write letters? Is it your preferred form of communication? If yes, describe

the what, how, when, and why. If no, describe the what, how, when, and why.

_____

_____

_____

_____

_____

_____

35. Do you enjoy, or would you enjoy, writing a novel or long story? If yes, describe the what, how, when, and why. If no, describe the what, how, when, and why.

_____

_____

_____

_____

_____

_____

36. Do you always have something to say and enjoy talking? If yes, describe the what, how, when, and why. If no, describe the what, how, when, and why.

_____

_____

_____

_____

_____

_____

37. Are books and reading material very important to you? If yes, describe the what, how, when, and why. If no, describe the what, how, when, and why.

_____

_____

_____

_____

_____

38. Do you hear words in your head before you speak, read, or write? If yes, describe the what, how, when, and why. If no, describe what happens, if anything, before you speak, read, or write. What, how, when, and why?

_____

_____

_____

_____

_____

39. Do you hear words in your head as you listen to someone or when you are watching something? For example, if you think of a cat, do you envision an actual cat or see the word *cat*? If yes, describe the what, how, when, and why. If no, describe what happens when you listen to someone. Describe the what, how, when, and why.

_____

_____

_____

_____

_____

40. Would you rather listen to the radio, an audiobook, or something similar than watch TV? If yes, describe the what, how, when, and why. If no, describe the what, how, when, and why.

_____

_____

_____

_____

_____

_____

41. Do you enjoy games like Scrabble and Trivial Pursuit? If yes, describe the what, how, when, and why. If no, describe the what, how, when, and why.

_____

_____

_____

_____

_____

42. Do you enjoy entertaining yourself and others with tongue twisters, puns, and nonsense rhymes? If yes, describe the what, how, when, and why. If no, describe the what, how, when, and why.

_____

_____

_____

_____

_____

_____

43. Do you like to use complex vocabulary and long sentence structures? If yes, describe the what, how, when, and why. If no, describe the what, how, when, and why.

_____

_____

_____

_____

_____

44. When you are in a car, do you pay more attention to signs, billboards, and anything written than the scenery? Or both? If you pay more attention to the written things, describe the what, how, when, and why. If no, describe the what, how, when, and why.

_____

_____

_____

_____

_____

45. Do you prefer subjects such as history, literature, integrated studies, and languages to math, science, and other technical studies? If yes, describe the what, how, when, and why. If no, describe the what, how, when, and why.

_____

_____

_____

_____

_____

46. In a conversation, do you refer a lot to what you have read or heard? If yes, describe the what, how, when, and why. If no, describe the what, how, when, and why.

47. Do you speak well? That is, do you find it easy to discuss topics or issues clearly and intelligently? If yes, describe the what, how, when, and why. If no, describe the what, how, when, and why.

48. Do you ask a lot of questions while learning new information in any setting—classroom, church, and so forth? If yes, describe the what, how, when, and why. If no, describe the what, how, when, and why.

49. Do you enjoy learning about grammar? If yes, describe the what, how, when, and why. If no, describe the what, how, when, and why.

_____

_____

_____

_____

_____

_____

50. Do you enjoy learning and using new vocabulary? If yes, describe the what, how, when, and why. If no, describe the what, how, when, and why.

_____

_____

_____

_____

_____

_____

Now take all your answers and in the space below write a summary of how you seem to be using the linguistic module. You might find that in this process you want to change or add to your answers. Go ahead, this is a normal self-regulatory process. Once you have done the summary, look it over to see if you agree with what you have written and if you can add more. Edit the summary, asking yourself the following questions: _Is this me? Do I really think this way? Is this a people-pleasing statement or am I being true to me?_ Don't be too hard on yourself. Add a few lines on how you can use the Linguistic Module to improve how you communicate and connect with people and to improve how you function in general. After all, you are you—but you get better at being you all the time.

Module 4: Logical/Mathematical Metacognitive Module— Thinking, Feeling, Choosing

Next up is the Logical/Mathematical Metacognitive Module, which deals with scientific reasoning, logic, and analysis. This type of thinking involves the raw computational capacities of understanding the underlying principles of a connecting system; recognizing logical and numerical patterns; handling long chains of reasoning in a precise manner; manipulating words, numbers, quantities, and operations; seeing the meaning in things; calculating; quantifying; reasoning things out; imagining; theorizing; pondering on paradoxes and inconsistencies; and recognizing and solving problems.

This mode of thought also includes but is not exclusively limited to the ability to strategize, mentally calculate, and process the logic of life and/or logical problems and equations, such as the types of problems most often found on multiple-choice and other standardized tests.

1. God made everything and science is a description of that everything. Science is how we understand how we as humans and all of God's creation works. Based on this conceptualization, are there certain areas of science that interest you? For example: the earth sciences, neuroscience, medical science, engineering science, the science of art, computer science, technological science, geology, music, teaching, liberal arts, philosophy, and so on. If yes, describe the what, how, when, and why. If no, describe the what, how, when, and why.

---

2. Does how the universe and consciousness and life work interest you? If yes, describe the what, how, when, and why. If no, describe the what, how, when, and why.

---

3. Do you like to understand the underlying principles of how things work? This could be anything from biology to bugs to machines to cooking—anything. If yes, describe the what,

how, when, and why. If no, describe the what, how, when, and why.

_____

_____

_____

_____

_____

_____

_____

4. Do you like things to be logical? Do you enjoy seeing logical patterns in the world around you? If yes, describe the what, how, when, and why. If no, describe the what, how, when, and why.

_____

_____

_____

_____

_____

5. Do you like asking questions related specifically to the "how" nature of reality? If yes, describe the what, how, when, and why. If no, describe the what, how, when, and why.

_____

_____

_____

_____

_____

6. Do you see order and meaning in everyday life, including everyday objects? If yes, describe the what, how, when, and why. If no, describe the what, how, when, and why.

_____

_____

_____

_____

_____

_____

7. Do things have to make sense to you? Is it distressing when you cannot logically understand something? If yes, describe the what, how, when, and why. If no, describe the what, how, when, and why.

_____

_____

_____

_____

_____

_____

8. Do you see numerical patterns as you go about everyday life? If yes, describe the what, how, when, and why. If no, describe the what, how, when, and why.

_____

_____

_____

_____

_____

9. Do you need long chains of reasoning to make sense of things? This can be about anything to do with living your life. If yes,

describe the what, how, when, and why. If no, describe the what, how, when, and why.

_____

_____

_____

_____

_____

_____

10. Do you need short or long chains of reasoning in order to make sense of things? If yes, describe the what, how, when, and why. If no, describe the what, how, when, and why.

_____

_____

_____

_____

_____

_____

11. Are you good at mathematical and/or statistical equations? If yes, describe the what, how, when, and why. If no, describe the what, how, when, and why.

_____

_____

_____

_____

_____

_____

12. Are you good with geometrical thinking? If yes, describe the what, how, when, and why. If no, describe the what, how, when, and why.

_____

_____

_____

_____

_____

_____

13. Are you good at time management? If yes, describe the what, how, when, and why. If no, describe the what, how, when, and why.

_____

_____

_____

_____

_____

_____

14. Do you generally find scientific concepts easy to understand? If yes, describe the what, how, when, and why. If no, describe the what, how, when, and why.

_____

_____

_____

_____

_____

_____

15. Can you shift back and forth easily between the big picture and the details of a situation, problem, or topic? If yes,

describe the what, how, when, and why. If no, describe the what, how, when, and why.

_____

_____

_____

_____

_____

_____

16. Do you mull things over in different ways until they make sense? If yes, describe the what, how, when, and why. If no, describe the what, how, when, and why.

_____

_____

_____

_____

_____

_____

17. Is your thinking generally disciplined? If yes, describe the what, how, when, and why. If no, describe the what, how, when, and why.

_____

_____

_____

_____

_____

_____

18. Do you enjoy calculating? If yes, describe the what, how, when, and why. If no, describe the what, how, when, and why.

_____

_____

_____

_____

_____

_____

19. Do you like quantifying? If yes, describe the what, how, when, and why. If no, describe the what, how, when, and why.

_____

_____

_____

_____

_____

_____

20. Do you want to know what is coming up next (such as during your day-to-day life or in a movie or book)? If yes, describe the what, how, when, and why. If no, describe the what, how, when, and why.

_____

_____

_____

_____

_____

_____

21. Do mathematical, statistical, and/or physics formulas speak to you? If yes, describe the what, how, when, and why. If no, describe the what, how, when, and why.

_____

_____

_____

_____

_____

_____

22. Do you see meaning in numbers? If yes, describe the what, how, when, and why. If no, describe the what, how, when, and why.

_____

_____

_____

_____

_____

_____

23. Do you like designing and conducting experiments? If yes, describe the what, how, when, and why. If no, describe the what, how, when, and why.

_____

_____

_____

_____

_____

24. Do you like creating strategy games like treasure hunts? If yes, describe the what, how, when, and why. If no, describe the what, how, when, and why.

_____

_____

_____

_____

_____

_____

_____

25. Do you like organizing your time? If yes, describe the what, how, when, and why. If no, describe the what, how, when, and why.

_____

_____

_____

_____

_____

_____

26. Do you enjoy interpreting data? If yes, describe the what, how, when, and why. If no, describe the what, how, when, and why.

_____

_____

_____

_____

_____

27. Do you enjoy hypothesizing and asking "What if?" If yes, describe the what, how, when, and why. If no, describe the what, how, when, and why.

_____

_____

_____

_____

_____

_____

28. Do you enjoy categorizing facts and information? If yes, describe the what, how, when, and why. If no, describe the what, how, when, and why.

_____

_____

_____

_____

_____

_____

29. Do you enjoy describing things in terms of symmetry and balance? If yes, describe the what, how, when, and why. If no, describe the what, how, when, and why.

_____

_____

_____

_____

_____

_____

30. Can you generally see the pros and cons of a situation? If yes, describe the what, how, when, and why. If no, describe the what, how, when, and why.

_____

_____

_____

_____

_____

_____

31. Do you like planning? If yes, describe the what, how, when, and why. If no, describe the what, how, when, and why.

_____

_____

_____

_____

_____

32. Do you like reasoning things out? If yes, describe the what, how, when, and why. If no, describe the what, how, when, and why.

_____

_____

_____

_____

_____

33. Do you like playing with numbers and doing complex mathematical operations? If yes, describe the what, how, when, and why. If no, describe the what, how, when, and why.

_____

_____

_____

_____

_____

_____

34. Do you like using technology? Do you enjoy trying to understand the technology you use? If yes, describe the what, how, when, and why. If no, describe the what, how, when, and why.

_____

_____

_____

_____

_____

_____

35. Can you easily compute numbers in your head? If yes, describe the what, how, when, and why. If no, describe the what, how, when, and why.

_____

_____

_____

_____

_____

_____

36. Are (or were) your favorite school subjects either the sciences, math, or computer science? If yes, describe the what, how, when, and why. If no, describe the what, how, when, and why.

_____

_____

_____

_____

_____

_____

37. Do you enjoy logical games such as chess and cards? If yes, describe the what, how, when, and why. If no, describe the what, how, when, and why.

_____

_____

_____

_____

_____

_____

38. Do you enjoy strategic computer or video games? If yes, describe the what, how, when, and why. If no, describe the what, how, when, and why.

_____

_____

_____

_____

_____

_____

39. Do you enjoy brainteasers? If yes, describe the what, how, when, and why. If no, describe the what, how, when, and why.

_____

_____

_____

_____

_____

_____

_____

40. Do you enjoy problem solving? If yes, describe the what, how, when, and why. If no, describe the what, how, when, and why.

_____

_____

_____

_____

_____

_____

41. Do you enjoy "what-if" games? If yes, describe the what, how, when, and why. If no, describe the what, how, when, and why.

_____

_____

_____

_____

_____

_____

42. Does your mind search for patterns, regularities, and logical sequences? If yes, describe the what, how, when, and why. If no, describe the what, how, when, and why.

_____

_____

_____

_____

_____

_____

43. Do new developments in science, technology, and the natural sciences interest and excite you? If yes, describe the what, how, when, and why. If no, describe the what, how, when, and why.

_____

_____

_____

_____

_____

_____

44. Do you like rational explanations for everything? If yes, describe the what, how, when, and why. If no, describe the what, how, when, and why.

_____

_____

_____

_____

_____

_____

45. Do you often think in abstract (wordless, imageless) concepts? If yes, describe the what, how, when, and why. If no, describe the what, how, when, and why.

_____

_____

_____

_____

_____

_____

46. Do you understand and desire order? If yes, describe the what, how, when, and why. If no, describe the what, how, when, and why.

_____

_____

_____

_____

_____

_____

47. Are you immediately aware of the logical flaws in a person's argument or conversation? If yes, describe the what, how, when, and why. If no, describe the what, how, when, and why.

_____

_____

_____

_____

_____

48. Do you notice illogical sequences in events or films, conversations, books, memes, and so forth? If yes, describe the what,

how, when, and why. If no, describe the what, how, when, and why.

_____

_____

_____

_____

_____

49. Do you like building puzzles, LEGOs, or anything of this nature? If yes, describe the what, how, when, and why. If no, describe the what, how, when, and why.

_____

_____

_____

_____

_____

50. Do you enjoy questioning, experimenting, exploring? If yes, describe the what, how, when, and why. If no, describe the what, how, when, and why.

_____

_____

_____

_____

_____

Now take all your answers and in the space below write a summary of how you seem to be using the Logical/Mathematical Module. You might find that in this process you want to change or add to your answers. Go ahead, this is a normal self-regulatory process. Once you have done the summary, look it over to see if you agree with what you have written and if you can add more.

Edit the summary, asking yourself the following questions: *Is this me? Do I really think this way? Is this a people-pleasing statement or am I being true to me?* Don't be too hard on yourself. Add a few lines on how you can use the Logical/Mathematical Module to improve how you communicate and connect with people and to improve how you function in general. After all, you are you—but you get better at being you all the time.

_____

_____

_____

_____

_____

_____

_____

_____

_____

Module 5: Kinesthetic Metacognitive Module—Thinking, Feeling, Choosing

The Kinesthetic Metacognitive Module includes movement, somatic sensation, and feeling life, emotions, and experiences through your physical body. Your Kinesthetic mode of thought involves raw computational capacities such as coordination, sense of timing, moving, dexterity, and balance, all of which help you play games like soccer, run around, sit in a chair without falling off, or navigate your way down an aisle. It includes integrating the sensations from inside your body as well.

In essence, this is a very tactile, energetic, multisensory type of capacity that involves the control of body movements, the ability

181

to coordinate yourself, and the capacity to handle objects around you skillfully. It involves the need to touch, feel, and move things around, to maneuver or experience while learning.

1. Do you need to experience and feel in order to understand something? For example, if someone is showing you something on their phone or in a book or magazine, do you need to hold it in your hand to process the information? If yes, describe the what, how, when, and why. If no, describe the what, how, when, and why.

_____

_____

_____

_____

_____

_____

2. Do you envision yourself carrying out a physical move or activity before you do it? In other words, do you imagine the whole sequence and see it before you actually carry it out, especially if it's a complex process? If yes, describe the what, how, when, and why. If no, describe the what, how, when, and why.

_____

_____

_____

_____

_____

_____

3. Do you need to hold a book to read, or see the information on a page, even touching it with your finger, in order to understand what you are reading? If yes, describe the what,

how, when, and why. If no, describe the what, how, when, and why.

_____

_____

_____

_____

_____

_____

4. Do you feel the need to touch, move around, and feel things to help you understand and retain information? If yes, describe the what, how, when, and why. If no, describe the what, how, when, and why.

_____

_____

_____

_____

_____

5. Do you need to experience what you are learning to make it part of you? (For example, if you are finding your way, do you need to be the one driving or following along with your smartphone GPS in order to learn the route, or can you learn the route by being a passenger or following someone?) If yes, describe the what, how, when, and why. If no, describe the what, how, when, and why.

_____

_____

_____

_____

_____

_____

6. Do you like to be shown how to do something rather than being told how to do something? If yes, describe the what, how, when, and why. If no, describe the what, how, when, and why.

_____

_____

_____

_____

_____

7. Do you like to teach yourself how to do new things, such as learning the piano, a new sport, a technique, or knowledge about something? If yes, describe the what, how, when, and why. If no, describe the what, how, when, and why.

_____

_____

_____

_____

_____

8. Would you consider your coordination to be fair, good, or excellent when it comes to sports, specialized activities, and life in general? If yes, describe the what, how, when, and why. If no, describe the what, how, when, and why.

_____

_____

_____

_____

_____

9. Do you consider yourself to have a good sense of timing when it comes to life in general, including sports, playing a musical instrument, or driving? If yes, describe the what,

how, when, and why. If no, describe the what, how, when, and why.

_____

_____

_____

_____

_____

_____

10. Do you find yourself needing to touch, feel, physically manipulate, or otherwise use objects when you are explaining something or trying to understand something? If yes, describe the what, how, when, and why. If no, describe the what, how, when, and why.

_____

_____

_____

_____

_____

_____

11. Do you need to use objects to explain things to people or to get your message across? Do you, for example, grab whatever is in front of you to explain your point? If yes, describe the what, how, when, and why. If no, describe the what, how, when, and why.

_____

_____

_____

_____

_____

12. Do you need to use lots of body movements to explain things or to get your message across? If yes, describe the what, how, when, and why. If no, describe the what, how, when, and why.

_____

_____

_____

_____

_____

13. Do you find yourself wanting to touch and move through a new environment that you haven't been in before? Does this help you process and understand the environment better, almost as though you are imprinting this into your memory? If yes, describe the what, how, when, and why. If no, describe the what, how, when, and why.

_____

_____

_____

_____

_____

14. Do you find yourself picking up objects and trying to figure them out? If yes, describe the what, how, when, and why. If no, describe the what, how, when, and why.

_____

_____

_____

_____

_____

15. Do you find you are always moving your hands, feet, body, or all of these when listening to, understanding, or explaining something? Are you a wiggle worm in the classroom—

someone who gets up and starts pacing while talking, explaining, processing, understanding, or learning? If yes, describe the what, how, when, and why. If no, describe the what, how, when, and why.

_____

_____

_____

_____

_____

16. Do you stretch a lot, especially when sitting still for long periods, as a means of focusing on new information? Do you feel that stretching or moving helps you understand information? If yes, describe the what, how, when, and why. If no, describe the what, how, when, and why.

_____

_____

_____

_____

_____

17. Do you need to get up and move around as you process information? Do you find yourself switching off or battling to concentrate when you don't move around? If yes, describe the what, how, when, and why. If no, describe the what, how, when, and why.

_____

_____

_____

_____

_____

18. Do you yawn a lot while listening and focusing deeply? (Yawning actually "reboots" the brain and helps concentration!) If yes, describe the what, how, when, and why. If no, describe the what, how, when, and why.

_____

_____

_____

_____

_____

_____

19. Do you enjoy role play, drama, charades, and theater? If yes, describe the what, how, when, and why. If no, describe the what, how, when, and why.

_____

_____

_____

_____

_____

_____

20. Do you like games that require movement, talking, and actions? If yes, describe the what, how, when, and why. If no, describe the what, how, when, and why.

_____

_____

_____

_____

_____

21. Do you need to explore an environment through touch and movement before you can settle down? If yes, describe the

what, how, when, and why. If no, describe the what, how, when, and why.

_____

_____

_____

_____

_____

_____

22. Do you like to touch or handle what you need to learn, instead of just looking at something? For example, in a lecture or watching an online learning program, do you find yourself needing to stop and write or draw pictures or get interactive in some other way to learn? If yes, describe the what, how, when, and why. If no, describe the what, how, when, and why.

_____

_____

_____

_____

23. Are you good at arranging furniture in a room and placing ornaments on a table or cushions on a couch? Can you see how to pull things together on a wall, in a room, in any area? Can you walk into a shop and know exactly what pieces to buy? If yes, describe the what, how, when, and why. If no, describe the what, how, when, and why.

_____

_____

_____

_____

24. Do you enjoy field trips, such as visiting a museum or the planetarium? If yes, describe the what, how, when, and why. If no, describe the what, how, when, and why.

_____

_____

_____

_____

_____

_____

25. Do you enjoy participating in plays or musicals? If yes, describe the what, how, when, and why. If no, describe the what, how, when, and why.

_____

_____

_____

_____

_____

26. Do you enjoy physical strategy games like catch, tag, and treasure hunts? If yes, describe the what, how, when, and why. If no, describe the what, how, when, and why.

_____

_____

_____

_____

_____

27. Do you notice when people have not color-coordinated their clothes or styles correctly? If yes, describe the what, how,

when, and why. If no, describe the what, how, when, and why.

_____

_____

_____

_____

_____

_____

28. Do you like symmetry in a room, such as putting two identical potted plants on either side of a couch? What do balance and symmetry mean to you? If yes, describe the what, how, when, and why. If no, describe the what, how, when, and why.

_____

_____

_____

_____

_____

29. Are you aware of your body and how you feel? If yes, describe the what, how, when, and why. If no, describe the what, how, when, and why.

_____

_____

_____

_____

30. Are you aware of and concerned about your physical health? Do you exercise regularly and try to eat a balanced, real-food diet? Are you aware of the dysfunctional food system and

the dangers of processed food and GMOs? If yes, describe the what, how, when, and why. If no, describe the what, how, when, and why.

_____

_____

_____

_____

_____

31. Do you find it easy to participate in a group activity that involves a coordinated sequence of movements, such as aerobics, dancing, Pilates, or soul cycle? If yes, describe the what, how, when, and why. If no, describe the what, how, when, and why.

_____

_____

_____

_____

32. Do you consider yourself to be fair, good, or excellent at activities involving your hands, such as sewing, surgery, painting, and so on? If yes, describe the what, how, when, and why. If no, describe the what, how, when, and why.

_____

_____

_____

_____

33. Do you enjoy handicrafts such as pottery, woodcarving, building things, painting, or other crafts? Is this something you

do to relax? If yes, describe the what, how, when, and why. If no, describe the what, how, when, and why.

_____

_____

_____

_____

_____

_____

34. Do you find it easy to create new forms of a sport, such as a new type of dance or a new version of basketball? If yes, describe the what, how, when, and why. If no, describe the what, how, when, and why.

_____

_____

_____

_____

_____

35. Do you enjoy playing soccer, baseball, football, tennis, and so on? This question is not about skill, it's about enjoying ball games. If yes, describe the what, how, when, and why. If no, describe the what, how, when, and why.

_____

_____

_____

_____

36. Do you feel you have good hand-eye coordination for life in general, such as dancing, sports, handicrafts, and so on? If

yes, describe the what, how, when, and why. If no, describe the what, how, when, and why.

_____

_____

_____

_____

_____

_____

37. Would you consider yourself to be good at cycling, motorbike riding, skiing—activities that require speed, balance, and coordination skills? If yes, describe the what, how, when, and why. If no, describe the what, how, when, and why.

_____

_____

_____

_____

_____

38. Do you like to jog or run for exercise or fun? If yes, describe the what, how, when, and why. If no, describe the what, how, when, and why.

_____

_____

_____

_____

_____

_____

39. Do you enjoy taking part in marathons, sports competitions, and so forth? If yes, describe the what, how, when, and why. If no, describe the what, how, when, and why.

_____

_____

_____

_____

_____

_____

_____

40. Do you prefer individual sports, group sports, or just exercising any way you see fit, such as walking or working out in the gym on your own? Describe the what, how, when, and why.

_____

_____

_____

_____

_____

_____

41. Do you love movement and sports but are not that proficient in any particular sport? If yes, describe the what, how, when, and why. If no, describe the what, how, when, and why.

_____

_____

_____

_____

_____

42. Do you like swimming or aqua aerobics, either for relaxation or competition? If yes, describe the what, how, when, and why. If no, describe the what, how, when, and why.

43. Do you like being in water? If yes, describe the what, how, when, and why. If no, describe the what, how, when, and why.

44. Do you often feel compelled to move when you are thinking deeply about something? If yes, describe the what, how, when, and why. If no, describe the what, how, when, and why.

45. Do you like making models of things with Play-Doh or modeling clay? If yes, describe the what, how, when, and why. If no, describe the what, how, when, and why.

_____

_____

_____

_____

_____

46. Do you enjoy watching sports—live and on TV—and recognize and appreciate the skill involved? If yes, describe the what, how, when, and why. If no, describe the what, how, when, and why.

_____

_____

_____

_____

47. Do you get a sense for things through your body? For example, when you walk through a place, or play a game or a sport, or go into new areas, do you feel your whole body responding? If yes, describe the what, how, when, and why. If no, describe the what, how, when, and why.

_____

_____

_____

_____

48. Do you find it difficult to sit still for long periods of time, especially in a classroom environment? If yes, describe the

what, how, when, and why. If no, describe the what, how, when, and why.

_____

_____

_____

_____

_____

_____

_____

49. Does movement or moving in some way relax you and/or make you feel at peace? If yes, describe the what, how, when, and why. If no, describe the what, how, when, and why.

_____

_____

_____

_____

_____

_____

_____

Now take all your answers and in the space below write a summary of how you seem to be using the Kinesthetic Module. You might find that in this process you want to change or add to your answers. Go ahead, this is a normal self-regulatory process. Once you have done the summary, look it over to see if you agree with what you have written and if you can add more. Edit the summary, asking yourself the following questions: *Is this me? Do I really think this way? Is this a people-pleasing statement or am I being true to me?* Don't be too hard on yourself. Add a few lines on how you can use the Kinesthetic Module to improve how you communicate and connect with people and to improve how you function in general.

After all, you are you—but you get better at being you all the time.

_____

_____

_____

_____

_____

_____

_____

_____

_____

_____

Module 6: Musical Metacognitive Module—Thinking, Feeling, Choosing

The Musical Metacognitive Module might seem like it is the ability to sing or play a musical instrument; seek sound; find peace, comfort, stimulation, and motivation in music; hum; and so on—that is obvious. But, surprisingly, it also involves the computational capacities to intuit, be instinctual, read patterns, identify rhythm, and, most importantly, read between the lines and experience when things, a place, or what a person is saying just "does not feel right," as well as sensitivity to surroundings, people, and the atmospheres they create.

It works very extensively with the part of your brain called the insula, which is responsible for the development of instinct, thereby allowing you to read between the lines. It also allows you to sense meaning and to verify it. For example, when you ask your friend, "Are you okay?" and she says, "Yes, I'm fine" (with a quiver in her voice), this mode of thinking warns you that there is more to the situation. It is therefore concerned with the ability to read people through their tone of voice and body language rather than just listening to their words.

Musical thinking incorporates sensitivity to pitch, melody, rhythm, and tuning in the sounds and movements you hear and see around you, as well as the ability to produce rhythm, pitch, and forms of musical expression. It is also the intelligence of intuition, "gut instinct," and reading body language. It is involved both in the type of thinking attributed to the interpretation of conversation and in the type of thinking seen in musical individuals such as Mozart.

1. We are all intuitive; it's part of the thinking process. However, some of us have more sensitivity in this area in that we almost see and know things before they happen. Does this sound like you? If yes, describe the what, how, when, and why. If no, describe the what, how, when, and why.

_____

_____

_____

_____

_____

2. Do you find yourself becoming absorbed, sometimes even consumed, in the joys or sorrows of other people? If yes, describe the what, how, when, and why. If no, describe the what, how, when, and why.

_____

_____

_____

_____

_____

3. Do you feel the pain of other people intensely? Does it affect your ability to function? Do you pull away or try to help in some way? If yes, describe the what, how, when, and why. If no, describe the what, how, when, and why.

_____

_____

_____

_____

_____

_____

4. Do you often cry in touching or sad movies? If yes, describe the what, how, when, and why. If no, describe the what, how, when, and why.

_____

_____

_____

_____

_____

_____

5. Do you find it hard to watch certain movies or certain stories because they become too real for you? Or do you love getting lost in them? If yes, describe the what, how, when, and why. If no, describe the what, how, when, and why.

_____

_____

_____

_____

_____

6. Do you have a sense for mathematical thinking? If yes, describe the what, how, when, and why. If no, describe the what, how, when, and why.

_____

_____

_____

_____

_____

_____

7. Generally, can you read other people's attitudes? If yes, describe the what, how, when, and why. If no, describe the what, how, when, and why.

_____

_____

_____

_____

_____

_____

8. Can you "read between the lines" of what someone is saying aloud, in written form, and/or through their body language? If yes, describe the what, how, when, and why. If no, describe the what, how, when, and why.

_____

_____

_____

_____

_____

_____

9. Are you very aware of how you feel mentally and emotionally? If yes, describe the what, how, when, and why. If no, describe the what, how, when, and why.

_____

_____

_____

_____

_____

_____

_____

10. Can you easily identify and describe pain in your body? If yes, describe the what, how, when, and why. If no, describe the what, how, when, and why.

_____

_____

_____

_____

_____

_____

_____

11. Can you easily feel the impact of negative thinking and emotions in your mind and body? If yes, describe the what, how, when, and why. If no, describe the what, how, when, and why.

_____

_____

_____

_____

_____

12. Do you find yourself intuitively predicting things? Are you usually correct? If yes, describe the what, how, when, and why. If no, describe the what, how, when, and why.

_____

_____

_____

_____

_____

_____

13. Do you find it easy to read other people? Are you good at reading their body language, expressions, and tone of voice? If yes, describe the what, how, when, and why. If no, describe the what, how, when, and why.

_____

_____

_____

_____

_____

14. Generally, are you a good judge of character? If yes, describe the what, how, when, and why. If no, describe the what, how, when, and why.

_____

_____

_____

_____

_____

_____

15. Do you find it easy to follow conversations and interpret the dynamics of conversations? If yes, describe the what, how, when, and why. If no, describe the what, how, when, and why.

_____

_____

_____

_____

_____

16. Do you often find yourself noticing other people who don't self-regulate their actions and conversations in social situations? If yes, describe the what, how, when, and why. If no, describe the what, how, when, and why.

_____

_____

_____

_____

_____

_____

17. Do you instinctively feel when something is right or wrong or that something in an environment is not right? If yes, describe the what, how, when, and why. If no, describe the what, how, when, and why.

_____

_____

_____

_____

_____

18. Do you find yourself not doing or saying something until it feels "right"? If yes, describe the what, how, when, and why. If no, describe the what, how, when, and why.

_____

_____

_____

_____

_____

_____

19. Do you find you can easily pick up whether or not to trust someone? If yes, describe the what, how, when, and why. If no, describe the what, how, when, and why.

_____

_____

_____

_____

_____

20. Do you find it easy to pick up the nuances in someone's speech, such as whether or not someone is being sarcastic? If yes, describe the what, how, when, and why. If no, describe the what, how, when, and why.

_____

_____

_____

_____

_____

21. Do you find yourself listening and responding to a variety of sounds, including the human voice, environmental sounds,

sounds in nature, and music? If yes, describe the what, how, when, and why. If no, describe the what, how, when, and why.

_____

_____

_____

_____

_____

_____

22. Do you enjoy music and find yourself needing it in a learning environment? If yes, describe the what, how, when, and why. If no, describe the what, how, when, and why.

_____

_____

_____

_____

_____

_____

23. Do you often create your own rhythm if you can't hear music, especially when you are concentrating—for example, clicking your pen, tapping your foot, and rocking in your chair when you are studying? If yes, describe the what, how, when, and why. If no, describe the what, how, when, and why.

_____

_____

_____

_____

24. Do you find yourself responding to music by humming along?
    If yes, describe the what, how, when, and why. If no, describe
    the what, how, when, and why.

    _____

    _____

    _____

    _____

    _____

    _____

25. Do you find yourself responding to music by moving in time
    to the music? If yes, describe the what, how, when, and why.
    If no, describe the what, how, when, and why.

    _____

    _____

    _____

    _____

    _____

    _____

26. Do you find that music and singing make you feel a variety
    of emotions? If yes, describe the what, how, when, and why.
    If no, describe the what, how, when, and why.

    _____

    _____

    _____

    _____

    _____

    _____

27. If you watch gymnastics, ballet, dancing, or any sport, can
    you "hear" the music in the performers' body movements? If

yes, describe the what, how, when, and why. If no, describe
the what, how, when, and why.

_____

_____

_____

_____

_____

28. Do you recognize different types of musical styles, notes,
    tones, genres, and cultural variations? If yes, describe the
    what, how, when, and why. If no, describe the what, how,
    when, and why.

_____

_____

_____

_____

_____

_____

29. Do you find the role music has played and continues to play in
    human life fascinating? If yes, describe the what, how, when,
    and why. If no, describe the what, how, when, and why.

_____

_____

_____

_____

_____

30. Do you collect recordings of different types of music? If yes, describe the what, how, when, and why. If no, describe the what, how, when, and why.

_____

_____

_____

_____

_____

_____

31. Can you sing? If yes, describe the what, how, when, and why. If no, describe the what, how, when, and why.

_____

_____

_____

_____

_____

_____

32. Do you play one or more musical instruments? If yes, describe the what, how, when, and why. If no, describe the what, how, when, and why.

_____

_____

_____

_____

_____

_____

33. Are you able and do you like to analyze and critique musical selections? If yes, describe the what, how, when, and why. If no, describe the what, how, when, and why.

_____

_____

_____

_____

_____

_____

34. Are you often able to interpret what a composer is communicating through music? If yes, describe the what, how, when, and why. If no, describe the what, how, when, and why.

_____

_____

_____

_____

_____

35. Do you remember the titles and words of songs? If yes, describe the what, how, when, and why. If no, describe the what, how, when, and why.

_____

_____

_____

_____

_____

36. Can you hear a song once or twice and then sing or hum most of it? If yes, describe the what, how, when, and why. If no, describe the what, how, when, and why.

_____

_____

_____

_____

_____

_____

_____

37. Do you have a desire to create, or have you created, a musical instrument? If yes, describe the what, how, when, and why. If no, describe the what, how, when, and why.

_____

_____

_____

_____

_____

_____

38. Do you like music? If yes, describe the what, how, when, and why. If no, describe the what, how, when, and why.

_____

_____

_____

_____

_____

_____

39. Would you love to be (or are you already) a sound engineer, conductor, or musician? If yes, describe the what, how, when, and why. If no, describe the what, how, when, and why.

_____

_____

_____

_____

_____

_____

40. Do you read and/or write music? If yes, describe the what, how, when, and why. If no, describe the what, how, when, and why.

_____

_____

_____

_____

_____

41. Do you like musical activities such as karaoke? If yes, describe the what, how, when, and why. If no, describe the what, how, when, and why.

_____

_____

_____

_____

_____

42. Do you often tap, sing, or hum while working or when learning something new? If yes, describe the what, how, when, and why. If no, describe the what, how, when, and why.

_____

_____

_____

_____

_____

_____

43. Do you like whistling? Can you whistle? If yes, describe the what, how, when, and why. If no, describe the what, how, when, and why.

_____

_____

_____

_____

44. Do you battle when you are in a negative environment or around people who have negative attitudes? Does their mood hang over you and influence you for long? If yes, describe the what, how, when, and why. If no, describe the what, how, when, and why.

_____

_____

_____

_____

45. Are you able to discern when someone is misleading you or being a negative influence in your life? If yes, describe the

what, how, when, and why. If no, describe the what, how, when, and why.

_____

_____

_____

_____

_____

_____

46. Do you find yourself asking a lot of questions about how and why something happened or is happening? Can you see the positive and negative sides? If yes, describe the what, how, when, and why. If no, describe the what, how, when, and why.

_____

_____

_____

_____

_____

_____

Now take all your answers and in the space below write a summary of how you seem to be using the Musical Module. You might find that in this process you want to change or add to your answers. Go ahead, this is a normal self-regulatory process. Once you have done the summary, look it over to see if you agree with what you have written and if you can add more. Edit the summary, asking yourself the following questions: *Is this me? Do I really think this way? Is this a people-pleasing statement or am I being true to me?* Don't be too hard on yourself. Add a few lines on how you can use the Musical Module to improve how you communicate and connect with people and to improve how you function in general. After all, you are you—but you get better at being you all the time.

_____

_____

_____

_____

_____

_____

_____

_____

_____

_____

_____

Module 7: Visual/Spatial Metacognitive Module—Thinking, Feeling, Choosing

The final module is the Visual/Spatial Metacognitive Module. Visual/spatial thinking involves the raw computational capacities to see color, light, shape, and depth; to navigate spaces; and to close your eyes and imagine objects, thereby visualizing things that are not actually in front of your eyes. Individuals with visual impairments have very well-developed visual/spatial thinking, since they rely on what they can see in their "mind's eye."

Hence the visual/spatial mode of thought is the ability to be able to see without seeing; for example, you can imagine a loved one and call up a visual image from your nonconscious into your conscious mind. This is the ability to visualize in pictures and/or images, to "see" with the mind's eye, to make mental maps, to perceive the visual/spatial world accurately, and to act on initial perceptions.

Visual/spatial thinking is about internally representing the spatial world in your mind and being able to orient yourself in three-dimensional space with ease. Artists have a high level of visual/spatial thinking, which expresses itself in great works such as the masterpieces of Leonardo da Vinci and Michelangelo.

Yet this type of thinking is not restricted to the arts. In the minds of Sir Isaac Newton and Albert Einstein, for example, the expression of their high visual/spatial thinking was more scientific. It also is not restricted to the physical sense of what something looks like.

1. Do you find yourself noticing color, light, depth, and forms around you? If yes, describe the what, how, when, and why. If no, describe the what, how, when, and why.

_____

_____

_____

_____

_____

2. Can you imagine and see an object, situation, or person as if it or they were right in front of you? If yes, describe the what, how, when, and why. If no, describe the what, how, when, and why.

_____

_____

_____

_____

_____

3. Can you orient yourself in a three-dimensional space with ease? That is, are you easily able to maneuver through complicated spaces, or do you bump into things? If yes, describe

the what, how, when, and why. If no, describe the what, how, when, and why.

_____

_____

_____

_____

_____

_____

4. Do you usually notice mess or dirt? How does it make you feel? If yes, describe the what, how, when, and why. If no, describe the what, how, when, and why.

_____

_____

_____

_____

_____

_____

5. Do you notice things out of alignment, such as a picture hanging askew on the wall? Do you want to automatically fix it or can you ignore it and carry on with what you are doing? If yes, describe the what, how, when, and why. If no, describe the what, how, when, and why.

_____

_____

_____

_____

_____

6. Do you notice when people have coordinated or matching outfits? If yes, describe the what, how, when, and why. If no, describe the what, how, when, and why.

_____

_____

_____

_____

_____

_____

7. Do you notice when people are well groomed or if they are disheveled? Does it worry you? How does it make you feel? If yes, describe the what, how, when, and why. If no, describe the what, how, when, and why.

_____

_____

_____

_____

_____

8. Do you notice people's hair color, clothing style, and/or level of health? If yes, describe the what, how, when, and why. If no, describe the what, how, when, and why.

_____

_____

_____

_____

9. Do you need to express yourself artistically in drawing, painting, diagrams, new theories, ideas, businesses, or any

other form of creativity? If yes, describe the what, how, when, and why. If no, describe the what, how, when, and why.

_____

_____

_____

_____

_____

_____

10. Do you have lots of ideas? What do you do with them? If yes, describe the what, how, when, and why. If no, describe the what, how, when, and why.

_____

_____

_____

_____

_____

11. Do you visualize what people are saying to you or stories they tell you or things you read as "little movies" in your mind's eye? If yes, describe the what, how, when, and why. If no, describe the what, how, when, and why.

_____

_____

_____

_____

_____

12. Do you often find yourself staring off into space while listening to someone? If yes, describe the what, how, when, and why. If no, describe the what, how, when, and why.

_____

_____

_____

_____

_____

13. Do you enjoy creating things—songs, music, games, clothes, furniture, whatever—even if it's just in your mind's eye? If yes, describe the what, how, when, and why. If no, describe the what, how, when, and why.

_____

_____

_____

_____

_____

14. Do you find it easy to follow a GPS and find your way around new places? Do you have confidence doing this? If yes, describe the what, how, when, and why. If no, describe the what, how, when, and why.

_____

_____

_____

_____

_____

15. Are you able to drive a route once and find your way back? If yes, describe the what, how, when, and why. If no, describe the what, how, when, and why.

_____

_____

_____

_____

_____

_____

16. Can you easily self-correct the route you have taken while driving if you missed a turn or something? Is it easy for you to readjust your smartphone map (or whatever you use to help you find your way)? If yes, describe the what, how, when, and why. If no, describe the what, how, when, and why.

_____

_____

_____

_____

_____

_____

17. Can you easily "see" in your mind's eye how to solve problems or issues? If yes, describe the what, how, when, and why. If no, describe the what, how, when, and why.

_____

_____

_____

_____

_____

_____

18. Can you easily translate ideas into a written or physical action? If yes, describe the what, how, when, and why. If no, describe the what, how, when, and why.

_____

_____

_____

_____

_____

_____

19. Do you find yourself thinking in pictures? For example, do you imagine the image of a cat or the word *cat* first? If yes, describe the what, how, when, and why. If no, describe the what, how, when, and why.

_____

_____

_____

_____

_____

_____

20. Are you able to move furniture, rooms, or physical things around in your head? If yes, describe the what, how, when, and why. If no, describe the what, how, when, and why.

_____

_____

_____

_____

_____

21. Do you think in 3-D—for example, can you mentally move or manipulate objects in space to see how they will interact

with other objects, such as gears turning in different parts of machinery? If yes, describe the what, how, when, and why. If no, describe the what, how, when, and why.

_____

_____

_____

_____

_____

_____

22. Do you understand and like to use and produce graphic information—for example, do you enjoy using graphs or charts to explain concepts? If yes, describe the what, how, when, and why. If no, describe the what, how, when, and why.

_____

_____

_____

_____

_____

23. Can you easily navigate your way through space—for example, when moving through apertures, moving a car through traffic, or parking a car? If yes, describe the what, how, when, and why. If no, describe the what, how, when, and why.

_____

_____

_____

_____

_____

_____

24. Can you easily read a map? Is paper easier than digital, or vice versa? If yes, describe the what, how, when, and why. If no, describe the what, how, when, and why.

_____

_____

_____

_____

_____

_____

25. Do you like building blocks, origami objects, LEGOs, and models? If yes, describe the what, how, when, and why. If no, describe the what, how, when, and why.

_____

_____

_____

_____

_____

26. Do you enjoy putting together puzzles, especially complicated ones? If yes, describe the what, how, when, and why. If no, describe the what, how, when, and why.

_____

_____

_____

_____

_____

27. Do you like creating photo collages and scrapbooking, selecting and planning photos for photo books, and so on? If

yes, describe the what, how, when, and why. If no, describe the what, how, when, and why.

_____

_____

_____

_____

_____

_____

28. Do you like creating slideshow presentations? If yes, describe the what, how, when, and why. If no, describe the what, how, when, and why.

_____

_____

_____

_____

_____

_____

29. Do you enjoy taking photos or creating videos of special occasions? If yes, describe the what, how, when, and why. If no, describe the what, how, when, and why.

_____

_____

_____

_____

_____

_____

30. Do you like designing posters, murals, bulletin boards, or websites? Are you attracted to them wherever you may see them, and do you notice their detail? If yes, describe the

what, how, when, and why. If no, describe the what, how, when, and why.

_____

_____

_____

_____

_____

_____

31. Do you find yourself visualizing (picturing and imagining) a lot, especially when you are listening and trying to understand something? If yes, describe the what, how, when, and why. If no, describe the what, how, when, and why.

_____

_____

_____

_____

_____

_____

32. Can you easily remember large chunks of information (for short periods of time) just from reading? If yes, describe the what, how, when, and why. If no, describe the what, how, when, and why.

_____

_____

_____

_____

_____

_____

33. Do you like creating complex, "architectural" type drawings? If yes, describe the what, how, when, and why. If no, describe the what, how, when, and why.

_____

_____

_____

_____

_____

_____

34. Would you like to make (or do you love to make) a film or an advertisement? If yes, describe the what, how, when, and why. If no, describe the what, how, when, and why.

_____

_____

_____

_____

_____

_____

35. Do you appreciate and notice variation in color, size, and shape—for example, do you notice the colors, furniture, and interior design in rooms? If yes, describe the what, how, when, and why. If no, describe the what, how, when, and why.

_____

_____

_____

_____

_____

_____

36. Do you naturally color code—for example, Sunday is red and Monday is blue? Maybe sounds or places or people have

colors in your mind? If yes, describe the what, how, when, and why. If no, describe the what, how, when, and why.

_____

_____

_____

_____

_____

37. Do you like board games such as Monopoly and Trivial Pursuit? If yes, describe the what, how, when, and why. If no, describe the what, how, when, and why.

_____

_____

_____

_____

_____

38. Do you like and do you consider yourself to be fair, good, or excellent at producing various art forms such as illustrations, drawings, sketches, paintings, or sculptures? If yes, describe the what, how, when, and why. If no, describe the what, how, when, and why.

_____

_____

_____

_____

_____

_____

39. Do you like using technology, such as computers, smart-phones, and tablets? If yes, describe the what, how, when, and why. If no, describe the what, how, when, and why.

_____

_____

_____

_____

_____

40. Do you like to do presentations and lecture or teach using computers and data projectors? If yes, describe the what, how, when, and why. If no, describe the what, how, when, and why.

_____

_____

_____

_____

_____

41. Do you like to write on a board, flip chart, paper, iPad, or anything you can get your hands on when you are explaining something, lecturing, or teaching? If yes, describe the what, how, when, and why. If no, describe the what, how, when, and why.

_____

_____

_____

_____

_____

42. Do you see clear visual images of what you are thinking or hearing when you close your eyes? If yes, describe the what,

how, when, and why. If no, describe the what, how, when, and why.

_____

_____

_____

_____

_____

43. We all dream, and what we are focusing on and watching and thinking about just before sleep will influence our dreams. However, some of us have more vivid dreams than others and recall them more easily, as though they were almost real. Do you have such vivid dreams and even nightmares, especially when going through "stuff"? If yes, describe the what, how, when, and why. If no, describe the what, how, when, and why.

_____

_____

_____

_____

_____

44. Do you like drawing and doodling, especially in situations where you have to concentrate, such as while on the phone or listening to a lecture? If yes, describe the what, how, when, and why. If no, describe the what, how, when, and why.

_____

_____

_____

_____

45. Do you prefer not to look at a lecturer's, teacher's, or any other person's face when you are trying to listen and concentrate, as this distracts you? If yes, describe the what, how, when, and why. If no, describe the what, how, when, and why.

_____

_____

_____

_____

_____

46. Do you find it easier to learn when you can see and observe something? If yes, describe the what, how, when, and why. If no, describe the what, how, when, and why.

_____

_____

_____

_____

_____

47. Do you often use visual images as an aid to recall detailed information? If yes, describe the what, how, when, and why. If no, describe the what, how, when, and why.

_____

_____

_____

_____

_____

48. Can you easily fold a piece of paper into a complex shape and visualize its new form? If yes, describe the what, how, when, and why. If no, describe the what, how, when, and why.

_____

_____

_____

_____

_____

49. Do you find it easy to see things—both concrete and linguistic— in different ways or from new perspectives; for example, detecting one form hidden in another or seeing the other angle of a problem? If yes, describe the what, how, when, and why. If no, describe the what, how, when, and why.

_____

_____

_____

_____

50. Can you perceive both obvious and subtle patterns in objects, furniture, clouds, and so on? If yes, describe the what, how, when, and why. If no, describe the what, how, when, and why.

_____

_____

_____

_____

Now take all your answers, and in the space below write a summary of how you seem to be using the Visual/Spatial Module. You might find that in this process you want to change or add to your answers. Go ahead, this is a normal self-regulatory process. Once you have done the summary, look it over to see if you agree with what you have written and if you can add more. Edit the summary, asking yourself the questions, *Is this me? Do I really think this way? Is this a people-pleasing statement or am I being true to me?* Don't be too hard on yourself. Add a few lines on how you can use the Visual/Spatial Module to improve how you communicate and connect with people and to improve how you function in general. After all, you are you—but you get better at being you all the time.

_____

_____

_____

_____

_____

_____

_____

_____

_____

_____

7

The Perfect You Checklist

In the great drama of existence we ourselves are both
actors and spectators.

Niels Bohr, quantum physicist

This Perfect You checklist is an extremely handy and simple but
powerful lifestyle tool that will help you become more mindful of
what you are thinking, feeling, choosing, saying, and doing in order
to stay in your Perfect You. You can use this checklist prior to,
during, and after the moment of decision making. This will keep
you in your Perfect You—which you have discovered more about
in the profile you just filled in—and will help you make right decisions. The quickest way to activate your Perfect You is to begin by
practicing, on a daily basis, *actively self-regulating your thinking
and being aware of your spirit, mind, and body.* As you do this
intentionally and deliberately, you will force active (conscious)
and dynamic (always happening on a nonconscious level) self-
regulation to interact, which is when you will be operating at a

very high intellectual level. Familiarize yourself with the checklist below and memorize it so you can use it as a lifestyle.

Practice this daily for sixty-three days and observe how your life turns around in every sphere—relationally, intellectually, career-wise, academically, socially, and emotionally. After sixty-three days, you should be doing this automatically and starting to develop your expertise and effectiveness in being mindfully aware of operating in your Perfect You—and you will have set up a constant internal dialogue with the Holy Spirit. In this way, you will literally be pray-ing continuously and thus operating in your godly, wired-for-love, Perfect You design. You will begin to be a serious image-bearer, reflecting God's glory! And, as you continue doing this for the rest of your life, you will develop your divine sense of purpose to produce evidence and substance in your life that is over, above, and beyond what you had ever hoped or imagined!

Multiple Perspective Advantage (MPA)

Our *multiple perspective advantage* (MPA) is our ability to stand outside ourselves and observe our own thinking. This happens when we are conscious, intentional, and mindful. It activates the brain's frontal lobe and the internal networks of the mind.

Consciously and deliberately activate your MPA, stand outside of yourself, and observe yourself going through the following steps:

☐ Am I self-aware of what I am thinking about, feeling, and choosing in my mind and how my body is reacting in this *now* moment?

☐ Am I intentionally and deliberately using my active self-regulation (my conscious thinking, feeling, and choosing) in this *now* moment?

☐ Am I actively self-regulating the *incoming* informa
this *now* moment?

☐ Am I actively self-regulating the *upcoming* internal memo-
ries/thoughts in this *now* moment?

☐ Am I actively choosing to ask the Holy Spirit to guide my
self-regulation in this *now* moment?

☐ Am I actively self-regulating my thinking about the *incoming and upcoming* information in this *now* moment?

☐ Am I actively self-regulating the *feelings I am experiencing*
at this moment that are part of the incoming and upcoming
information in this *now* moment?

☐ Am I actively self-regulating my tone of voice, facial expressions, and body language in this *now* moment?

☐ Am I self-regulating *how I am choosing to listen* to the
Holy Spirit in this *now* moment?

☐ Now, before you choose, do the long or short version
of the thanksgiving, praise, and worship exercise (see
below).

☐ Now *choose* and create with your power, love, and sound
mind!

Thanksgiving, Praise, and Worship Exercise

Long Version

1. Ask God to show you what issue you need to work on for
the next sixty-three days.

2. Visualize the issue as a toxic tree in your hands and now carry
it to God's feet. You can do this in your imagination and/or
carry out the actual actions however you want to.

3. Acknowledge, confess, and receive your forgiveness.

4. Now kneel down and place that toxic tree down at the throne of grace and *don't* pick it back up.

5. While kneeling, say five sentences beginning with "Lord, I thank you. . . ." Be as specific as you can. Research says the more specific you are, the quicker your healing will come.

6. Now stand up, clasp your hands tightly together, and imagine that Jesus is holding your hands, because he inhabits our praises. Say five sentences beginning with "Lord, I praise you for. . . ." Once again, be as specific as you can be, and stick with the same issue. Don't be tempted to swap issues.

7. Now raise your hands and enter into worship. Focus 100 percent on God and not on your issues.

Three-Second Short Version

1. Thank God that he is helping.

2. Praise God that he is right there with you at this moment.

3. Worship God to activate the wisdom you need.

PART
FOUR

8

The Discomfort Zones

If you put yourself in a position where you have to
stretch outside your comfort zone, then you are forced
to expand your consciousness.

Les Brown, author

An important lesson in physic is here to be learnt,
the wonderful and powerful influence of the passions
of the mind upon the state and disorder of the body.

John Haygarth, physician

I hope that you are filled with expectancy and excitement because
you are starting to understand how you think, feel, and choose in
your Perfect You! Along the way, you have probably also learned
more about your spouse, your children, your friends and neighbors,
and maybe even your boss. Now, when you wonder, *Does anyone
out there understand me?* you can see in Scripture, philosophy,
and science that God does. He created you with care. You were

created with intention, purpose, and greatness. You were designed to be the Perfect You.

In this section we will take the Perfect You one step further and explore how to identify when you have moved out of your Perfect You. You have been reading about the spirit-mind-body/ brain connection throughout this book, and now you will discover how your spirit, mind, and body respond to your choices through the "discomfort zones."

As you have been learning in this book, your Perfect You is your unique way of thinking, feeling, and choosing. The UQ profile helps you understand your Perfect You: your particular mindset and the ways you think, feel, and choose. As you go through your day, you will be reacting to the events and circumstances of your life and building these reactions into your brain as real, physical thoughts. The way you think, feel, and choose to react—and subsequently build thoughts—will either develop or block your Perfect You. Your UQ profile has a threefold purpose: to help you understand how you uniquely think, feel, and choose; to increase your ability to mindfully and deliberately self-regulate your thinking, feeling, and choosing to keep you in alignment with the Holy Spirit; and to help you understand how you think, feel, and choose when you are operating in your Perfect You so that you can recognize when you are operating outside of it. To this end, the discomfort zones help facilitate these three purposes. Let's take a closer look at how this happens.

Discomfort Zones Sounding the Alarm

Evidence of the power of the mind is all around us, in stories of our own lives and those "overcoming the odds" narratives we love to hear about. In fact, we as humans have an endless fascination with how we can use our minds to change things. God has designed us to be victors of the flesh and conquer it, but there is a catch; the conquering of the flesh only has sustainability *in Christ* (Rom. 7:24–25; 8:37; Gal. 2:19–21).

As I mentioned at the beginning of this book, we have a mind, we live in a body, and we are a spirit. Our spirit has three parts. First, our *intuition*, where the Holy Spirit speaks truth to us and leads us, is where our "gut instinct" to think, feel, and choose in the Perfect You mode resides. Second, our *conscience* is where our awareness of right and wrong resides. Third, our *worship* is where we recognize our need to be immersed in the love of God—we are designed to be addicted to God.

Our minds—our souls—are also comprised of three parts: our intellect, emotions, and free will (thinking, feeling, and choosing). The body includes both the brain and the rest of the physical body. As we have already seen, the mind and brain are separate. Through the mind we change the brain. The brain and body simply do what the mind and spirit tell them to do.

If the mind is out of alignment with the natural design of the Perfect You, through incorrect reactions and trauma, then the brain and body can get damaged in various ways, which will be expressed through damaged genes and biology. Subsequently, minds have to work through areas of damage in the brain and body, and a toxic feedback loop is set up. However, this can be changed because the mind is more powerful than the brain. This ability of the brain to change as a result of mind work is called neuroplasticity.

Discomfort zones are zones in our spirits, minds, and bodies that alert us to when we are stepping out of our Perfect You. In other words, they sound the "alarm" in our consciousness when we step out of the love zone and into the damaging fear zone (see chapter 3). These discomfort zones are more evidence of God's bottomless love for us, since they are prompts that remind us to stay in our Perfect You. When we use the discomfort zones, we immerse ourselves in an environment of love, which on a physical level changes our brain chemistry *and* changes all 75–100 trillion cells of our bodies. In turn, this gives us courage to deal with our issues and develop our minds.

In this chapter we are going to briefly track a few of these discomfort zone levels so you can use them to recognize when you are out of your Perfect You. Discomfort zones are gracious "prompts" from God to keep us in his love zone by increasing our awareness of our thoughts, feelings, and choices so we can self-regulate them.

There are four main **discomfort zone levels** that we sequence through. These include but are not limited to the following:

1. The "just aware" discomfort zone level—when you are just becoming aware of the information and your reaction.
2. The "adrenaline-pumping, heart-pounding" discomfort zone level—when the stress reaction kicks in, which we can make work for us (or against us) through our choices, which I will explain in more depth further on.
3. The "attitudes" discomfort zone level—these are the actual physical thoughts, with information and emotions, which cannot be hidden because they are real, alive, and generating either healthy or toxic energy that is affecting you, your loved ones, and the world we live in. They are the roots of all your words and actions.
4. The "about to choose" discomfort zone level—when you are consciously aware of all thoughts, attached emotions, the incoming stimulus, and your attitude. This is also the point at which you consciously choose to interact with the Holy Spirit and ask for advice or choose to ignore his advice.

These four levels of discomfort zones incorporate elements of the spirit, mind, and body.

The Spiritual Element of the Discomfort Zones

The spiritual element of the discomfort zones is when the opposites of the fruit of the Spirit (Gal. 5:22–23) activate in our minds. They form our spiritual alarms—they help us recognize we are in a discomfort zone and need to increase our mindfulness. Their information is so useful that we should memorize them.

1. *Love*, which conquers all and casts out fear (1 John 4:18), is the first fruit of the Spirit. When its opposite occurs—when we feel conquered, hopeless, and consumed with life in the fear zone—we need to increase our mindfulness of whether we are operating in love.

2. *Joy* is our strength (Neh. 8:10). Its opposite is when we are feeling mentally and physically weak and lacking joy.

3. *Peace* will guard our minds in Christ Jesus (Phil. 4:8). Its opposite is when we do not have peace, or if we feel vulnerable and exposed.

4. *Patience* is a perfect work (James 1:4–8). When we are feeling impatient with ourselves and others, it can inhibit our actions.

5. *Goodness* should be reflected out of every part of us as God's image-bearers (Ps. 136:1). When we gossip, are judgmental, take offense, are jealous, and so on, we do not reflect his goodness.

6. *Kindness* is a key characteristic of Jesus (Eph. 4:32). If we are not being genuinely kind to our spouse, family, work colleagues, friends, traffic buddy, and even shopping line partner, we are not following the way Jesus showed us.

7. *Gentleness* does not speak evil to or of anyone (Titus 3:2). How gentle was your response to your loved ones today? Gentleness is endearing and uplifting, but a lack of gentleness is hurtful and will spark a response of emotional shame.

8. *Faithfulness* is something God shows throughout the Old and New Testaments (Deut. 7:9; John 3:16). Are you

245

reliable? Do you run away when challenged? Hiding from issues, hard work, or your fears will make you unhappy and uncomfortable.

9. *Self-control* is an expression of wisdom (Prov. 29:11). A lack of self-control can inhibit perseverance (2 Pet. 1:5–9) and lead to a sense of irritation and failure.

The Mind Element of the Discomfort Zones

The mind level of discomfort zones occurs in superposition, from being just aware, as in discomfort level 1, to the about-to-choose level of discomfort zone 4. Superposition is the point when you are consciously aware of the incoming information (events and circumstances of life coming at you through your five senses) and upcoming information (your existing memories or thoughts), until the point at which you deliberately, actively, and dynamically self-regulate your thinking, feeling, and choosing and build the physical memory (see the summary chart in chapter 9).

As you go into superposition, you start evaluating the spiritual elements in an increasing level of depth and in essence are using your mind to evaluate your spiritual state in the four discomfort zones. You become "just aware" of whether or not you are operating in the fruit of the Spirit, respond to the strong physical reaction of whether or not you are in the fruit of the Spirit, check whether your attitude aligns with the fruit of the Spirit, and see if your choices are guided by the fruit of the Spirit. This is a lot of self-regulation in superposition, which is essentially bringing those thoughts into captivity to Christ Jesus.

The Body Element of the Discomfort Zones

The body level of discomfort zones directly reflects the spirit and mind. These discomfort zones are the physical responses to

Discomfort Zones Prompts

1. Go into superposition and use your multiple perspective advantage (MPA).
2. How are the fruit of the Spirit operating:
    on the just-aware level?
    on the adrenaline-pumping level?
    on the attitude level?
    on the about to choose level?
3. How are you feeling physically? Is this different than how you were feeling?

the spirit and mind in action. For example, you feel physically sick or as though you have had a blow to your stomach, or you actually do develop a sickness. They become evident in your lifestyle because both the spirit and mind express *through* the body. They can easily be felt because of the discomfort caused by the interruption in the regular, consistent, and comfortable level of your body's millions of minute and complex electrical, chemical, and quantum reactions and transactions taking place at any one time.

The Sequence of the Discomfort Zones through the Four Levels

The spirit, mind, and body discomfort elements above are encompassed in the four discomfort zones. If we can train ourselves to identify and use the four discomfort zones, we are well on the way to being freed from the chains of toxicity and the fear attitudes they produce. We will lock up when out of the Perfect You, but we will unlock our true selves when we are in the Perfect You. One of the simplest ways to train ourselves to stay in the Perfect You is to intimately familiarize ourselves with these four discomfort zones and how they appear along the route that thinking, feeling, and

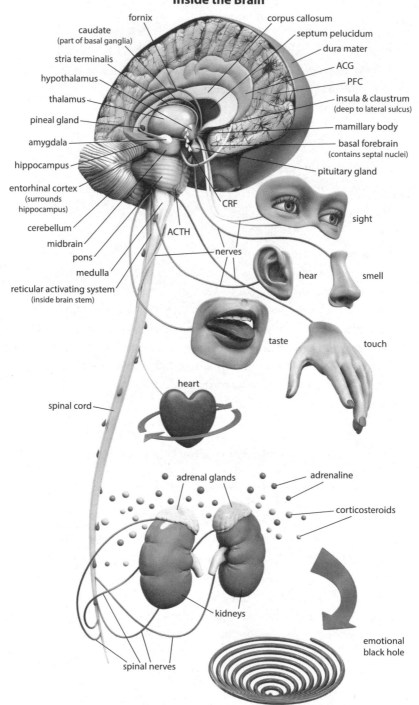

Illustration 8.1
Inside the Brain

choosing pass through in the process of building physical thoughts (which, as you will recall, become the root of our words and actions). In order to visualize this route, it will be a good idea to reference the "Inside the Brain" diagram below, which will show you these parts of the brain as I describe them.

The discomfort zones go into action when we get input from the environment through the events and circumstances of life. This input comes through our senses, our bodies, and our thoughts—it is both internal and external. The information enters the brain and passes into the entorhinal cortex and is transmitted via a structure called the thalamus to the outer cortex of the brain, where memories (thoughts) are stored. This is a literal quantum cloud of spreading activity through the brain, which on a quantum level is called a "smeared wave of probabilities."[1]

The neurons and dendrites of the brain have an arbor-like structure and look like a massive entangled forest of trees. Thoughts actually look like trees and are often referred to by scientists as the "magic trees of the mind," since they keep changing and growing in response to our moment-by-moment experiences. The internal and external information flies through these "trees" at speeds so fast that they are quantum in nature, and scientists estimate these speeds to be around 10^{27}. This is the first place where an attitude (a cluster of thoughts with information and emotions) is activated. The attitude is literally "switched on" as the information sweeps through the memory like "the breeze through the trees."

Your brain is now able to make sense of new information. Your thinking and feeling drives a process of referencing connections with previous experiences and memories. This metacognitive action is orchestrated by dynamic and active self-regulation (see chapter 5). A memory that is similar or linked in some way to the incoming information will be experienced as a subtly warm and happy feeling if it is a good memory, or a warning or sense of uneasiness if it is a bad memory.

Discomfort Zone 1: Just-Aware

If the memory is negative, you will have feelings of unrest and the peace of the spiritual element of the discomfort zone will be disturbed. This is the first point where your self-regulating spiritual discomfort zone is alerted on a nonconscious level. The discomfort will develop, gaining enough energy to impinge on your conscious mind and influence it. You can't quite place "it" yet, but something is starting to happen in your brain on a nonconscious level and is moving into your conscious awareness. This spiritual element activates the just-aware level, the first discomfort zone.

We need to respond in our minds to these just-aware moments, which are like spiritual taps on the shoulder reminding us to self-regulate and ask ourselves, *Am I operating in love, joy, peace, patience, kindness, gentleness, and self-control?* Never ignore these spiritual taps on the shoulder, because thoughts are alive, real, and dynamic and will produce either healthy fruit or toxic fruit. Bring that thought into captivity before it catches you, so you don't have to do extra work to get out of its clutches later! This step is important because it is on the epigenetic level (in other words, over and above the genetic expression of something). This means there is an environment developing outside of the new memory about to be built that is going to influence exactly how the memory is going to look and feel—healthy (love-based) or toxic (fear-based)—and you are able to control this process. Your mind affects which genes in your neurons are expressed as well as when and how they are expressed.

A memory is built when genetic expression happens, which occurs as we *choose.* Choosing makes physical thoughts come into being. Your brain is designed to respond to knowledge, and you need to detect whether this information is good or bad for you, otherwise you will build toxic knowledge into your brain with your mind. Essentially this just-aware level is almost like a

Discomfort Zone 1 (Just-Aware) Tip

Analyze this quickening of love or fear that you are just becoming aware of in your conscious mind, this witness in your Perfect You, and bring it into your conscious awareness. This is an anticipation built into your Perfect You—the regulatory part of you—that is responding to incoming and existing knowledge. It is a fear or love anticipation starting to build up in you.

What spiritual discomfort zone—what fruit of the Spirit—is going awry? Are you feeling slightly disturbed or is your joy starting to fade? Using your mind discomfort zone, what thoughts are you becoming aware of right at this moment? What feelings are they bringing with them? Now quickly focus on your body. Is your heart rate just starting to increase, and are you starting to feel tense? Deliberately and intentionally tune in to your spirit, mind, and body to see what they are telling you.

preview of how the information will influence your feelings about the information, but it is very subtle; it is not quite a conscious thought yet.

The just-aware zone has the purpose of starting the process of protecting and guarding your mind. The spiritual element shows us whether we are in love or fear, joy or peace, and so on. The mind element is the self-regulating awareness of the incoming and upcoming information. The body element incorporates the physical accompaniment to the spiritual and mind elements.

As we have seen throughout this book, "toxic in, toxic out." You will step out of your Perfect You if you have a toxic mindset, which comes from not controlling what you are thinking. If the incoming knowledge and thoughts are good, healthy, and based on love, your gift and wisdom will be further developed. But if information is negative and fear-based, neurophysiological damage can ensue, producing toxic stress, which manifests in some way physically, mentally, or both.

251

We need to remember that every thought has an emotional component attached to it, a "chemical signature." These peptides, small proteins that are chemical messengers, are initiated by the part of the brain I call the chemical factory—the hypothalamus, found deep in the middle of the brain. The hypothalamus has a host of "recipes" for attitudes, made up of the chemical signature of the thoughts and the attached emotion. It uses the peptides to make a chemical signature for each attitude. So the hypothalamus translates the attitude into a physical reality in the body via the neurochemicals. If the attitude is love-based, this is great; but if it is toxic, this will cascade the body into chemical chaos, because we are wired for love and have no real "recipes" for toxicity. And when we catch the possible growth of a toxic thought before an attitude is formed, this is the best way to prevent a lock on our Perfect You.

But what happens when a toxic thought takes root and does grow, because you didn't catch it at the just-aware discomfort zone? After discomfort zone 1, the chemicals are flowing, the electrical and quantum levels increase in energy, and the adrenaline-pumping, heart-pounding discomfort zone 2 begins.

Discomfort Zone 2: Adrenaline-Pumping and Heart-Pounding

These chemicals are called "molecules of emotion and information,"[2] and they are responsible, along with the dynamics of quantum physics, for carrying the emotions you are feeling into another part of your brain, the amygdala, which is close to the chemical factory. So once again, we see a physical reaction to mind activity. These signals activate the amygdala, which is like a library in the brain that holds the emotional perceptions you have built with your mind. The two amygdalae are about the size of almonds. They work very closely with the hypothalamus, which responds to the mind, monitoring the flow of chemicals and attitudes. Indeed, even here we see our uniqueness since we each have our own balance and our own internal chemical design, which is affected by nature, nurture, and, most importantly, our own unique way of thinking—our Perfect You. We can enhance or upset our own balanced state just by our thoughts. Isn't that amazing?

Once the electrochemical and quantum signature that is activated by a thought in the outer part of the brain arrives at the library of emotional perceptions, the amygdala, you will feel a strong physical reaction because this is when the stress reaction begins. Stress chemicals start flowing in this discomfort zone. They make your heart pump faster and send adrenaline flowing through your body. You feel a rush of alert focus and awareness that almost gets you off your feet. Cortisol is also released, sharpening cognition; your muscles tense and your breathing becomes shallow and rapid. This breathing pushes extra oxygen into your brain to improve your thinking and memory retrieval. You are being prepared to think clearly and make a good choice—*however, only if you perceive the way you feel in that moment as being good for you.*

Yes, stress can actually be good for you! It only becomes toxic when you think it's bad for you.[3]

What do I mean by this? Well, as I have pointed out throughout this book, there is extensive research on the connection between body and mind, between the physical and the emotional, and studies show that psychological trauma affects the activity of many genes. Research has found a link between microRNA (the regulatory RNA I spoke of earlier) and stressful situations—stress and anxiety will result in an inflammatory response and dramatically increase the expression levels of microRNA regulators of inflammation in both the brain and the gut, so that the inflammation increases.[4]

This stress reaction in and of itself is not bad. Your perception of stress is what makes it work for or against you, which means you can control your body's reactions with your mind—even the stress reaction! This is where the spiritual (fruit of the Spirit), mind (superposition), and body (physical reactions) elements of discomfort zone 2 kick in. Use them to help you develop the correct perception of stress, and read on to find out why this is so important.

According to research, if you change your mind about stress you can change your body's response to stress. One study has shown that if you believe stress is harmful for your health, your fears can increase your chance of illness and death by 43 percent.[5] This study estimated that an average of twenty thousand people die each year because of the belief that stress itself is toxic. Yet there is good news! Individuals who did not believe stress was bad for them decreased their risk of dying. Similarly, another study

Discomfort Zone 2
(Adrenaline-Pumping and Heart-Pounding) Tip

When in stress, choose to see your increased heart rate as a way of getting more blood, oxygen, and nutrients to your brain so you can think more clearly. View your pounding heart as getting more oxygen and blood into your brain to increase your depth of thought and, hence, wisdom. View the increased tension in your muscles as preparing you for action. View the adrenaline rush as decreasing your response time and increasing your sharpness of mind. Thus, in superposition, choose to see the stress response as a loving design by God to help you rise to the challenges of life, and do what it says in James 1:2–4, which is to rejoice despite the circumstances. Choose in superposition to let the fruit of the Spirit grow into pillars in your mind. Choose to remember the nature of God, which is to love and guide you through the issues of life. Consciously and deliberately practice this, using your active and dynamic self-regulation every day, and in sixty-three days you will have actualized a pattern or a habit for handling stress in this way. When you find yourself in a stressful situation, reach out immediately and serve others, while choosing to see your situation as something you can handle, since you are more than a conqueror in Christ (Rom. 8:37).

showed that when you see the stress response as something positive, it actually changes you body's physical responses.[6] For example, if you see stress as good for you, then the blood vessels around your heart will dilate instead of constrict, thereby increasing blood flow and oxygen to your brain instead of decreasing them. The former will increase the fruit of the Spirit and cognitive clarity, confidence, and intelligence; the latter will potentially put you at risk for a cardiovascular event, maybe even a stroke. At the least, your cognitive fluency will decrease and you will become confused.

More research has shown that caring for others in your state of need increases your resilience and reduces your risk of dying. So instead of a major stressful experience (such as financial difficulties or family issues) increasing the risk of dying by 30 percent, caring for others reduced that risk.[7] A belief about stress can make a huge difference in someone's life expectancy.[8] These studies have also found that how you perceive and react to stressful events is more important to your health than how *frequently* you encounter stress.[9] Minor hassles can build up to influence your health if you stay in toxic stress for too long, and this can cause nerve cells and memory to disintegrate. Toxic stress can set off a cascade of destructive reactions inside a nerve cell, sometimes even causing "cell suicide." These reactions can manifest in symptoms of anxiety, depression, or even physical illness (recall the Fear Tree on page 55). Such symptoms lock up your Perfect You. Other research shows that we have genes in the hippocampus (part of the brain involved in the conversion of short-term memory to long-term memory) that are activated when we are in a stress mode to help us cope with stress. But if we see the stress reaction as negative, the genes switch off instead of switching on.[10]

In fact, during periods of stress, research shows that one of the best things we can do is act like Jesus and care for others![11] This is not surprising, since compassion is a key feature of a wired-for-love mindset, which cannot coexist with a self-centered fear mindset.

It is, after all, how we have been created to live: in community, entangled in each other's lives (Mark 9:35; Acts 20:35; Phil. 2:1–11; 1 Pet. 4:10). As Paul says in Galatians 5:14, "For all the law is fulfilled in one word, . . . 'You shall love your neighbor as yourself.'"

Our Perfect You locks down in isolation but flourishes as part of God's body (1 Cor. 12:12; Rom. 12:4; Eph. 4:16). If you want to live the good life, you have to learn to follow the servant model of Christ (Matt. 20:28). There truly is no point in being "talented" or "unique" (your Perfect You) if you live in a one-person universe.

Discomfort Zone 3: Attitude

The third discomfort zone deals with established *attitudes*, which are long-term memories with their intertwined emotions. These attitudes move into the conscious mind so that you become aware of them. Remember, these are real physical thoughts with information and emotions, so tune in to the spiritual (fruit of the Spirit), mind (superposition), and body (physical reactions). They cannot be

Discomfort Zone 3 (Attitude) Tip

Don't just react to the upwelling attitude (a thought with intertwined emotions) *but use the spiritual (fruit of the Spirit), mind (superposition), and body (physical reactions) to self-regulate that attitude—keep it if it is healthy or eliminate it if it is toxic.* Because an attitude is a cluster of thoughts with their related emotions, it's extremely important to evaluate it; a toxic attitude will take you out of your Perfect You and will affect your ability to choose well with wisdom. If necessary, reconceptualize the toxic attitude. And if it doesn't work the first time, do it again—and again and again. Science demonstrates that you need to practice using something or studying something at least seven times per day over sixty-three days before you are going to be able to use the information or perform the skill.[12]

hidden because they are alive and generating energy that is either healthy or toxic. They are the roots of all your words and actions and are swirling around your nonconscious mind, gaining momentum and energy as you, while thinking deeply, activate them.

But, as I have emphasized throughout this book, you do not have to let your thoughts control you. You are not a victim of your thoughts and their biology; you are a victor over them. This means you can change these thoughts! You may have been nursing these negative mindsets for so long that they are so familiar to you that you think they are normal. This mistake is often made. However, only the thoughts formed when you are in your Perfect You, from God's perspective, are normal, while the rest need redesigning or, to use the scientific term, *reconceptualization*. You can analyze your thoughts and, because of the neuroplasticity of the brain, redesign and rewire them. This is "renewing the mind" in action, and with the guidance of the Holy Spirit it is an essential part of a healthy, good life. Indeed, it is grace meeting science, since research shows that conscious awareness of thoughts makes the thoughts amenable to change because they are physically weakened![13]

For example, you may have been abused as a child and find that your emotions are awakened each time you move into a new relationship, affecting your ability to connect with your partner. Or you may have been scared of math for years, and as soon as you walk into the math class, emotions of anxiety and fear well up in you, resulting in a negative attitude, decreased concentration, and poor performance that perpetuate the negative cycle of hating math. In these cases it is imperative that you deal with the activated thought or it will submerge back into the nonconscious mind even stronger than before and become part of your dynamic and powerful belief system. This will affect your Perfect You and your ability to lead a normal life.

It may of course sound daunting to try to capture all of your attitudes in this way. But when you understand how you can scientifically choose what becomes *a part of who you are*, you will also understand that you have an amazing opportunity to be the person you want to be.

Discomfort Zone 4: About to Choose

This process of developing an awareness of the impact of our established attitudes (habits/entrenched belief systems) helps us understand what a bad habit really does to us. And this is where discomfort zone 4 enters the picture: it is the "about to choose" discomfort zone where you are in very active superposition and essentially basing your choices off the upwelling attitudes (discomfort zone 3), the incoming information, *and* wisdom from the Holy Spirit through the spiritual (fruit of the Spirit) and body (physical reactions). So discomfort zone 4 works hand in hand with discomfort zones 1, 2, and 3.

Mindful awareness of what is going on in your mind at this point—that is, a willing and intentional awareness to turn toward your inner spirit, mind, and body experiences—is a far more effective way to handle toxic stress than trying to change your toxic reactions in a mindless way. So in discomfort zone 4, when you are very intentional, conscious, and aware in your spirit, mind, and body, you have to be particularly mindful of what you are going to choose based on the incoming information, upwelling thoughts, and conversation with the Holy Spirit.

Studies using fMRI show that the self-referential network of the brain, called the default mode network (DFM), is active all the time, but particularly so when we switch off the external and switch on the internal during deep meditative thinking. This area gets activated when we get absorbed—caught up in our thoughts and consumed by them. When in this superposition or "about to choose" state, which is the fourth discomfort zone, if we choose to ask the Holy Spirit to help us focus, we can calm down, let go, and step back and out of the process by being aware of the need for his wisdom and guidance. We increase our intuitive powers and seem to stand outside of ourselves, the crazy chaos of our thinking calms down, and this same region, the DFM, responds accordingly.[14]

When we make a choice, the emotional perceptual library (the amygdala, mentioned above) does not always provide the accurate truth, because it works on perceptions we have built into our minds through our choices and reactions, and human perceptions are sometimes false. In fact, the emotions stored in this amygdala library can be quite dangerous if we allow them to control us.

So what should we do to choose well? We need to mindfully and intentionally remind ourselves that God has given us everything we need (2 Pet. 1:3). He has given us a way to handle every situation, so we should not make choices without him. In superposition we need to consciously ask God for wisdom and focus on the fruit of the Spirit. Practice this over sixty-three days and it will become a habit. By doing so, we take advantage of a circuit God has built into our brains that runs between the amygdala and the front part of the brain called the prefrontal cortex (PFC), which is situated more or less behind the eyebrows. Operating much like a scale, this circuit responds to balance reason and emotion. This is because the frontal lobe, of which the PFC is a part, is directly

---

Discomfort Zone 4 (About to Choose) Tip

You are in active superposition. You choose well by intentionally and deliberately observing your own thoughts, feelings, and bodily responses. You intuitively and deliberately choose to ask the Holy Spirit to help you make decisions about your thoughts and emotions. Become aware of what is going on in your mind and body at the moment of choosing. This is how you bring all thoughts into captivity!

---

connected to all the other parts of the brain and therefore becomes very active when we mindfully self-regulate. The PFC also has at its command the basal forebrain that activates all the processing loops through the brain. It manages, coordinates, and integrates all other brain regions when the mind is in action through thinking, feeling, and choosing.

The PFC is very active when we reason and understand our own thoughts about ourselves.[15] We use this PFC-amygdala circuit to control the raging emotions and stress responses in our bodies; it is part of the love circuit described earlier. We do this by reasoning out the situation facing us, in our minds or out loud, almost as though we were standing outside of ourselves *thinking about our thinking*. If we don't do this we will fall prey to the fear zone described earlier. If we do control the fear, however, the corpus striatum is activated. This causes us to feel calm, peaceful, and confident, thereby enabling us to rejoice despite our circumstances. So acknowledging our thoughts, feelings, existing memories, and bodily reactions is of paramount importance, because the emotions are dynamic chemicals that flow in the bloodstream between cells and deposit information about the memory into cells. This also happens through quantum action because the brain is like a biological quantum computer. If you suppress an emotion, it will explode somewhere. This is because the hypothalamic-pituitary-adrenal (HPA) axis will be disrupted and function abnormally. This HPA[16] axis involves the hypothalamus and pituitary glands in the brain and the adrenal glands just above the kidneys. It is the circuit that is activated in a complex, cyclic way of tension and release as we are responding to life all day long.

When we become aware of our four discomfort zones, we will become less interested in the bad attitude/habit/belief system and more interested in what the Holy Spirit has to say about situations in our lives and our existing attitudes. We learn, by mindfully listening to our spirit and body, to see the full impact toxic thinking, feeling, and choosing have on our lives.[17] We literally become disenchanted with the wrong way of thinking, feeling, and choosing, making it easier to let go of our pain and toxic thinking and step into our true perfect selves—the Perfect You. Once we realize that we control our pain, toxic thinking, and wrong feelings and reactions, once we truly understand that these do not control us, we are set free to start running God's race and reflecting his glorious image.

We all have the opportunity to choose to walk in the Perfect You God has given us, despite our circumstances.

9

The Perfect You Chart

In this chapter you will find a summary of what you have been reading up to this point, as a way of helping you pull all of the concepts together into a whole picture. It tracks the process from the point at which you focus on information to the point at which choices are being made. You will see four columns that you read from left to right. Column one deals with the five stages of the incoming signal of the events, circumstances of life, and upcoming existing memories. Column two tracks the philosophy and science of this. Column three provides a few examples, and column four shows how to use the discomfort zones to stay in your Perfect You.

Input:

External and Internal	Perfect You Science and Philosophy	Example	Discomfort Zones
1. Stimulus—from external world (events and circumstances of life); internal world (thoughts/memories), or both—sets the mind into action and activates the brain.	The quantum signal moves through the filter of the unique design of your brain, and you are attuned to respond in your exclusive way. You are the causal agent of the changes that are about to happen in your brain and be expressed through your words and/or actions.	1. You get a diagnosis from the doctor. 2. You get into an argument with a family member. 3. You receive an email from your boss. 4. You have to make a choice in a relationship.	Discomfort zone 1 (just-aware level) Your unique processing of the events and circumstances is activated. It passes through your Perfect You filter, so your perception and specialized interpretation that kick in is the lens through which you start becoming aware of the incoming and upcoming information. This Perfect You awareness results in a feeling of either peace or discomfort.
2. Nonconscious action in response to the stimulus; memories that are related in some way to the incoming information are selected.	Perfect You metacognitive action on nonconscious level is first orchestrated by Perfect You dynamic self-regulation. Your nonconscious mind looks for related (pattern-making and identification) Perfect You descriptive systems (thoughts/memories) to try to make sense of the incoming signal. These memories will provide knowledge about the situation and are the belief systems and attitudes that the incoming information will be filtered through. Your brain's and body's stress response kicks in and your whole brain and body responds at quantum speeds. If you were connected to brain imaging there would be evidence of nonconscious action about 350–550 milliseconds before you are consciously aware of your thinking.	You are in a superposition (just-aware discomfort zone 1) where you are becoming aware but are not yet *fully* aware of the incoming and upwelling information.	1. Use discomfort zone 1 to become mindful of your spirit, mind, and body responses and start evaluating what you are thinking and feeling. 2. Remind yourself that stress is good for you and makes you more focused and alert to be able to get through the situation. Train yourself over sixty-three days to make the stress response work for you and not against you.

Input: External and Internal	Perfect You Science and Philosophy	Example	Discomfort Zones
3. Thoughts start moving to the conscious mind.	1. This happens by pattern recognition and results in the activation of the related descriptive system (thoughts that have enough energy to move into the conscious mind because they were implanted deeply). Whatever you think about repeatedly over sixty-three days (three cycles of twenty-one) becomes automatized (a habit). 2. Active and dynamic self-regulation interact and you become fully aware of the upcoming and incoming information. Your mind action increases as you think and feel. This is called *superposition* in quantum physics, where the particles are in both states of 1 and 0 at the same time, so nothing has yet happened because no choice has yet been made. There is an infinite number of probabilities, both good and bad, that can be chosen from. These probabilities can be described by Schrödinger's wave of probabilities. 3. As you make the choice, genes are expressed and you build a new memory/thought of this experience, which is becoming a real physical thing in your brain made of proteins.	You begin to feel the impact of the stress response. You may feel all or some of these: your heart beats faster, adrenaline pumps through you, your pupils dilate, you are extremely alert, you feel like you have just been hit in the stomach, you feel nauseated, or you have muscular tension in your neck, throat, and back. You may think *Oh no!* as memories of the math class, the incident, the place, discussions, and so on bubble up into your conscious mind. These become the probabilities that you can choose from, and as you choose you create realities.	You are in the adrenaline-pumping, heart-pounding discomfort zone 2. 1. Remember to see the stress response as a good thing, and make all the physical reactions work for you and not against you. 2. Develop a Perfect You active reach, which is something you can automatically fall back on to anchor and reorient you. I suggest the thanksgiving, praise, and worship exercise (see pp. 237–38).

Input: External and Internal	Perfect You Science and Philosophy	Example	Discomfort Zones
4. Active free will: intentional choices are being made.	As a choice is made, a signal is generated that causes genetic expression, proteins are formed, and the memory is imprinted into the brain, causing structural change. In quantum physics terms, the wave collapses as a probability is chosen and a reality is created.	1. You choose to stay calm and reasonably work out a solution or you freak out and yell, a whole argument ensues, and a pattern of responses is set up. 2. You collapse with fear under the weight of all the negative things that can happen as a result of your diagnosis or you hang on to the healing Scriptures once again until a habit forms. At any point this thinking can be changed.	You are in discomfort zones 3 (attitude) and 4 (about to choose). For example, maybe you jump out of bed and verbalize "Oh no!" in response to a situation—now: 1. Become mindfully aware of your upwelling internal thoughts and feelings. 2. Become mindfully aware of your words and behaviors, especially your habits. 3. Evaluate the probabilities with the Holy Spirit. Draw on Scriptures you have memorized. 4. Use the discomfort zones to stay in the Perfect You and make stress work for you and not against you. 5. Do a discomfort zone 3 (attitude) check. Mindfully become aware of what attitudes you are expressing.

Input:

External and Internal	Perfect You Science and Philosophy	Example	Discomfort Zones
5. The impact of the stimulus is now being consciously processed and cycles of choices are being made every few seconds.	This is the cycle of thinking, feeling, and choosing that happens continually. Conscious cognitive action driven by metacognitive action is in full swing. Your brain is fired up with lots of activity and you are moving through thinking, feeling, and choosing every few seconds as you expand the memory with the new information coming in. This is the collapsing of the wave function through your thinking, feeling, and choosing—and it's changing your brain. You need to increase your mindfulness and thereby ramp up your active and dynamic self-regulation.	For example, a telephone or face-to-face discussion provides you with more information that you are adding to your thoughts about this incident. Whatever you think about the most will grow in your brain, so if you ruminate daily, you will build this into a long-term memory. If the memory is all toxic worry and fearful thinking about all the bad things that can happen to that person, your discernment to think, feel, and choose well will be compromised. If you think healthy thoughts and rejoice despite the circumstances, then you will build healthy thoughts and therefore realities into your brain as you consciously and intentionally ramp up your mindful appraisal of the situation.	1. Become mindfully aware of your thinking, feeling, choosing, words, behaviors, and habits. 2. The more deliberate you become at this point about objectively—with the help of the Holy Spirit—considering all the probabilities and disciplining yourself to slow down and evaluate each, the more you will move into your Perfect You.

10

Perfect You Metacognitive Module Exercises

Every time you think, it actively changes your brain and body for better (within your Perfect You) or worse (outside your Perfect You). When you make bad choices, toxic thought clusters with their attached emotions cause you to step out of your Perfect You, and this slippage affects your thoughts, words, and actions. Every time you operate according to your Perfect You, you are operating in your perfect design, reflecting a particular part of God's image. This is what you discovered when you did your UQ profile.

You can choose whether you would like to grow a healthy love attitude tree that brings health and life into your brain or a toxic, thorny fear attitude tree that will bring death into your brain. It all has to do with your Perfect You.

In my practice, I always made a point of focusing on the uniqueness of my patients, as I mostly saw children, teenagers, and adults who had given up all hope in their ability to learn or achieve anything in life. My greatest joy was seeing patients walk out of my practice with hope in their eyes and the message in their hearts that it is a scientific fact that they have an amazing mind they can develop and that they truly do have something to contribute to the world that no one else has. Some of my favorite experiences were receiving messages from angry teenagers who originally only came to see me because their parents were at their wit's end when it came to dealing with them, but by the end of our time together they considered me a friend. I remember one young man even gave me a hug, introducing me to his friends when we bumped into him at the movies and sending me this text: "Dr. Leaf, you have changed my life; I have hope again."

One of my favorite stories of hope comes out of my time working in South Africa among the poorest of schools, where my goal was to try to help twelfth graders pass their exams. The conditions were abysmal—no decent facilities, a few textbooks among a hundred students, a broken chalkboard, many hungry and hurting children.

One particular young man always stands out in my mind, because when I arrived in his classroom he was angry with life, hungry, tired, weighed down with the burdens of sickness, living in extreme poverty, involved in many dangerous activities that made the students and teachers very wary of him, and a whole host of other toxic things in his life that I didn't know about. I remember him glaring at me as I got up to teach him and his classmates how to learn. I remember thinking that this young man had no hope, just pain, and I asked God to help me touch his heart. Well, at the end of a long six-hour day, the teachers asked who wanted to thank me. Holding up a pen, this young man rushed to the front, tears pouring from his eyes, and said to me, "Dr. Leaf, thank you, thank you. Now I know what to do with my pen." That young man found meaning and value and God that day, and his face will always be in my mind. He went on to change his community and impact his world.

I treasure these memories and am blessed to have many, many more like them. The changes I saw in these people inspired me to study more about the mind and the brain, and my studies have given me a deeper sense of how great our God is. It will always be the mission of my heart to build this hope into people, because it makes people come alive. As Scripture says, "Hope deferred makes the heart sick, but a longing fulfilled is a tree of life" (Prov. 13:12 NIV). I want to stimulate a hope in you to find, develop, and use your Perfect You. I want you to be so filled with hope and love that you will pour this into someone else who, in turn, will also pour it into someone else. I want this message of hope to go viral!

The exercises below are designed to help you develop a more conscious awareness of what it feels like when you operate in your Perfect You and inspire you to hope again. Alongside developing an awareness of operating in your Perfect You, based on your UQ profile, and an awareness of what is blocking your Perfect You, you are going to develop the intellectual side of thinking, and therefore your intelligence.

The Purpose of the Perfect You Exercises

The Perfect You exercises are designed:

- To help you become aware of how you think, feel, and choose in your Perfect You state.
- To improve how you use the seven metacognitive modules, as well as to increase their interaction. (Remember, the strength of your Perfect You is in the sum of the parts operating as a whole system. We cannot single out one metacognitive module and describe it as our "strength.")
- To help you recognize when you step out of your Perfect You.
- To develop your intellect.

How to Use the Perfect You Exercises

When it comes to using the Perfect You exercises, I recommend you work through them in the sequence below, spending as many days on each as you feel necessary. Use the Perfect You checklist (see page 235) *every day* and, in addition, carve out minutes in your day to work on these exercises. My best recommendation is to do one per day or one per week—whatever works best for you—until you have done them all, and then repeat them. These are not exercises you do once and then forget about them; they are actually deliberate lifestyle changes you are going to be making to develop and stay in your Perfect You. They are part of a lifestyle of continual growth.

So, on a practical level, you could read through an exercise first thing in the morning, type it into your smartphone or write it on a card, and practice it through the day. If you are already doing my twenty-one-day brain detox (see www.21daybraindetox.com and my book *Switch On Your Brain*), you can use these exercises as part of your *active reaches*.

Intrapersonal Exercises

Here are ways you can enhance your intrapersonal mode of thought by taking quiet time to evaluate the knowledge you are receiving, by being aware of what is going on inside your mind, and by thinking deeply.

1. Practice listening to what you say. For example, be very aware of how you sound, your tone of voice. Focus on the choice of words you are using to communicate what you say. Be aware of your facial expressions as you communicate, as well as the reactions of other people. You may find it helpful to write down your observations in a journal.

2. Practice being aware of what you are thinking. Practice bringing all thoughts into captivity. Don't let any thoughts go unchecked through your mind. Stop randomly thinking and be intentional in what you choose to think about.

3. Practice analyzing your intuition, your gut feeling about things. Ask yourself, when you feel led by intuition, what actually is happening in your thinking. How does it feel when your intuition proves to be correct? Do you think your mind is sharper with this awareness?

4. Find seven periods of alone time, just for thinking—no phone, iPad, computer, people, or other distractions—just you sitting still, thinking. Do this for at least one to two minutes each day. It may be a bit of a challenge at first, but stick with it! As you quietly think deeply, you are building your intrapersonal thinking pillar, which is fundamental to introspection, self-knowledge, and understanding your own feelings, thoughts, and intuitions.

5. Try writing down your dreams and listening to what the Holy Spirit tells you about them. This may require putting away distractions and asking the Lord to speak to you through dreams. If this is new territory for you, simply pray about it this week. You can continue to work on this exercise over the coming weeks as well.

6. Practice comparing new and unique ideas with old ideas. For example, if you are reading about someone's new business idea, compare this to how you would normally see a business of that nature running. If you have always thought you should eat three meals a day, think about fasting from one of them every second day. If you have a strong opinion about something, argue it from another angle. Look at things from different points of view.

7. Practice mental self-examination by learning about yourself and examining your UQ profile. Look back at your profile. See how God created you unique in how you process thoughts. This is a simple exercise. You do not need to spend hours studying your profile. Simply recognize that God made you wonderfully, uniquely, perfectly *you*: this is your Perfect You!

Interpersonal Exercises

Here are ways you can enhance your interpersonal mode of thought by bouncing ideas off other people, communicating, and having interactive discussion with others.

1. Practice retelling stories. For example, tell someone, in as much detail as possible, about a film you have seen or a book or article you have read or are reading. Share your thoughts and have an interactive discussion about the topic. This doesn't have to be time-consuming. Simply share your experience with someone. As you engage in interactive discussion, you will be building your interpersonal thinking.

2. Practice making people feel at ease in challenging situations. For example, maybe there is a friend or work colleague who is battling with a situation. Talk to her, encourage her, and help her think through her feelings and what to do.

3. Practice spending *quality* time with people. For example, book a lunch or coffee date with a friend you haven't seen in a while. Get into an intense text conversation with someone. Call someone for a deep chat.

4. Practice listening without interrupting and without planning your own response. Try to do this at least twice each day. Simply listen actively to what another person is saying and take in what he has to say.

5. Practice listening twice as much as you talk. So, in a conversation, the other person will do the bulk of the talking. Listen intently to her and not to the thoughts in your head. Put yourself in another's position and try to think how he thinks.

6. Play "what if" games with yourself and others. "What if" games are an open-ended exploration of where your mind wants to go. They are creative in that you can go in any direction, but at the same time they are a disciplined activity since you observe what you are saying and therefore thinking about. You can even try to think of answers. You can move from the simple *What if I drove another way to work; what would be different about my day?* to the wild *What if I could go to work on a magic carpet?* The idea is to play and fantasize, to explore ideas and concepts.

7. Take a bit of time to coach or mentor others in something you are good at. You have gifts, talents, and skills that others would benefit from. Find someone who is looking for coaching or mentoring and share your experience and expertise with them. This doesn't have to be time-consuming. Simply connect with another person and pass on what you know.

Linguistic Exercises

Enhancing the linguistic mode of thought can be done by using words—talking in your head and out loud, asking questions, repeating statements, writing down thoughts, thinking in words, reading, and so forth.

1. Practice repeating statements you hear as you listen to people, the TV, and so on. Try repeating phrases or even complete sentences. Use your linguistic thinking to take in the information

in the form of words, then repeat it back. You may want to make this an exercise you do with another person. This simple exercise shouldn't take hours and hours. Simply add the exercise into your daily life.

2. Practice writing down thoughts while learning and concentrating. Take notes during lectures, meetings, or sermons. Take notes as you are reading an informative book or article. Don't only write down the information that is being presented; write down your thoughts as well. This may be a change from your normal routine, but it will help to build your linguistic mode of thought.

3. Read! This is the quickest and most effective way of building linguistic thinking and should become a lifestyle habit. Find a good book—maybe one you haven't read yet or a favorite you have read many times. Carve out some time each day to immerse yourself in your book. Simply enjoy reading the story or information.

4. Read a variety of literature, from the newspaper to novels, news magazines, and even comics! Read across a variety of different subjects. Read, read, and read some more! Try reading from a source you would not normally choose. Expand your literature base. This does not need to be time-consuming. Simply add some reading from a variety of sources each day.

5. Practice increasing your vocabulary. Try learning one new word each day. Within a year, you will have increased your vocabulary by 365 words. Practice using these words in different contexts. Do not overcomplicate this simple exercise. Simply use the new words you learn throughout your daily routine.

6. Practice playing word games like Trivial Pursuit, Scrabble, Clue, General Knowledge, and so on. Have fun with this simple exercise! Play with the twenty-six letters of the alphabet, as they are the foundation of language.

7. Practice doing crossword puzzles. Challenge yourself by working on a crossword puzzle a little every day this week. Exercise your linguistic mode of thought by learning new words in the puzzle and writing down the letters. Have fun as you expand your vocabulary!

Logical/Mathematical Exercises

Reasoning, analyzing, and strategizing can enhance the logical/mathematical mode of thought.

1. Practice quantifying everything you do. Analyze the time you use for various activities. What percentage of your day do you spend on eating, talking, social networks, and so forth? This is a simple yet profound exercise. You may be surprised at the answers to the questions you ask yourself.

2. Practice asking a lot of questions about whatever interests you and whatever doesn't interest you until you understand the topic deeply. Ask many questions this week! Encourage your curiosity. Find out answers. Work on recognizing logical and numerical patterns. Try to follow long chains of reasoning in a precise manner. Do not overcomplicate this exercise. It should be a simple addition to your daily life.

3. Practice estimating. For example, how long will it take you to get to a certain place, do your hair, or finish a task? How much time is left until lunch or before work is over? Then time yourself to see if you were correct.

4. Practice remembering statistics related to your favorite sports team. Try to recall statistics that you already know and also memorize and learn new statistics. If you don't know sports statistics, try asking someone in your household or looking at a sports website.

5. Play mental calculation games. For example, if you are a passenger in a car, add up the numbers you see on license plates of other vehicles on the road. You could also play Sudoku or a similar numbers game.

6. Practice breaking apart information you want to remember. Ask questions, to others or to yourself, until you understand the information. Analyze the information from different angles until it is clear. This doesn't have to be complicated; keep this exercise simple and as quick as possible.

7. Play games that are an effective mind sport, such as backgammon, chess, or bridge. If you do not already know how to play one of these games, learn. Strategize and think through the moves as you challenge your opponent. Maybe find a group of people who meet on a regular basis to play these games. Enjoy building your logical/mathematical thinking!

Kinesthetic Exercises

Enhancing the kinesthetic mode of thought can be done by touching, building, creating, and just about anything to do with movement.

1. Practice sitting on something other than a chair when learning, at your computer, reading, watching TV, and so on. For example, sitting on an exercise ball is an experience of actively engaging your body, whereas sitting in your chair is a passive activity. Make it fun! You can sit on an exercise ball at your desk, at the kitchen table, instead of on a couch—get creative with this exercise.

2. Stretch frequently, go for walks, or do some form of exercise. Get up and go! When you move your body, you will experience a positive sense of action in actually doing something.

3. Play around with drama, including formal theater, role play, and simulations. Maybe get the whole family involved by creating and performing a family skit. This does not have to be complicated or time-consuming. Get creative with this week's exercise.

4. Practice doing creative movement, dance, or stretching routines. This may be something you already do regularly, but you may not realize the positive effects the movement has on your thinking process. If you don't do this regularly, this week you have an opportunity to try something new. Have fun with the exercise!

5. Practice engaging in small tasks. For example, use flash cards and rubber stamps, build with LEGOs, and make things. You can get creative with this exercise. By definition, this is a very tactile, energetic, multisensory type of thinking that involves the control of body movements, the ability to coordinate yourself, and the capacity to handle objects and things around you skillfully. This week's exercise is a fun way to put your kinesthetic thinking into practice.

6. Rearrange a room in your house, your closet, or your office to make it more visually appealing. This simple exercise will help you build memory through sensory perceptions and movement. Do not overcomplicate the exercise. You do not need to spend hours and hours doing it. Simply rearranging something to improve the arrangement will suffice.

Musical Exercises

You can enhance your musical thinking via rhythm, melodies, and intuition, as well as by creating.

1. Practice playing your favorite music in the background when working. If you already do this, change your genre. There is

a powerful, scientifically established link between music and our emotions. This link is responsible for memory building. Enjoy listening to music in the background as you work this week. This is an exercise that should simply fit into the pattern of your daily life.

2. Practice using available musical instruments (or make them) and play them periodically. If you can't actually play a musical instrument, improvise by using pots as drums or something like that, or start learning! It's never too late to learn to play an instrument. As you experiment with playing an instrument, you will also build your ability to have instinct, which allows you to "read between the lines." Your musical thinking will also allow you to sense meaning and to verify it.

3. Practice some aerobic routines, stretch, or walk to music. Do your movements to the rhythm of the music you are listening to. Pay attention to the beat and melody. Don't overcomplicate this simple exercise. Simply moving your body to the rhythm of the music is enough to build your musical thinking.

4. Practice tapping a rhythm with your feet in time to your fingers. This may take some practice, but it should be a fun exercise that stretches you. This does not need to be time-consuming or complicated. Simply add the exercise into your normal daily routine.

5. Practice singing or humming while you work, even if it's under your breath so as not to disturb others. No matter whether your musical thinking is high or low, music can still help you learn. Classical music, in particular, has proven to be beneficial in classrooms and other learning environments.

6. Practice reading poetry and learning about poetic structure. Find a book on poetry and enjoy reading the poems out loud or silently. Use a good rhythm while reading. Do a little research in order to learn more about poetic structure. Don't

overcomplicate the exercise. You don't need to spend hours reading poetry. Simply enjoy poetry.

7. Practice consciously reading between the lines of what people are saying and doing and try to fathom people's attitudes by observing their body language. This can be done any time you interact with other people. Notice their facial expressions and the stance of their bodies. Try to interpret what they are saying through nonverbal communication. Use your intuition as you listen to what they are saying.

8. Practice noticing inflection in other people's voices. As you are having conversations, notice what other people are saying through their use of voice inflection. Notice the rise and fall of your voice inflection, as well as theirs. Simply work this exercise into your daily routine as you interact with people.

Visual/Spatial Exercises

Enhancing the visual/spatial mode of thought can be done by thinking in images and pictures, using your imagination, and visualizing while learning.

1. Practice reading cartoons and/or creating your own cartoons. Get creative with this simple and fun exercise! Exercising your visual/spatial thinking encourages mental operations not usually performed in a verbal mode. Reading and creating cartoons may turn out to be an activity that you really enjoy, while at the same time it strengthens and builds this way of thinking.

2. Practice making poster displays in your office, class, or house to help you think and express ideas—even Pinterest works. These can be simple, on small pieces of paper, or as elaborate as you want. The point is to express yourself visually in some form.

279

3. Practice drawing pictures or doodling when thinking. It doesn't matter what the pictures look like; it's the exercise that counts. Have fun with this exercise! Be free to draw or doodle whatever you would like.

4. Practice being aware of and differentiating between colors in nature, around your house—everywhere. Become aware of the different shades of color. Notice color as you drive through your neighborhood, as you are at work, as you are in school, as you take a walk—wherever you are throughout the week.

5. Practice developing your visual memory. Do this by doing the da Vinci exercise. That is, stare at a complex object, memorize it, then close your eyes and try to recall it in as much detail as possible. This may take some practice, but don't give up! This exercise shouldn't be time-consuming. Simply take a few minutes to practice this exercise throughout the week.

6. Study decorating and fashion magazines and be more aware of furniture and home decor, as well as what people are wearing. Wherever you go each day, notice the decor of the places you see. Take note of how different people use fashion in different ways. Flip through the pages of a fashion or decorating magazine while you are in a waiting room or grocery store line. This simple exercise can be done as you are going about your daily life.

7. Practice trying to take artistic pictures, whether or not you share them with others. Try to see things from different perspectives and photograph them from different angles than you would normally use. Don't overcomplicate this simple exercise. Simply taking artistic pictures while you go about your normal daily routine is sufficient.

Epilogue

How do we grasp the concept of human uniqueness? It is so vast and profoundly mysterious, made more so by the fact that we are image-bearers of the Creator. I wrote this book for all of us, including myself, to stimulate in us the recognition of the need to start unlocking the wonderful mystery of our Perfect You and to embrace our exceptionality. We need to recognize that we are beyond an IQ or SQ or EQ or a category in a questionnaire!

When we begin to see who we are, our blueprint for identity, we begin to discover the meaning of our lives. Meaning is not just something that happens inside our brains. It is something that evolves through the Perfect You and provides context to the things that come into our lives. Think of a painting. The meaning of the work does not arise from the chemical analysis of the materials used to create it. Nor does meaning arise from the multiple levels of neurophysiological processes from the photons of light striking the retina at the back of the eye or the resultant electrical impulses passing along the optic nerve to the different parts of the brain. Meaning arises from *your* interpretation of the painting—your exclusive perspective, your context, your Perfect You.

Our thoughts, feelings, choices, words, experiences, lives—these all have meaning, which is beautifully shaped and expressed through the special way each of us thinks, feels, and chooses. Through our Perfect You, we grow as human beings, learning more about ourselves and others.

The uniqueness of your Perfect You cannot merely be measured and locked in by the numbers and categories of intelligence, or emotional and social quotients. You are so much more; you have the properties of eternity. You are one of a kind. You have your own blueprint for identity. You are designed to operate in the currency of love, power, and soundness. You are *type-you*. And, as type-you, you can do something that no one else can do; the world would not be the same without you.

Once you really understand your Perfect You, you will start operating in your type-you. You will be set free from low self-esteem, self-doubt, envy, jealousy, and self-preoccupation, which can destroy brain tissue. You will find yourself celebrating the success of others because you will recognize how each of their unique experiences adds to, rather than detracts from, your own success in achieving the purpose God has fixed in each of us as different parts of his body. And, in doing so, you will grow healthy brain tissue instead of destroying it, thereby bringing health to your mind, spirit, and soul.

You will stop comparing yourself to others, looking for that elusive key to success in the achievements of others, because you will be set free to look within to the success that is already yours to activate. You will no longer hurt your self-esteem by trying to reshape your fingerprint to match someone else's. You will hold up your hands with a humble pride for all the world to see.

When you read about someone else's accomplishments you will find yourself celebrating their road map, learning from their perseverance and drive and commitment to their own Perfect You. In doing this, you will take the limits off where your Perfect You can take *you*. You can only be you. You'd make a lousy someone else. The Perfect You in you is meant to glorify, to love, and to reach beyond yourself, but you cannot grow into the fullest expression of God's creation if you live in doubt or unrest. You lose God's view of yourself in the quest to be someone else. You also lose sight of yourself when you allow yourself to get consumed with guilt for your past issues and wrongdoings.

In this book you have discovered your value, your meaning, and how *not* to live in doubt and unrest. You have activated a quest that will begin the process of identifying the blueprint for your Perfect You—the unique way you think, feel, and choose. You have started learning how to become mindfully aware and more interested in what is going on in your body and mind, which will help you stay in your Perfect You. You have begun to develop a willingness to turn toward your experience rather than trying to forcefully change it to be something it cannot be.

The world is about probabilities. You, with your Perfect You, are at the intersection of making your unique probabilities real and meaningful because no one can see what you see. It is your personal experience. And as you create a unique reality with your brilliant Perfect You, you are updating your knowledge of the world and adding a quality to the world that only you can add.

You are not designed to collide with everyone else's experience. You are designed to walk alongside everyone else in your uniqueness. It is not the world or us—but *us within the world*. Your unique mind, expressed through your Perfect You, reflects God's glory, bringing heaven to earth and making the world a more beautiful place.

YOU ARE BRILLIANT.

Every being cries out silently to be read differently.

Simone Weil, French philosopher

Afterword

by Dr. Avery M. Jackson

> Guard and keep safe the deposit [of godly truth] entrusted to you, turn away from worldly and godless chatter [with its profane, empty words], and the contradictions of what is falsely called "knowledge"—which some have professed and by doing so have erred (missed the mark) and strayed from the faith.
>
> 1 Timothy 6:20–21 AMP

The power of the mind, as Dr. Caroline Leaf demonstrates, is limitless when we have the mind of Christ and operate in love—and, therefore, in the Perfect You. The Lord God purposed me to function as a neurosurgeon who displays his manifested love through my hands when performing brain and spine surgeries. I walk in my Perfect You as I am led by the Lord, using the mind of Christ and the wisdom of God during surgical procedures, in order to have the best outcomes.

Dr. Leaf also emphasizes that we can unlearn negative toxic thoughts when we operate in love as we walk in the Perfect You. Science is purported to give final answers regarding medical problems.

Yet we can apply scientific method and still miss some of the practical applications of basic science (especially concerning how the mind and environment affect the brain and body in epigenetics). We draw conclusions about best practices in how to treat a unique, individual patient using population-based statistical methods, and that patient can receive medical care that is not tailored to their idiosyncratic needs as a result.

Not so with God's perfect will for you individually as you walk in your Perfect You. Your mindful decisions, based on how God has truly made you to be, will create right situations based on right actions based on right thoughts from a mind that is free of toxic thought. Your brain responds to what you do, so if there is communication—and behavioral and intellectual change—then the brain has been changed by the mind, and this change is expressed through words and actions, which as Dr. Leaf points out is relatively new thinking about the brain in science.

This book will help you unlock your true potential, once you have worked through and applied its principles. You can discover what your Perfect You is by learning its structure and how to begin living in it. Your purpose is to live beyond yourself through reflecting God's glory to a broken world. As you learn to operate in your Perfect You, you will be able to negotiate life more successfully.

Dr. Caroline Leaf is a passionate "cognitist" who "sees" and eloquently describes the Lord's heart in the quantum mechanics of how he purposed our unique souls to function together and "enrich each other's Perfect You, by walking alongside each other and *celebrating our differences.*" We will be the agent of change as we walk in our Perfect You in this world, and we will reflect the Lord's glory.

Avery M. Jackson III, MD, FACS, FAANS,
board certified neurosurgeon
CEO/founder of Michigan Neurosurgical Institute PC
CEO/founder of Optical Spine LLC
Grand Blanc, Michigan, USA

Afterword

by Dr. Peter Amua-Quarshie

Then I said, "Behold, I come; in the scroll of the book
it is written of me."

Psalm 40:7

The above verse is quoted in Hebrews 10:7 in reference to Jesus
Christ's mission on earth. Just like our Savior, our unique per-
sonalities, gifts, and purposes are already written by God "in the
scroll of the book" before we are born into this world. In other
words, our "Perfect You" is already written in "the book." In this
book, *The Perfect You*, Dr. Leaf helps us to peer into what has
been written about us so that we can live the life we have been
ordained to live by our Creator.

Having known Dr. Leaf for almost a decade now, and having
discussed the principles and practices in this book over countless
hours, I can truly say that *The Perfect You* comes out of what God
has revealed to her from his Word. These revelations have been

rigorously researched, tested, and applied with amazing success in multitudes of people around the world.

I would suggest, dear reader, to be like the Bereans (Acts 17:10–11), who considered what Paul told them with an open mind and did their research to verify what they heard. Dr. Leaf has provided ample references, both scriptural and academic, for further study. She has given you practical steps to apply what you have read.

Above all, rise up and become the Perfect You God created you to be.

Peter Amua-Quarshie, MD, MPH, MS

Notes

Prologue

1. S. McDowell and Jonathan Morrow, *Is God Just a Human Invention? And Seventeen Other Questions Raised by the New Atheists* (Grand Rapids: Kregel, 2011), Kindle loc. 1525.
2. Keith Ward, *The God Conclusion: God and the Western Philosophical Tradition* (London: Darton, Longman and Todd, 2009), Kindle loc. 843.
3. David Brooks, *The Road to Character* (New York: Random House, 2015).

Chapter 1 The Big Picture

1. J. M. Schwartz and S. Begley, *The Mind and the Brain* (New York: Harper-Collins, 2009), Kindle loc. 377.
2. Caroline Leaf, "The Mind Mapping Approach: A Model and Framework for Geodesic Learning," unpublished DPhil dissertation (Pretoria, South Africa: University of Pretoria, 1997).
3. H. P. Stapp, "Quantum Interactive-Dualism: An Alternative to Materialism," *Journal of Religion and Science* 3 (2006), doi:10.1111/j.1467–9744.2005.00762.x, http://www-atlas.lbl.gov/~stapp/QID.pdf.
4. Jeffrey M. Schwartz, Henry P. Stapp, and Mario Beauregard, "Quantum Physics in Neuroscience and Psychology: A Neurophysical Model of Mind-Brain Interaction." *Philosophical Transactions of the Royal Society B* 360, no. 1458 (2005): 1309–27, doi:10.1098/rstb.2004.1598.
5. Leaf, "The Mind Mapping Approach"; Caroline Leaf, "Mind Mapping: A Therapeutic Technique for Closed Head Injury," Master's dissertation (University of Pretoria, 1990); Caroline Leaf, "The Mind Mapping Approach (MMA): A Culture and Language-Free Technique," *The South African Journal of Communication Disorders* 40: 35–43; Caroline Leaf, "The Development of a Model for Geodesic Learning: The Geodesic Information Processing Model," *The South African Journal of Communication Disorders* 44 (1997): 53–70; C. M. Leaf, I. C. Uys, and B. Louw, "An Alternative Non-Traditional Approach to Learning: The

Metacognitive-Mapping Approach," *The South African Journal of Communication Disorders* 45 (1998): 87–102; C. M. Leaf, I. C. Uys, and B. Louw, "The Development of a Model for Geodesic Learning: The Geodesic Information Processing Model," *The South African Journal of Communication Disorders* 44 (1997).

6. Leaf, "Mind Mapping."

7. Schwartz and Begley, *The Mind and the Brain*, 27.

8. William R. Uttal, "The Two Faces of MRI," *Cerebrum*, Dana Foundation, July 1, 2002, http://www.dana.org/Cerebrum/Default.aspx?id=39300.

9. Brian Resnick, "There's a Lot of Junk FMRI Research Out There. Here's What Top Neuroscientists Want You to Know," *Vox*, September 9, 2016, http://www.vox.com/2016/9/8/12189784/fmri-studies-explained; A. Eklund et al., "Cluster Failure: Why FMRI Inferences for Spatial Extent Have Inflated False-Positive Rates," *Proceedings of the National Academy of Sciences* 113, no. 28 (2016): 7900–7905.

10. Alexis Madrigal, "Scanning Dead Salmon in FMRI Machine Highlights Risk of Red Herrings," *Wired.com*, September 19, 2009, https://www.wired.com/2009/09/fmrisalmon/.

11. J. R. Middleton, *The Liberating Image: The Imago Dei in Genesis 1* (Grand Rapids: Brazos, 2005).

Chapter 2 The Perfect You

1. J. Cairns, J. Overbaugh, et al. "The Origin of Mutants," *Nature* 35 (1988): 142–45.

2. Binghamton University, "Researchers Can Identify You by Your Brain Waves with 100 Percent Accuracy," *Science Daily*, April 18, 2016, https://www.sciencedaily.com/releases/2016/04/160418120608.htm; Maria V. Ruiz-Blondet et al., "A Novel Method for Very High Accuracy Event-Related Potential Biometric Identification," *CEREBRE: IEEE Transactions on Information Forensics and Security* 11, no. 7 (2016): 1618, doi:10.1109/TIFS.2016.2543524.

3. Weizmann Institute of Science, "Smell Fingerprints? Each Person May Have a Unique Sense of Smell," *Science Daily*, June 30, 2015, www.sciencedaily.com/releases/2015/06/150630100509.htm.

4. Wellcome Trust, "Brain's Architecture Makes Our View of the World Unique," *Science Daily*, Dec. 6, 2010, www.sciencedaily.com/releases/2010/12/101205202512.htm.

5. "Professor Keith Ward—Religion and the Quantum World," YouTube video, 50:05, uploaded by Mystical Theosis on Jan. 9, 2013, https://youtu.be/z4VjaoVHqNk, run time 18:00–18:25.

6. Christine Sutton, "Fifty Years of Bell's Theorem," CERN, Nov. 4, 2014, https://home.cern/about/updates/2014/11/fifty-years-bells-theorem; J. S. Bell, "On the Einstein Podolsky Rosen Paradox," *Physics* 1, no. 3 (1964): 195–200, https://cds.cern.ch/record/111654/files/vol1p195-200_001.pdf?version=1; J. S. Bell, *Speakable and Unspeakable in Quantum Mechanics: Collected Papers on Quantum Philosophy* (Cambridge: Cambridge University Press, 2004), Kindle ed.

7. "Mental Health: A State of Well-Being," World Health Organization, August 2014, http://www.who.int/features/factfiles/mental_health/en/.

Chapter 3 Discovering the Potential of Our Blueprint for Identity

1. Middleton, *The Liberating Image*.

2. Stanton Peele and Archie Brodsky, *Love and Addiction* (New York: Taplinger, 1975); Stanton Peele, "The 7 Hardest Addictions to Quit—Love is the Worst," *Psychology Today*, December 15, 2008, https://www.psychologytoday.com/blog /addiction-in-society/200812/the-7-hardest-addictions-quit-love-is-the-worst; Stan Tatkin, *Wired for Love: How Understanding Your Partner's Brain and Attachment Style Can Help You Defuse Conflict and Build a Secure Relationship* (New York: New Harbinger, 2011); E. R. Kandel, *In Search of Memory: The Emergence of a New Science of Mind* (New York: Norton, 2008); Elizabeth Seto and Joshua A. Hicks, "Disassociating the Agent from the Self: Undermining Belief in Free Will Diminishes True Self-Knowledge," *Social Psychological and Personality Science* 7 (2016): 726–34, doi:http://dx.doi.org/10.1177/1948550616653810; A. G. Christy et al., "Straying from the Righteous Path and from Ourselves: The Interplay between Perceptions of Morality and Self-Knowledge," *Personality and Social Psychology Bulletin* 1, no. 42 (2016): 1538–1550; F. Gino et al., "The Moral Virtue of Authenticity," *Psychological Science* 26, no. 7 (2015): 983–86.

3. Candace B. Pert, *Molecules of Emotion: The Science behind Mind-Body Medicine* (New York: Scribner, 2010), Kindle ed.; Bruce H. Lipton, *The Biology of Belief* (New York: Hay House, 2008) Kindle ed., loc. 115 ff.; Michael A. Ferguson et al., "Reward, Salience, and Attentional Networks Are Activated by Religious Experience in Devout Mormons," *Social Neuroscience* 1 (2016), doi:10.1080 /17470919.2016.1257437; Angela Jones et al., "Relationships between Negative Spiritual Beliefs and Health Outcomes for Individuals with Heterogeneous Medical Conditions," *Journal of Spirituality in Mental Health* 17, no. 2 (2015): 135, doi:10.1080/19349637.2015.1023679; Society for Neuroscience, "Be Afraid, Be Very Afraid, If You Learned To: Study on Fear Responses Suggests New Understanding of Anxiety Disorders," *Science Daily* (January 24, 2007), www .sciencedaily.com/releases/2007/01/070123182010.htm; M. A. Penzo, V. Robert, and B. Li, "Fear Conditioning Potentiates Synaptic Transmission onto Long-Range Projection Neurons in the Lateral Subdivision of Central Amygdala," *Journal of Neuroscience* 34, no. 7 (2014): 2432, doi:10.1523/JNEUROSCI.4166-13.2014.

4. Yomayra F Guzmán et al., "Fear-Enhancing Effects of Septal Oxytocin Receptors," *Nature Neuroscience* (2013), doi:10.1038/nn.3465; Patty Van Cappellen et al., "Effects of Oxytocin Administration on Spirituality and Emotional Responses to Meditation," *Social Cognitive and Affective Neuroscience* (2016), doi:10.1093 /scan/nsw078; Don Wei et al., "Endocannabinoid Signaling Mediates Oxytocin-Driven Social Reward," *PNAS* (October 26, 2015), doi:10.1073/pnas.1509795112.

5. Medical University of Vienna, "Dopamine: Far More Than Just the 'Happy Hormone,'" *Science Daily* (August 31, 2016), https://www.sciencedaily.com/releases /2016/08/160831085320.htm; John D. Salamone and Mercè Correa, "The Mysterious Motivational Functions of Mesolimbic Dopamine," *Neuron* 76, no. 3 (2012): 470, doi:10.1016/j.neuron.2012.10.021.

6. M. J. Poulin et al., "Giving to Others and the Association between Stress and Mortality," *Am J Public Health* 103, no. 9 (September 2013): 1649–55, doi:10.2105

/AJPH.2012.300876; E. B. Raposa, H. B. Laws, and E. B. Ansell, "Prosocial Behavior Mitigates the Negative Effects of Stress in Everyday Life," *Clinical Psychological Science* (2015), doi:10.1177/2167702615611073.

7. British Neuroscience Association, "How Our Bodies Interact with Our Minds in Response to Fear and Other Emotions," *Science Daily* 7 (April 2013), www.sciencedaily.com/releases/2013/04/130407211558.htm; Damian Refojo et al., "Glutamatergic and Dopaminergic Neurons Mediate Anxiogenic and Anxiolytic Effects of CRHR1," *Science* 333, no. 6051 (September 30, 2011): 1903–7, doi: 10.1126/science.1202107; T. Steimer, "The Biology of Fear and Anxiety-Related Disorders," *Dialogues in Clinical Neurosciences* 4, no. 3 (2002): 231–49.

8. Peele, "7 Hardest Addictions"; Seto and Hicks, "Disassociating the Agent," 726–34; Christy et.al. "Straying from the Righteous Path;" Gino et al., "Moral Virtue."

9. S. Satel and S. O. Lillienfield, *Brainwashed: The Seductive Appeal of Mindless Neuroscience* (New York: Basic Books, 2013), 49–72.

10. B. H. Lipton, "Insight into Cellular Consciousness," *Bridges* 12, no. 1 (2012): 5; M. Gutschner, "Discovery of Quantum Vibrations in Microtubules Inside Neurons Corroborates Controversial 20-Year-Old Theory of Consciousness," *Elsevier* (January 16, 2014), https://www.elsevier.com/about/press-releases/research-and-journals/discovery-of-quantum-vibrations-in-microtubules-inside-brain-neurons-corroborates-controversial-20-year-old-theory-of-consciousness; Deepak Chopra, *How Consciousness Became the Universe: Quantum Physics, Cosmology, Relativity, Evolution, Neuroscience, Parallel Universes* (Cambridge: Cosmology Science Publishers, 2015).

11. Peter Kinderman, *The New Laws of Psychology: Why Nature and Nurture Alone Can't Explain Human Behavior* (London: Robinson, 2014).

12. See my web page www.drleaf.com for multiple references on this subject; on mental health specifically see http://drleaf.com/blog/a-brief-history-of-mental-health-care-in-the-twentieth-century/; see replays of my TV show series on mental health at http://drleaf.com/broadcast/; P. R. Breggin, "Rational Principles of Psychopharmacology for Therapists, Healthcare Providers and Clients," *Journal of Contemporary Psychotherapy* 46 (2016): 1–13; P. R. Breggin, "The Biological Evolution of Guilt, Shame and Anxiety: A New Theory of Negative Legacy Emotions," *Elsevier Medical Hypotheses* 85 (2015): 17–24.

13. Lipton, "Insight into Cellular Consciousness," 5; B. H. Lipton, *The Biology of Belief: Unleashing the Power of Consciousness* (Santa Rosa, CA: Mountain of Love/Elite Books, 2005).

14. Caroline Leaf, *Switch On Your Brain. The Keys to Peak Thinking, Happiness, and Health* (Grand Rapids: Baker, 2013); Caroline Leaf, "21-Day Brain Detox," www.21daybraindetox.com.

15. Cosmas D. Arnold et al., "Genome-Wide Quantitative Enhancer Activity Maps Identified by STARR=Seq," *Science* 339, no. 6123 (March 1, 2013): 1074–77, doi:10.1126/science.1232542; I. I. Patrushev, T. F. Kovalenko, "Functions of Noncoding Sequences in Mammalian Genomes," *Biochemistry* (Mosc.) 79, no. 13 (December 2014): 1442–69; Manolis Kellis et al., "Defining Functional DNA Elements in the Human Genome," *Proc Natl Acad Sci USA* 111, no. 17 (April 29,

2014): 6131–38; Perla Kaliman et al., "Rapid Changes in Histone Deacetylases and Inflammatory Gene Expression in Expert Meditators," *Psychoneuroendocrinology* 40 (February 2014): 96–107.

16. Robin Holliday, "Epigenetics: A Historical Overview," *Epigenetics* 1, no. 2 (2006): 76–80; Adrian Bird, "Perceptions of Epigenetics," *Nature* 447, no. 7143 (2007): 396398.

17. J. J. Day and J. D. Sweatt, "Epigenetic Mechanisms in Cognition," *Neuron* 70, no. 5 (2011): 813–29.

18. Trygve Tollefsbol, ed., *Handbook of Epigenetics: The New Molecular and Medical Genetics* (New York: Elsevier/Academic Press, 2011).

19. Bob Weinhold, "Epigenetics: the Science of Change," *Environmental Health Perspectives* 114, no. 3 (2006): A160; Kaliman et al., "Rapid Changes."

20. John Cairns, Julie Overbaugh, and Stephan Miller, "The Origin of Mutants," *Nature* 335 (1988): 142–45; H. F. Nijhout, "Metaphors and the Role of Genes in Development," *Bioessays* 12, no. 9 (1990): 441–46.

21. Henry Stapp, "Minds and Values in the Quantum Universe," *Information and the Nature of Reality from Physics to Metaphysics*, ed. P. C. W. Davies and Niels Henrik Gregersen (Cambridge, UK: Cambridge University Press, 2014): 157.

22. Middleton, *The Liberating Image*, 14–89.

23. S. A. McGee, *Heaven's Reality: Lifting the Quantum Veil* (Denver, CO: Glistening Prospect Bookhouse, 2016).

24. Stapp, "Minds and Values in the Quantum Universe."

Chapter 4 The Philosophy of the Perfect You

1. J. A. Wheeler, *A Journey into Gravity and Spacetime* (New York: W. H. Freeman, 1990).

2. Keith Ward, *The Evidence for God: The Case for the Existence of the Spiritual Dimension* (London: Darton, Longman and Todd, 2014), Kindle ed.; Keith Ward, "The New Atheists," YouTube video, 37:32, uploaded by ObjectiveBob, August 29, 2012, https://www.youtube.com/watch?v=fkJshx-7l5w; Ward, *God Conclusion*, Kindle loc. 759–60.

3. Keith Ward, *The Big Questions in Science and Religion* (West Conshohocken, PA: Templeton Press, 2008), Kindle ed.

4. J. C. Eccles and K. Popper, *The Self and Its Brain: An Argument for Interactionism* (London: Taylor and Francis, 2014), Kindle ed.

5. Satel and Lilienfeld, *Brainwashed*; J. Kulnych, "Psychiatric Neuroimaging Evidence: A High-Tech Crystal Ball?" *Stanford Law Review* 49 (1997): 1249–70; E. Monterosso et al., "Explaining Away Responsibility: Effects of Scientific Explanations on Perceived Culpability," *Ethics and Behavior* 15, no. 2 (2005): 139–53.

6. A. Keller et al., "Does the Perception That Stress Affects Health Matter? The Association with Health and Mortality," *Health Psychology* 31, no. 5 (September 2012): 677–84, https://www.ncbi.nlm.nih.gov/pubmed/22201278; Bianca Nogrady, "Chronic Stress Enhances Cancer Spread through Lymphatic System," *ABC News*, March 2, 2016, http://mobile.abc.net.au/news/2016-03-02/chronic-stress-enhances-spread-of-cancer-through-lymph-system/7211536; M. J.

Poulin et al., "Giving to Others and the Association between Stress and Mortality," *American Journal of Public Health* 103, no. 9 (September 2013): 1649–55, http:// www.ncbi.nlm.nih.gov/pubmed/23327269; N. L. Sin and R. P. Sloan, "Linking Daily Stress Processes and Laboratory-Based Heart Rate Variability in a National Sample of Midlife and Older Adults," *Psychosomatic Medicine* (2016): 1, doi: 10.1097/PSY.0000000000000306; C. C. Wolford et al., "Transcription Factor ATF3 Links Host Adaptive Response to Breast Cancer Metastasis," *Journal of Clinical Investigation* 123, no. 7 (2013): 2893, doi:10.1172/JCI64410.

7. R. Swinburne, *Mind, Brain and Free Will* (London: Oxford University Press, 2013).

8. Sabrina Tavernise, "First Rise in U.S. Death Rate in Years Surprises Experts," *The New York Times*, June 1, 2016, http://mobile.nytimes.com/2016/06/01 /health/american-death-rate-rises-for-first-time-in-a-decade.html?_r=2&referer=; CDC, "Vital Statistics Rapid Release: Quarterly Provisional Estimates," *National Center for Health Statistics*, http://www.cdc.gov/nchs/products/vsrr/mortality -dashboard.htm.

9. Mark Rapley, Joanna Moncrieff, and Jacqui Dillon, *De-Medicalizing Misery: Psychiatry, Psychology and the Human Condition* (New York: Palgrave Macmillan, 2011).

10. Axel Cleeremans, "Radical Plasticity Thesis: How the Brain Learns to Be Conscious," *Frontiers in Psychology* 2, no. 86 (May 9, 2011), doi:10.3389/fpsyg .2011.00086; Olivia Goldhill, "A Civil Servant Missing Most of His Brain Challenges Our Most Basic Theories of Consciousness," *Quartz* (July 2, 2016), http:// qz.com/722614/a-civil-servant-missing-most-of-his-brain-challenges-our-most -basic-theories-of-consciousness/.

11. J. C. Eccles and K. Popper, *The Self and Its Brain: An Argument for Interactionism* (London: Taylor and Francis, 2014), Kindle loc. 241.

12. Ward, *Big Questions in Science and Religion*.

13. Ibid.

14. Ibid.

15. Ibid.

16. Stapp, "Minds and Values in the Quantum Universe."

17. Richard Dawkins, *River Out of Eden: A Darwinian View of Life* (New York: Basic Books, 1995).

Chapter 5 The Science of the Perfect You

1. Kinderman, *The New Laws of Psychology*.

2. B. Draganski et al., "Neuroplasticity: Changes in Grey Matter Induced by Training," *Nature* 427, no. 6972 (2004): 311–12; H. K. Manji and R. S. Duman, "Impairments of Neuroplasticity and Cellular Resilience in Severe Mood Disorders: Implications for the Development of Novel Therapeutics," *Psychopharmacology Bulletin* 5, no. 2 (2000): 5–49; T. F. Münte, E. Altenmüller, and L. Jäncke, "The Musician's Brain as a Model of Neuroplasticity," *Nature Reviews Neuroscience* 3, no. 6 (2002): 473–78.

3. See the recommended reading list for more information on my research.

4. H. Gardner, *Frames of Mind* (New York: Basic Books, 2011); J. M. Shine et al., "The Dynamics of Functional Brain Networks: Integrated Network States during Cognitive Task Performance," *Neuron* 92, no. 2 (October 19, 2016): 544–54, doi:10.1016/j.neuron.2016.09.018.

5. Leaf, *Switch On Your Brain*; P. Lally, "How Are Habits Formed: Modelling Habit Formation in the Real World," *European Journal of Social Psychology* 40, no. 6 (2010): 998–1009; James Clear, "How Long Does It Actually Take to Form a New Habit (Backed by Science)," *James Clear*, http://jamesclear.com/new-habit.

6. M. M. Merzenich et al., "Some Neurological Principles Relevant to the Origins of—and the Cortical Plasticity Based Remediation of—Language Learning Impairments," *Neuroplasticity: Building a Bridge from the Laboratory to the Clinic*, J. Grafman, ed. (Amsterdam: Elsevier, 1999), 169–87; M. Merzenich, *Soft-Wired. How the New Science of Brain Plasticity Can Change Your Life* (San Francisco: Parnassus, 2013).

7. "Libet Experiments," *The Information Philosopher*, retrieved October 28, 2016, http://www.informationphilosopher.com/freedom/libet_experiments.html; Benjamin Libet, Anthony Freeman, and Keith Sutherland, *The Volitional Brain: Towards a Neuroscience of Free Will* (Exeter, UK: Imprint Academic, 1999); Benjamin Libet, "Mind Time: The Temporal Factor in Consciousness," *Perspectives in Cognitive Neuroscience* (Cambridge, MA: Harvard University Press, 2004); M. Pauen, "Does Free Will Arise Freely?" *Scientific American Mind* 14, no. 1 (2004); in his virtual Nobel acceptance speech, Libet summarized his life's research and highlighted his work on conscious volitional acts and the antedating of sensory awareness.

8. C. S. Soon et al., "Unconscious Determinants of Free Decisions in the Human Brain," *Nature Neuroscience* 11, no. 5 (April 13, 2008): 543–45, doi: 10.1038/nn.2112.

9. "Libet Experiments."

10. C. S. Herrmann et al., "Analysis of a Choice-Reaction Task Yields a New Interpretation of Libet's Experiments," *International Journal of Psychophysiology* 67 (2008): 156, http://www.fflch.usp.br/df/opessoa/Hermann%20-%20New%20inter pretation%20-%20%202008.pdf.

11. Benjamin Libet, *Mind Time: The Temporal Factor in Consciousness* (Cambridge, MA: Harvard University Press, 2004).

12. D. Denett et al., *Neuroscience and Philosophy: Brain, Mind, and Language* (New York: Columbia University Press, 2007).

13. C. S. Keener, *The Mind of the Spirit: Paul's Approach to Transformed Thinking* (Grand Rapids: Baker Academic, 2016).

14. C. M. Caves et al., "Unknown Quantum States: The de Finetti Representation," *Journal of Mathematical Physics* 43, no. 9 (2002): 4537–59; C. Fuchs and R. Schack, "Quantum-Bayesian Coherence," *Reviews of Modern Physics* 85, no. 4 (2013): 1693; Amanda Gefter, "A Private View of Quantum Reality," *Quanta Magazine*, June 4, 2015, https://www.quantamagazine.org/20150604-quantum-bayesianism-qbism/.

15. Henry P. Stapp, "Quantum Interactive-Dualism: An Alternative to Materialism," *Journal of Religion and Science* (September 6, 2003): 3, http://www-atlas .lbl.gov/~stapp/QID.pdf, doi:10.1111/j.1467–9744.2005.00762.x.

16. Ibid.

17. Werner Heisenberg, *Physics and Philosophy: the Revolution in Modern Science* (New York: Harper and Row, 1958); David C. Cassidy, *Werner Heisenberg: A Bibliography of His Writings*, 2nd ed. (New York: Whittier, 2001).

18. John von Neumann, *Mathematical Foundations of Quantum Mechanics*, trans. Robert T. Beyer (Princeton: Princeton University Press, 1955).

19. Stapp, "Quantum Interactive-Dualism," 2.

20. Henry P. Stapp, "Quantum Interactive Dualism: An Alternative to Materialism," *Journal of Consciousness Studies* 12, no. 11 (2005): 43–59.

21. M. Beauregard et al., "Quantum Physics in Neuroscience and Psychology: A Neurophysical Model of Mind-Brain Interaction," *Philosophical Transactions of the Royal Society of London* Series B, *Biological Sciences* 360, no. 1458 (2005): 1309–27.

22. Gefter, "A Private View of Quantum Reality."

23. "Keith Ward—The New Atheists," YouTube video.

24. Gefter, "A Private View of Quantum Reality."

25. P. C. W. Davies and Niels Henrik Gregersen, *Information and the Nature of Reality: From Physics to Metaphysics* (Cambridge, UK: Cambridge University Press, 2010), 85.

26. Beauregard et al., "Quantum Physics in Neuroscience and Psychology."

27. Leon Gmeindl et al., "Tracking the Will to Attend: Cortical Activity Indexes Self-Generated, Voluntary Shifts of Attention," *Attention, Perception & Psychophysics* (2016), doi:10.3758/s13414-016-1159-7.

28. M. J. Poulin et al., "Giving to Others and the Association between Stress and Mortality."

29. M. J. Poulin, "Volunteering Predicts Health among Those Who Value Others: Two National Studies," *Health Psychology* 33, no. 2 (February 2014): 120–29, doi:10.1037/a0031620.

30. University of Chicago, "Loneliness Affects How the Brain Operates," *Science Daily*, Feb. 17 2009, www.sciencedaily.com/releases/2009/02/090215151800.htm.

31. J. S. Bell, *Speakable and Unspeakable in Quantum Mechanics*.

Chapter 6 Profiling the Perfect You

1. G. N. Fleming, "The Actualization of Potentialities in Contemporary Quantum Theory," *The Journal of Speculative Philosophy* 4 (1992): 259–76.

Chapter 8 The Discomfort Zones

1. Stapp, "Mind and Values in the Quantum Universe."

2. C. B. Pert, *Molecules of Emotion: Why You Feel the Way You Feel* (New York: Scribner, 1997).

3. S. T. Charles et al., "The Wear and Tear of Daily Stressors on Mental Health," *Psychological Science* (2013), doi:10.1177/0956797612462222.

4. C. Meydan et al., "MicroRNA Regulators of Anxiety and Metabolic Disorders," *Trends in Molecular Medicine* 22, no. 9 (2016): 798, doi: 0.1016/j.molmed.2016.07.001; D. Colbert, *Deadly Emotions: Understand the Mind-Body-Spirit Connection That Can Heal You or Destroy You* (Nashville: Thomas Nelson, 2003).

5. A. Keller et al., "Does the Perception that Stress Affects Health Matter? The Association with Health and Mortality," *Health Psychology* 5 (2012): 677–84, doi:10.1037/a0026743.

6. M. Miller, "Laughter Helps Blood Vessels Function Better," presentation conducted at the meeting of the American College of Cardiology Scientific Session, Orlando, FL, 2005.

7. M. J. Poulin et al., "Giving to Others and the Association Between Stress and Mortality."

8. Kelly McGonigal, "How to Make Stress Your Friend," YouTube video, 14:28, uploaded by TED Talks on September 4, 2013, https://www.youtube.com/watch?v=RcGyVTAoXEU&noredirect=1.

9. Penn State, "Let It Go: Reaction to Stress More Important Than Its Frequency," *Science Daily*, February 25, 2016, www.sciencedaily.com/releases/2016/02/16022514 0246.htm.

10. Church Dawson, *The Genie in Your Genes: Epigenetic Medicine and the New Science of Intention* (Santa Rosa, CA: Energy Psychology Press, 2009).

11. E. B. Raposa, H. B. Laws, and E. B. Ansell, "Prosocial Behavior Mitigates the Negative Effects of Stress in Everyday Life," *Clinical Psychological Science* (2015), doi:10.1177/2167702615611073.

12. You can discover exactly how to do this through my twenty-one-day detox program, found in my book *Switch On Your Brain*.

13. K. Nader, G. E. Schafe, and J. E. LeDoux, "Reply—Reconsolidation: The Labile Nature of Consolidation Theory," *Nature Reviews Neuroscience* 1, no. 3 (2000): 216–19.

14. Judson Brewer, "A Simple Way to Break a Bad Habit," *TED.com*, November 2015, http://www.ted.com/talks/judson_brewer_a_simple_way_to_break_a _bad_habit; Kalina Christoff et al., "Mind-Wandering as Spontaneous Thought: A Dynamic Framework," *Nature Reviews Neuroscience* 17, no. 11 (2016): 718, doi:10.1038/nrn.2016.113; Xiang Wang et al., "Cognitive Vulnerability to Major Depression," *Harvard Review of Psychiatry* 24, no. 3 (2016): 188, doi:10.1097 /HRP.0000000000000081; Jonas T. Kaplan et al., "Processing Narratives Concerning Protected Values: A Cross-Cultural Investigation of Neural Correlates," *Cerebral Cortex* (January 2016) doi:10.1093/cercor/bhv325.

15. K. Christoff et al., "Rostrolateral Prefrontal Cortex Involvement in Relational Integration During Reasoning," *Neuroimage* 14, no. 5 (2001): 1136–49; M. Donoso et al., "Foundations of Human Reasoning in the Prefrontal Cortex," *Science* 344, no. 6191 (2014): 1481–86.

16. B. M. Kudielka et al., "HPA Axis Responses to Laboratory Psychosocial Stress in Healthy Elderly Adults, Younger Adults, and Children: Impact of Age and Gender," *Psychoneuroendocrinology* 29, no. 1 (2004): 83–98.

17. J. A. Brewer et al., "Craving to Quit: Psychological Models and Neurobiological Mechanisms of Mindfulness Training as Treatment for Addictions," *Psychology of Addictive Behaviors* 27, no. 2 (2012): 366–79; K. M. Garrison et al., "Real-Time fMRI Links Subjective Experience with Brain Activity During Focused Attention," *NeuroImage* 81 (2013): 110–18.

Recommended Reading

The concepts I teach in this book cover a very wide spectrum and years of reading, researching, and working with clients in private practice, schools, and business corporations. If I had to provide all the citations for complete scientific scholarship to document the origin of each fact that I have used, there would be almost as many citations as words. So I have used a little flexibility to write this book in a more popular style, helping me to communicate my message as effectively as I can.

There are only a few citations in the actual text that are more general, and the book list that follows is less of a bibliography (which would also be too long) and more of a recommended reading list of some of the great books and scientific articles I have used in my research.

Adams, H. B., and B. Wallace. "A Model for Curriculum Development: TASC." *Gifted Education International* 7 (1991): 194–213.

Alavi, A., and L. J. Hirsch. "Studies of Central Nervous System Disorders with Single Photon Emission Computed Tomography and Positron Emission Tomography: Evolution Over the Past 2 Decades." *Seminars in Nuclear Medicine* 21, no. 1 (January 1991): 51–58.

Alesandrini, K. L. "Imagery: Eliciting Strategies and Meaningful

Learning." *Journal of Educational Psychology* 62 (1982): 526–30.

Allport, D. A. "Patterns and Actions: Cognitive Mechanisms and Content Specific." In *Cognitive Psychology: New Directions*, edited by G. L. Claxton. London: Routledge & Kegan Paul, 1980.

Amen, D. G. *Change Your Brain, Change Your Life*. New York: Three Rivers Press, 1998.

———. *Magnificent Mind at Any Age*. New York: Harmony Books, 2008.

Amend, A. E. "Defining and Demystifying Baroque, Classic and Romantic Music." *Journal of the Society for Accelerative Learning and Teaching* 14, no. 2 (1989): 91–112.

Amua-Quarshie, P. "Basalo-Cortical Interactions: The Role of the Basal Forebrain in Attention and Alzheimer's Disease." Unpublished Master's thesis. Newark: Rutgers University, 2009.

Anastasi, M. W., and A. B. Newberg. "A Preliminary Study of the Acute Effects of Religious Ritual on Anxiety." *The Journal of Alternative and Complementary Medicine* 14, no. 2 (March 2008): 163–65. doi:10.1089/acm.2007.0675.

Anderson, J. R. *Cognitive Psychology and Its Complications*. 2nd ed. New York: W. H. Freeman, 1985.

Arnheim, R. "Visual Thinking in Education." In *The Potential of Fantasy and Imagination*, edited by

A. Sheikll and J. Shaffer, 215–25. New York: Brandon House, 1979.

Atkins, R. C. *Dr. Atkins Health Revolution*. Boston: Houghton Mifflin Company, 1990.

———. *Dr. Atkins New Diet Revolution*. London: Ebury Press, 2003.

———. *New Diet Cook Book*. London: Ebury Press, 2003.

Bach-y-Rita, P., et al. "Vision Substitution by Tactile Image Projection." *Nature* 221, no. 5184 (1969): 963–64.

Bancroft, W. J. "Accelerated Learning Techniques for the Foreign Language Classroom." *Per Linguam* 1, no. 2 (1985): 20–24.

Barker, J. A. *Discovering the Future: The Business of Paradigms*. Minneapolis: ILI Press, 1986.

Bartlett, F. C. *Remembering: A Study in Experimental and Social Psychology*. Cambridge, UK: Cambridge, 1932.

Baxter, R., S. B. Cohen, and M. Ylvisaker. "Comprehensive Cognitive Assessment." In *Head Injury Rehabilitation: Children and Adolescents*, edited by M. Ylvisaker, 247–75. San Diego: College-Hill Press, 1985.

Beauregard, M., and D. O'Leary. *The Spiritual Brain*. New York: Harper Collins, 2007.

Bereiter, L. "Toward a Solution of the Learning Paradox." *Review of Educational Research* 55 (1985): 201–25.

Berninger, V., A. Chen, and R. Abbot. "A Test of the Multiple

Connections Model of Reading Acquisition." *International Journal of Neuroscience* 42 (1988): 283–95.

Bishop, J. H. "Why the Apathy in American High Schools?" *Educational Researcher* 18, no. 1 (1989): 6–10.

Block, N., and G. Dworkin. *The I.Q. Controversy*. New York: Pantheon, 1976.

Bloom, B. S. "The Z Sigma Problem: The Search for Methods of Group Instruction as Effective as One-to-One Tutoring." *Educational Researcher* 13, no. 6 (1984): 4–16.

Bloom, F. E., ed. *The Best of the Brain from Scientific American: Mind, Matter and Tomorrow's Brain*. New York: Dana Press, 2007.

Bloom, F. E., et al., eds. *The Dana Guide to Brain Health*. New York: Dana Press, 2003.

Bloom, L., and M. Lahey. *Language Development and Language Disorders*. Mississauga, ON, Canada: Wiley & Sons, 1978.

Boller, K., and C. Rovee-Collier. "Contextual Coding and Recording of Infants' Memories." *Journal of Experimental Child Psychology* 53, no. 1 (1992): 1–23.

Borkowski, J. G., W. Schneider, and M. Pressley. "The Challenges of Teaching Good Information Processing to the Learning Disabled Student." *International Journal of Disability, Development and Education* 3, no. 3 (1989): 169–85.

Botha, L. "SALT in Practice: A Report on Progress." *Journal of the Society for Accelerative Learning and Teaching* 10, no. 3 (1985): 197–99.

Botkin, J. W., M. Elmandjra, and M. Malitza. *No Limits to Learning: Bridging the Human Gap; A Report to the Club of Rome*. New York: Pergamon Press, 1979.

Boyle, P. "Having a Higher Purpose in Life Reduces Risk of Death Among Older Adults." *(e)Science News* (June 15, 2009). http:// esciencenews.com/articles /2009/06/15/having.a.higher .purpose.life.reduces.risk.death .among.older.adults.

"Brain and Mind Symposium." Columbia University (2004). http:// c250.columbia.edu/c250_events /symposia/brain_mind/brain _mind_vid_archive.html.

Bransford, J. D. *Human Cognition*. Belmont, CA: Wadsworth, 1979.

Braten, I. "Vygotsky as Precursor to Metacognitive Theory, II: Vygotsky as Metacognitivist." *Scandinavian Journal of Educational Research* 35, no. 4 (1991): 305–20.

Braun, A. "The New Neuropsychology of Sleep Commentary." *Neuro-Psychoanalysis* 1 (1999): 196–201.

Briggs, M. H. "Team Talk: Communication Skills for Early Intervention Teams." *Journal of Childhood Communication Disorders* 15, no. 1 (1993): 33–40.

Broadbent, D. E. *Perception and Communication*. London: Pergamon Press, 1958.

Brown, A. L. "Knowing When, Where and How to Remember: A Problem of Meta-Cognition." In *Advances in Instructional Psychology*, edited by R. Glaser. Hillsdale, NJ: Lawrence/Erlbaum, 1978.

Bunker, V. J., W. M. McBurnett, and D. L. Fenimore. "Integrating Language Intervention throughout the School Community." *Journal of Childhood Communication Disorders* 11, no. 1 (1987): 185–92.

Buzan, T. *Head First*. London: Thorsons, 2000.

———. *Use Both Sides of Your Brain*. New York: Plume, 1991.

Buzan, T., and T. Dixon. *The Evolving Brain*. Exeter, UK: Wheaten & Co., 1976.

Buzan, T., and R. Keene. *The Age Heresy*. London: Ebury Press, 1996.

Bynum, J. *Matters of the Heart*. Lake Mary, FL: Charisma House, 2002.

Byron, R. *Behavior in Organizations: Understanding and Managing the Human Side of Work*. 2nd ed. Boston: Allyn & Bacon, 1986.

Byron, R., and D. Byrne. *Social Psychology: Understanding Human Interaction*. 4th ed. Boston: Allyn & Bacon, 1984.

Calvin, W., and G. Ojemann. *Conversations with Neil's Brain*. Reading, MA: Addison-Wesley, 1994.

Campbell, B., L. Campbell, and D. Dickinson. "Teaching and Learning through Multiple Intelligences." Seattle: New Horizons for Learning, 1992.

Campione, J. C., A. L. Brown, and N. R. Bryant. "Individual Differences in Learning and Memory." In *Human Abilities: An Information Processing Approach*, edited by R. J. Sternberg, 103–26. New York: West Freeman, 1985.

Capra, F. "The Turning Point: A New Vision of Reality." *The Futurist* 16, no. 6 (1982): 19–24.

Caskey, O. "Accelerating Concept Formation." *Journal of the Society for Accelerative Learning and Teaching* 11, no. 3 (1986): 137–45.

Chi, M. "Interactive Roles of Knowledge and Strategies in the Development of Organized Sorting and Recall." In *Thinking and Learning Skills* 2. Edited by S. F. Chipman, J. W. Segal, and R. Glaser. Hillsdale, NJ: Lawrence Erlbaum, 1985.

Childre, D., and H. Martin. *The Heartmath Solution*. San Francisco: Harper-Collins, 1999.

Clancey, W. "Why Today's Computers Don't Learn the Way People Do." Paper presented at the Annual Meeting of the American Educational Research Association. Boston, MA, 1990.

Clark, A. J. "Forgiveness: A Neurological Model." *Medical Hypotheses* 65 (2005): 649–54.

Colbert, D. *The Bible Cure for Memory Loss*. Lake Mary, FL: Siloam Press, 2001.

———. *Deadly Emotions: Understand the Mind-Body-Spirit Connection that Can Heal or Destroy*

You. Nashville: Thomas Nelson, 2003.

Concise Oxford Dictionary. 9th ed. Oxford: Oxford University Press, 1995.

Cook, N. D. "Colossal Inhibition: The Key to the Brain Code." *Behavioral Science* 29 (1984): 98–110.

Costa, A. L. "Mediating the Metacognitive." *Educational Leadership* 42, no. 3 (1984): 57–62.

Cousins, N. "Anatomy of an Illness as Perceived by the Patient." *New England Journal of Medicine* 295 (1976): 1458–63.

———. *Anatomy of an Illness as Perceived by the Patient.* New York: Bantam, 1981.

Crick, F. *The Astonishing Hypothesis: The Scientific Search for the Soul.* New York: Charles Scribner & Sons, 1979.

Crick, F. H. C. "Thinking about the Brain." *Scientific American* 241, no. 3 (1981): 228–49.

Cromie, William J. "Aging Brains Lose Less Than Thought." *Harvard University Gazette* (October 3, 1996). https://news.harvard.edu/gazette/1996/10.03/AgingBrains.html.

Damasio, A. R. *The Feeling of What Happens: Body and Motion in the Making of Consciousness.* New York: Harcourt Brace, 1999.

Damico, J. S. "Addressing Language Concerns in the Schools: The SLP as Consultant." *Journal of Childhood Communication Disorders* 11, no. 1 (1987): 17–40.

Dartigues, J. F. "Use It or Lose It." *Omni* (February 1994): 34.

De Andrade, L. M. "Intelligence's Secret: The Limbic System and How to Mobilize It Through Suggestopedy." *Journal of the Society for Accelerative Learning and Teaching* 11, no. 2 (1986): 103–13.

De Capdevielle, B. "An Overview of Project Intelligence." *Per Linguam* 2, no. 2 (1986): 31–38.

Decety, J., and J. Grezes. "The Power of Simulation: Imagining One's Own and Others' Behavior." *Brain Research* 1079 (2006): 4–14.

Decety, J., and P. L. Jackson. "A Social Neuroscience Perspective of Empathy." *Current Directions in Psychological Science* 15 (2006): 54–58.

Derry, S. J. "Remediating Academic Difficulties through Strategy Training: The Acquisition of Useful Knowledge." *Remedial and Special Education* 11, no. 6 (1990): 19–31.

Dhority, L. *The ACT Approach: The Artful Use of Suggestion for Integrative Learning.* Bremen, West Germany: PLS Verlag GmbH, AnderWeide, 1991.

Diamond, M. *Enriching Heredity: The Impact of the Environment on the Brain.* New York: Free Press, 1988.

Diamond, M., and J. Hopson. "How to Nurture Your Child's Intelligence, Creativity and Healthy

Emotions from Birth through Adolescence." In *Magic Trees of the Mind: How to Nurture Your Child's Intelligence, Creativity and Healthy Emotions from Birth through Adolescence*. New York: Penguin, 1999.

Diamond, M., A. Scheibel, G. Murphy, Jr., and T. Harvey. "On the Brain of a Scientist: Albert Einstein." *Experimental Neurology* 88, no. 1 (1985): 198–204.

Dienstbier, R. "Periodic Adrenaline Arousal Boosts Health Coping." *Brain-Mind Bulletin* 14, no. 9a (1989).

Diamond, S., and J. Beaumont, eds. *Hemisphere Function in the Human Brain*. New York: Halstead, 1977, 264–78.

Dispenza, J. *Evolve Your Brain: The Science of Changing Your Brain*. Deerfield Beach, FL: Health Communications, 2007.

Dobson, J. *How to Build Confidence in Your Child*. London: Hodder & Stoughton, 1997.

Doidge, N. *The Brain That Changes Itself: Stories of Personal Triumph from the Frontiers of Brain Science*. New York: Penguin, 2007.

Duncan, J., et al. "A Neural Basis for General Intelligence." *Science* 289 (2000): 457–60.

Edelman, G. M., and V. B. Mountcastle, eds. *The Mindful Brain*. Cambridge, MA: MIT Press, 1978.

Edelman, G. M., and G. Tononi. *A Universe of Consciousness: How Matter Becomes Imagination*. New York: Basic Books, 2000.

Edmonds, M. "How Albert Einstein's Brain Worked." *HowStuffWorks* (accessed December 15, 2016). http://health.howstuffworks.com /einsteins-brain1.htm.

Edwards, B. *Drawing on the Right Side of the Brain*. Los Angeles: J. P. Torcher, 1979.

Einstein, A. *Albert Einstein, the Human Side: New Glimpses from His Archives*. Edited by Helen Dukas and Banesh Hoffmann. Princeton, NJ: Princeton University Press, 1979.

Eisenburger, N. "Understanding the Moderators of Physical and Emotional Pain: A Neural Systems-Based Approach." *Psychological Inquiry* 19 (2008): 189–95.

Entwistle, N. "Motivational Factors in Students' Approaches in Learning." In *Learning Strategies and Learning Styles*, edited by R. R. Schmeck, 21–51. New York: Plenum, 1988.

Entwistle, N. J., and P. Ramsden. *Understanding Student Learning*. London: Croom Helm, 1983.

Eriksen, C. W., and J. Botella. "Filtering Versus Parallel Processing in RSVP Tasks." *Perception and Psychophysics* 51, no. 4 (1992): 334–43.

Erskine, R. "A Suggestopedic Math Project Using Non Learning Disabled Students." *Journal of the Society for Accelerative Learning and Teaching* 11, no. 4 (1986): 225–47.

Farah, M. J., et al. "Brain Activity Underlying Visual Imagery: Event Related Potentials during Mental Image Generation." *Journal of Cognitive Neuroscience* 1 (1990): 302–16.

Faure, C. *Learning to Be: The World of Education Today and Tomorrow.* Paris: UNESCO, 1972.

Feldman, D. *Beyond Universals in Cognitive Development.* Norwood, NJ: Ablex Publishers, 1980.

Feuerstein, R. *Instrumental Enrichment: An Intervention Program for Cognitive Modifiability.* Baltimore: University Park Press, 1980.

Feuerstein, R., M. Jensen, S. Roniel, and N. Shachor. "Learning Potential Assessment." *Assessment of Exceptional Children.* Philadelphia: Haworth Press, 1986.

Flavell, J. H. "Metacognitive Development." In *Structural/Process Theories of Complete Human Behaviour,* edited by J. M. Scandura and C. J. Brainerd. Amsterdam: Sijthoff & Noordoff, 1978.

Flavell, P. *The Developmental Psychology of Jean Piaget.* New York: Basic Books, 1963.

Fodor, J. *The Modularity of Mind.* Cambridge, MA: MIT/Bradford, 1983.

Fountain, D. *God, Medicine, and Miracles: The Spiritual Factors in Healing.* New York: Random House, 2000.

Frassinelli, L., K. Superior, and J. Meyers. "A Consultation Model for Speech and Language Intervention." *American Speech-Language-Hearing Association* 25, no. 4 (1983): 25–30.

Freeman, W. J. *Societies of Brains: A Study in the Neuroscience of Love and Hate.* Hillsdale, NJ: Lawrence Erlbaum, 1995.

Fuster, J. M. *The Prefrontal Cortex.* 4th ed. London: Academic Press, 2008.

Galaburda, A. "Albert Einstein's Brain." *Lancet* 354 (1999): 182.

Galton, F. *Inquiries into Human Faculty and Its Development.* London: L. M. Dent, 1907.

Gardner, H. *Frames of Mind.* New York: Basic Books, 1985.

———. *The Quest for Mind: Piaget, Levi-Strauss, and the Structuralist Movement.* Chicago: University of Chicago Press, 1981.

Gardner, H., and D. P. Wolfe. "Waves and Streams of Symbolization." In *The Acquisition of Symbolic Skills,* edited by D. Rogers and J. A. Slabada. London: Plenum Press, 1983.

Gazzaniga, M. S. *Handbook of Neuropsychology.* New York: Plenum, 1977.

———, ed. *The New Cognitive Neurosciences.* Cambridge, MA: MIT/Bradford, 2004.

Gelb, M. *Present Yourself.* Los Angeles: Jalmar Press, 1988.

Gerber, A. "Collaboration Between SLP's and Educators: A

Continuity Education Process."
*Journal of Childhood Commu-
nication Disorders* 11, no. 1–2
(1987): 107–25.

"Ghost in Your Genes." *Nova*. Produced and directed by Sarah Holt
and Nigel Paterson. BBC, 2006.
http://www.pbs.org/wgbh/nova
/genes/.

Glaser, R. *Adaptive Education: In-
dividual Diversity and Learning*.
New York: Holt, Rinehart and
Winston, 1977.

Glasser, M. D. *Control Theory in the
Classroom*. New York: Harper &
Row, 1986.

Goldberg, E., and L. D. Costa.
"Hemisphere Differences in the
Acquisition and Use of Descriptive Systems." *Brain and Language*
14 (1981): 144–73.

Golden, F. "Albert Einstein: Person of
the Century." *Time* (December 31,
1999). http://content.time.com
/time/magazine/article/0,9171
,993017,00.html.

Gould, S. *The Mismeasure of Man*.
New York: W. W. Norton, 1981.

Griffiths, D. E. "Behavioural Science
and Educational Administration."
*63rd Yearbook of the National
Society for the Study of Education*. Chicago: National Society
for the Study of Education, 1964.

Gungor, E. *There Is More to the Secret*.
Nashville: Thomas Nelson, 2007.

Guyton, A. C., and J. E. Halle. *Text-
book of Medical Physiology*. 9th
ed. Philadelphia: W. D. Saunders,
2006.

Haber, R. N. "The Power of Visual
Perceiving." *Journal of Mental
Imagery* 5 (1981): 1–40.

Halpern, S., and L. Savary. *Sound
Health: The Music and Sounds
That Make Us Whole*. San Fran-
cisco: Harper & Row, 1985.

Hand, J. D. "The Brain and Accelerative Learning." *Per Linguam* 2, no.
2 (1986): 2–14.

Hand, J. D., and B. L. Stein. "The
Brain and Accelerative Learning,
Part II: The Brain and Its Func-
tions." *Journal of the Society for
Accelerative Learning and Teach-
ing* 11, no. 3 (1986): 149–63.

Harrell, K. D. *Attitude Is Everything:
A Tune-up to Enhance Your Life*.
Dubuque, IA: Kendall/Hunt Pub-
lishing, 1995.

Harrison, C. J. "Metacognition and
Motivation." *Reading Improvement* 28, no. 1 (1993): 35–39.

Hart, L. *Human Brain and Human
Learning*. New York: Longman,
1983.

Hatton, G. I. "Function-Related
Plasticity in the Hypothalamus."
Annual Review of Neuroscience
20 (1997): 375–97.

Hawkins, D. B. *When Life Makes
You Nervous: New and Effective
Treatments for Anxiety*. Colorado
Springs: Cook Communications,
2001.

Healy, J. "Why Kids Can't Think."
Bottom Line Personal 13, no. 8
(1992): 1–3.

Hinton, G. E., and J. A. Anderson.
Parallel Models of Associate

Memory. Hillsdale, NJ: Erlbaum, 1981.

Hobson, J. A. *Dreaming: An Introduction to the Science of Sleep.* New York: Oxford University Press, 2002.

Hochberg, L. R., et al. "Neuronal Ensemble Control of Prosthetic Devices by a Human with Tetraplegia." *Nature* 442, no. 7099 (2006): 164–71.

Holden, C. "Child Development: Small Refugees Suffer the Effects of Early Neglect." *Science* 305 (1996): 1076–77.

Holford, P. *The 30-Day Fat Burner Diet.* London: Piatkus, 1999.

———. *The Optimum Nutrition Bible.* London: Piatkus, 1997.

———. *Optimum Nutrition for the Mind.* London: Piatkus, 2003.

Holt, J. *How Children Fail.* New York: Pitman, 1964.

Horstman, J. *The Scientific American Day in the Life of Your Brain.* San Francisco: Jossey-Bass, 2009.

Hubel, D. H. "The Brain." *Scientific American* 24, no. 13 (1979): 45–53.

Hunter, C., and F. Hunter. *Laugh Yourself Healthy.* Lake Mary, FL: Christian Life, 2008.

Hyden, H. "The Differentiation of Brain Cell Protein, Learning and Memory." *Biosystems* 8, no. 4 (1977): 22–30.

Hyman, S. E. "Addiction: A Disease of Learning and Memory." *American Journal of Psychiatry* 162 (2005): 1414–22.

Iaccino, J. *Left Brain–Right Brain Differences: Inquiries, Evidence and New Approaches.* Hillsdale, NJ: Lawrence Erlbaum, 1993.

Iran-Nejad, A. "Active and Dynamic Self-Regulation of Learning Processes." *Review of Educational Research* 60, no. 4 (1990): 573–602.

———. "Associative & Nonassociative Schema Theories of Learning." *Bulletin of the Psychonomic Society* 27 (1989): 1–4.

———. "The Schema: A Long-Term Memory Structure of a Transient Functional Pattern." In *Understanding Reader Is Understanding,* edited by R. J. Teireny, P. Anders, and J. N. Mitchell, 109–28. Hillsdale, NJ: Lawrence Erlbaum, 1987.

Iran-Nejad, A., and B. Chissom. "Active and Dynamic Sources of Self-Regulation." Paper presented at the Annual Meeting of the American Psychological Association. Atlanta, GA, 1988.

Iran-Nejad, A., and A. Ortony. "A Biofunctional Model of Distributed Mental Content, Mental Structures, Awareness and Attention." *The Journal of Mind and Behaviour* 5 (1984): 171–210.

Iran-Nejad, A., A. Ortony, and R. K. Rittenhouse. "The Comprehension of Metaphonical Uses of English by Deaf Children." *American Speech-Language Association* 24 (1989): 551–56.

Jacobs, B., M. Schall, and A. B. Scheibel. "A Quantitative Dendritic

Analysis of Wernickes Area in Humans: Gender, Hemispheric and Environmental Factors." *Journal of Comparative Neurology* 327, no. 1 (1993): 97–111.

Jacobs, B. L., et al. "Depression and the Birth and Death of Brain Cells." *American Scientist* 88, no. 4 (2000): 340–46.

Jensen, A. *Bias in Mental Testing.* New York: Free Press, 1980.

Jensen, E. *Brain-Based Learning and Teaching.* South Africa: Process Graphix, 1995.

Johnson, D. W., R. T. Johnson, and E. Holubec. *Circles of Learning: Co-operation in the Classroom.* Edina, MN: Interaction Book Company, 1986.

Johnson, J. M. "A Case History of Professional Evolution from SLP to Communication Instructor." *Journal of Childhood Communication Disorders* 11, no. 4 (1987): 225–34.

Jorgensen, C. C., and W. Kintsch. "The Role of Imagery in the Evaluation of Sentences." *Cognitive Psychology* 4 (1973): 110–16.

Jouvet, M. "Working on a Dream." *Nature Neuroscience* 12 (2009): 811.

Kagan, A., and M. Saling. *An Introduction to Luria's Aphasiology Theory and Application.* Johannesburg, South Africa: Witwatersrand University Press, 1988.

Kalivas, P. W., and N. D. Volkow. "The Neural Basis of Addiction: A Pathology of Motivation and Choice." *American Journal of Psychiatry* 162 (2005): 1403–13.

Kandel, E. R. *In Search of Memory: The Emergence of a New Science of Mind.* New York: W. W. Norton, 2006.

———. "The Molecular Biology of Memory Storage: A Dialog Between Genes and Synapses." Nobel Lecture, December 8, 2000. http://nobelprize.org/nobel_prizes /medicine/laureates/2000/kandel -lecture.pdf.

———. "A New Intellectual Framework for Psychiatry." *American Journal of Psychiatry* 155, no. 4 (1998): 457–69.

Kandel, E. R., J. H. Schwartz, and T. M. Jessell, eds. *Principles of Neural Science.* 4th ed. New York: McGraw-Hill, 2000.

Kane, D. "How Your Brain Handles Love and Pain." *NBCNews.com,* February 19, 2004. http://www .msnbc.msn.com/id/4313263.

Kaniels, S., and R. Feuerstein. "Special Needs of Children with Learning Difficulties." *Oxford Review of Education* 15, no. 2 (1989): 165–79.

Kaplan-Solms, K., and M. Solms. *Clinical Studies in Neuro-Psychoanalysis.* New York: Karnac, 2002.

Kazdin, A. E. "Covert Modelling, Imagery Assessment and Assertive Behaviour." *Journal of Consulting and Clinical Psychology* 43 (1975): 716–24.

Kimura, D. "The Asymmetry of the Human Brain." *Scientific*

American 228, no. 3 (1973): 70–80.

———. "Sex Differences in the Brain." *Scientific American* 267, no. 3 (September 1992): 119–25.

King, D. F., and K. S. Goodman. "Whole Language Learning, Cherishing Learners and Their Language." *Language, Speech and Hearing Sciences in Schools* 21 (1990): 221–29.

Kintsch, W. "Learning from Text, Levels of Comprehension, or Why Anyone Would Read a Story Anyway?" *Poetics* 9 (1980): 87–98.

Kline, P. *Everyday Genius*. Arlington, VA: Great Ocean Publishers, 1990.

Kluger, J. "The Biology of Belief," *Time*, February 12, 2009. http://content.time.com/time/magazine/article/0,9171,1879179,00.html.

Knowles, M. *The Adult Learner: A Neglected Species*. Houston: Gulf Publishing Company, 1990.

Kopp, M. S., and J. Rethelyi. "Where Psychology Meets Physiology: Chronic Stress and Premature Mortality—the Central-Eastern European Health Paradox." *Brain Research Bulletin* 62 (2004): 351–67.

Kosslyn, S. M., and O. Koenig. *Wet Mind: The New Cognitive Neuroscience*. New York: Free Press, 1995.

Kruszelnicki, Karl S. "Einstein Failed School." *ABC Science* (June 23, 2004). http://www.abc.net.au/science/articles/2004/06/23/1115185.htm.

Kubzansky, L. D., et al. "Is Worrying Bad for Your Heart? A Prospective Study of Worry and Coronary Heart Disease in the Normative Aging Study." *Circulation* 94 (1997): 818–24.

LaHaye, T., and D. Noebel. *Mind Siege: The Battle for Truth in the New Millennium*. Nashville: Word Publishing, 2000.

Larsson, G., and B. Starrin. "Effect of Relaxation Training on Verbal Ability, Sequential Thinking, and Spatial Ability." *Journal of the Society of Accelerative Learning and Teaching* 13, no. 2 (1988): 147–59.

Lazar, C. "A Review and Appraisal of Current Information on Speech/Language Alternative Service Delivery Models in Schools." *Communiphon* 308 (1994): 8–11.

Lazar, S. W., and C. E. Kerr. "Meditation Experience Is Associated with Increased Cortical Thickness." *NeuroReport* 16, no. 17 (2005): 189–97.

Lea, L. *Wisdom: Don't Live Life without It*. Guilford, Surrey, UK: Highland Books, 1980.

Leaf, C. M. "An Altered Perception of Learning: Geodesic Learning." *Therapy Africa* 1 (October 1997). 7.

———. "An Altered Perception of Learning: Geodesic Learning: Part 2." *Therapy Africa* 2, no. 1 (January/February 1998): 4.

———. "The Development of a Model for Geodesic Learning:

The Geodesic Information Processing Model." *The South African Journal of Communication Disorders* 44 (1997): 53–70.

———. "Evaluation and Remediation of High School Children's Problems Using the Mind Mapping Therapeutic Approach." *Remedial Teaching* 7/8 (September 1992).

———. "The Mind Mapping Approach (MMA): Open the Door to Your Brain Power: Learn How to Learn." *Transvaal Association of Educators Journal* (TAT), 1993.

———. "The Mind Mapping Approach: A Model and Framework for Geodesic Learning." Unpublished DPhil dissertation, University of Pretoria, South Africa, 1997.

———. "Mind Mapping as a Therapeutic Intervention Technique." Unpublished workshop manual, 1985.

———. "Mind Mapping as a Therapeutic Technique." *Communiphon* 296 (1989): 11–15. South African Speech-Language-Hearing Association.

———. "Mind Mapping: A Therapeutic Technique for Closed Head Injury." Masters dissertation, University of Pretoria, South Africa, 1990.

———. "The Move from Institution Based Rehabilitation (IBR) to Community Based Rehabilitation (CBR): A Paradigm Shift." *Therapy Africa* 1 (August 1997): 4.

———. *Switch On Your Brain: Understand Your Unique Intelligence Profile and Maximize Your Potential.* Cape Town, South Africa: Tafelberg, 2005.

———. "Teaching Children to Make the Most of Their Minds: Mind Mapping." *Journal for Technical and Vocational Education in South Africa* 121 (1990): 11–13.

———. *Who Switched Off My Brain? Controlling Toxic Thoughts and Emotions.* Revised edition. Dallas: Inprov, 2009.

———. *Who Switched Off My Brain? Controlling Toxic Thoughts and Emotions.* DVD series. Johannesburg, South Africa: Switch on Your Brain, 2007.

Leaf, C. M., M. Copeland, and J. Maccaro. *Your Body His Temple: God's 233 Plan for Achieving Emotional Wholeness.* DVD series. Dallas: Life Outreach International, 2007.

Leaf, C. M., I. C. Uys, and B. Louw. "An Alternative Non-Traditional Approach to Learning: The Metacognitive-Mapping Approach." *The South African Journal of Communication Disorders* 45 (1998): 87–102.

———. "The Development of a Model for Geodesic Learning: The Geodesic Information Processing Model." *The South African Journal of Communication Disorders* 44 (1997): 53–70.

———. "The Mind Mapping Approach (MMA): A Culture and

Language-Free Technique." *The South African Journal of Communication Disorders* 40 (1992): 35–43.

LeDoux, J. *Synaptic Self: How Our Brains Become Who We Are.* New York: Viking, 2002.

Leedy, P. D. *Practical Research: Planning and Design.* New York: Macmillan, 1989.

Lehmann, E. L. *Non-Parametric: Statistical Methods Based on Ranks.* Oxford: Holden-Day, 1975.

Lepore, F. E. "Dissecting Genius: Einstein's Brain and the Search for the Neural Basis of Intellect." *Cerebrum.* January 2001. http://www.dana.org/news/cerebrum/detail.aspx?id=3032.

Leuchter, A. F., et al. "Changes in Brain Function of Depressed Subject during Treatment with Placebo." *American Journal of Psychiatry* 159, no. 1 (2002): 122–29.

Levy, J. "Research Synthesis on Right and Left Hemispheres: We Think with Both Sides of the Brain." *Educational Leadership* 40, no. 4 (1983): 66–71.

Lewis, R. "Report Back on the Workshop: Speech/Language/Hearing Therapy in Transition." *Communiphon* 308 (1994): 6–7.

Liebertz, C. "Want Clear Thinking? Relax." *Scientific American*, October 2005. http://www.scientificamerican.com/article.cfm?id=want-clear-thinking-relax&page=2.

Lipton, B. *The Biology of Belief: Unleashing the Power of Consciousness, Matter and Miracles.* Santa Cruz, CA: Mountain of Love Productions, 2008.

Lipton, B. H., et al. "Microvessel Endothelial Cell Transdifferentiation: Phenotypic Characterization." *Differentiation* 46 (1991): 117–33.

Lozanov, G. *Suggestology and Outlines of Suggestopedy.* New York: Gordon and Breach Science Publishers, 1978.

Lozanov, G., and G. Gateva. *The Foreign Language Educator's Suggestopaedic Manual.* New York: Gordon and Breach Science Publishers, 1989.

L. T. F. A. "Brain-Based Learning." Unpublished lecture series. South Africa: Lead the Field Africa, 1995.

Luria, A. R. *Higher Cortical Functions in Man.* 2nd ed. New York: Basic Books, 1980.

Lutz, K. A., and J. W. Rigney. *The Memory Book.* New York: Skin and Day, 1977.

MacLean, P. "A Mind of Three Minds: Educating the Triune Brain." In *77th Yearbook of the National Society for the Study of Education*, 308–42. Chicago: University of Chicago Press, 1978.

Marvin, C. A. "Consultation Services: Changing Roles for the SLPs." *Journal of Childhood Communication Disorders* 11, no. 1 (1987): 1–15.

Maslow, A. H. *Motivation and Personality.* New York: Harper & Row, 1970.

Mastropieri, M. A., and J. P. Bakken. "Applications of Metacognition." *Remedial and Special Education* 11, no. 6 (1990): 32–35.

Matheny, K. B., and J. McCarthy. *Prescription for Stress.* Oakland, CA: New Harbinger Publications, 2000.

McEwan, B. S. "Stress and Hippocampal Plasticity." *Annual Review of Neuroscience* 22 (1999): 105–22.

McEwan, B. S., and E. N. Lasley. *The End of Stress as We Know It.* Washington, DC: National Academies Press, 2002.

McEwan, B. S., and T. Seeman. "Protective and Damaging Effects of Mediators of Stress: Elaborating and Testing the Concepts of Allostasis and Allostatic Load." *Annals of the New York Academy of Sciences* 896 (1999): 30–47.

McGaugh, J. L., and I. B. Intrioni-Collision. "Involvement of the Amygdaloidal Complex in Neuromodulatory Influences on Memory Storage." *Neuroscience and Behavioral Reviews* 14, no. 4 (1990): 425–31.

Merzenich, M. M. "Cortical Plasticity Contributing to Childhood Development." In *Mechanisms of Cognitive Development: Behavioral and Neural Perspectives*, edited by J. L. McClelland and R. S. Siegler. Mahwah, NJ: Lawrence Erlbaum, 2001.

Meyer, J. *The Battlefield of the Mind.* Nashville: Faith Words, 1995.

———. *Life without Strife: How God Can Heal and Restore Troubled Relationships.* Lake Mary, FL: Charisma House, 2000.

Miller, G. A. "The Magical Number Seven, Plus or Minus Two: Some Limits on Our Capacity for Processing Information." *Psychological Review* 63 (1956): 81–97.

"Mind/Body Connection: How Emotions Affect Your Health." *Family Doctor.org* (May 2016). http://familydoctor.org/online/famdocen/home/healthy/mental/782.html.

Mogilner, A., et al. "Somatosensory Cortical Plasticity in Adult Humans Revealed by Magneto Encephalography." *Proceedings of the National Academy of Sciences* 90, no. 8 (1993): 3593–97.

Montessori, M. *The Absorbent Mind.* Amsterdam: Clio Press, 1989.

Moscowitz, Clara. "Scientists Get First Image of Memory Being Made." *Fox News* (June 29, 2009). http://www.foxnews.com/story/0,2933,529187,00.html.

Nader, K., et al. "Fear Memories Require Protein Synthesis in the Amygdala for Reconsolidation after Retrieval." *Nature* 406, no. 6797 (2000): 722–26.

Nelson, A. "Imagery's Physiological Base: The Limbic System. A Review Paper." *Journal of the Society for Accelerative Learning and Teaching* 13, no. 4 (1988): 363–71.

Nelson, R., ed. *Metacognition Core Readings.* Needham Heights, MA: Allyn & Bacon, 1992.

Newberg, A., et al. *Why God Won't Go Away: Brain Science and the Biology of Belief*. New York: Ballantine, 2001.

Novak, J. D., and B. Gowin. *Learning How to Learn*. Cambridge, UK: Cambridge University Press, 1984.

Nummela, R. M., and T. M. Rosengren. "Orchestration of Internal Processing." *Journal for the Society of Accelerated Learning and Teaching* 10, no. 2 (1985): 89–97.

Odendaal, M. S. "Needs Analysis of Higher Primary Educators in KwaZulu." *Per Linguam* special issue, no. 1 (1985): 5–99.

Okebukola, P. A. "Attitudes of Educators Towards Concept Mapping and Vee-Diagramming as Metalearning Tools in Science and Mathematics." *Educational Research* 34, no. 3 (1992): 201–12.

O'Keefe, J., and L. Nadel. *The Hippocampus as a Cognitive Map*. New York: Oxford University Press, 1978.

Olivier, C. *Let's Educate, Train and Learn Outcomes-Based*. Pretoria, South Africa: Benedic, 1999.

Ornstein, R. *The Right Mind*. Orlando: Harcourt, Brace, 1997.

Ornstein, R. E. *The Psychology of Consciousness*. New York: Penguin, 1975.

Palincsar, A. S., and A. L. Brown. "Reciprocal Teaching of Comprehension Fostering and Monitoring Activities." *Cognition and Instruction* 1 (1984): 117–75.

Palmer, L. L., M. Alexander, and N. Ellis. "Elementary School Achievement Results Following In-Service Training of an Entire School Staff in Accelerative Learning and Teaching: An Interim Report." *Journal of the Society for Accelerative Learning and Teaching* 14, no. 1 (1989): 55–79.

Paris, S. G., and P. Winograd. "Promoting Metacognition and Motivation of Exceptional Children." *Remedial and Special Education* 11, no. 6 (1990): 7–15.

Pascuale-Leone, A., and R. Hamilton. "The Metamodal Organization of the Brain." In *Progress in Brain Research* 134, edited by C. Casanova and P. Tito, 427–45. San Diego: Elsevier Science, 2001.

Paterniti, M. *Driving Mr. Albert: A Trip across America with Einstein's Brain*. New York: The Dial Press, 2000.

Perlmutter, D., and C. Coleman. *The Better Brain Book*. New York: Penguin, 2004.

Pert, C. B. *Molecules of Emotion: Why You Feel the Way You Feel*. London: Simon and Schuster, 1997.

Pert, C., et al. "Opiate Agonists and Antagonists Discriminated by Receptor Binding in the Brain." *Science* 182 (1973): 1359–61.

Peters, T. *Playing God? Genetic Determinism and Human Freedom*. 2nd ed. New York: Routledge, 2003.

"The Pleasure Centres Affected by Drugs." *The Brain from Top to*

Bottom (accessed December 15, 2016). http://thebrain.mcgill.ca/flash/i/i_03/i_03_cr/i_03_cr_par/i_03_cr_par.html.

Plotsky, P. M., and M. J. Meaney. "Early Postnatal Experience Alters Hypothalamic Corticotrophin-Releasing Factor (CRF) mRNA, Median Eminence CRF Content and Stress-Induced Release in Adult Rats." *Molecular Brain Research* 18 (1993): 195–200.

"Power of Forgiveness—Forgive Others." *Harvard Health Publications*. Boston: Harvard Medical School, 2004, https://www.health.harvard.edu/press_releases/power_of_forgiveness.

Praag, A. F., et al. "Functional Neurogenesis in the Adult Hippocampus." *Nature* 415, no. 6875 (2002): 1030–34.

Pribram, K. H. *Languages of the Brain*. Monterey, CA: Brooks/Cole, 1971.

Pulvermuller, F. *The Neuroscience of Language*. Cambridge, UK: Cambridge University Press, 2002.

Rajechi, D. W. *Attitudes: Themes and Advances*. Sunderland, MA: Sinauer Associates, 1982.

Ramachandran, V. S., and S. Blakeslee. *Phantoms in the Brain*. New York: William Morrow, 1998.

Redding, R. E. "Metacognitive Instruction: Trainers Teaching Thinking Skills." *Performance Improvement Quarterly* 3, no. 1 (1990): 27–41.

Restak, K. *The Brain: The Last Frontier*. New York: Doubleday, 1979.

Restak, R. "Hemisphere Disconnection and Unity in Conscious Awareness." *American Psychologist* 23 (1988): 723–33.

———. *Think Smart: A Neuroscientist's Prescription for Improving Your Brain Performance*. New York: Riverhead, 2009.

"Revised National Curriculum Statement Grades R-9." Policy document. Pretoria, South Africa: Department of Education, 2002.

Rizzolotti, G., and M. F. Destro. "Mirror Neurons." *Scholarpedia* 3, no. 1 (2008): 2055. http://www.scholarpedia.org/article/Mirror_neurons.

Rogers, C. R. *Freedom to Learn*. Columbus: Merrill, 1969.

Roizen, M. F., and C. O. Mehmet. *You: The Owner's Manual*. New York: HarperCollins, 2008.

Rosenfield, I. *The Invention of Memory*. New York: Basic Books, 1988.

Rosenzweig, E. S., C. A. Barnes, and B. L. McNaughton. "Making Room for New Memories." *Nature Neuroscience* 5, no. 1 (2002): 6–8.

Rosenzweig, M. R., and E. L. Bennet. *Neuronal Mechanisms of Learning and Memory*. Cambridge, MA: MIT Press, 1976.

Rozin, P. "The Evolution of Intelligence and Access to the Cognitive Unconscious." *Progress in Psychobiology and Physiological Psychology* 6 (1975): 245–80.

Russell, P. *The Brain Book*. London: Routledge and Kegan Paul, 1986.

Rutherford, R., and K. Neethling. *Am I Clever or Am I Stupid?* Vanderbijlpark, South Africa: Carpe Diem Books, 2001.

Sagan, C. *The Dragons of Eden*. New York: Random House, 1977.

Saloman, G. *Interaction of Media, Cognition and Learning*. San Francisco: Jossey-Bass, 1979.

Samples, R. E. "Learning with the Whole Brain." *Human Behavior* 4 (1975): 16–23.

Sapolsky, R. M. "Why Stress Is Bad for Your Brain." *Science* 273, no. 5276 (1996): 749–50.

Sarno, J. *The Mind-Body Prescription*. New York: Werner Books, 1999.

Sarter, M., M. E. Hasselmo, J. P. Bruno, and B. Givens. "Unraveling the Attentional Functions of Cortical Cholinergic Inputs: Interactions Between Signal-Driven and Cognitive Modulation of Signal Detection." *Brain Research Reviews* 48, no. 1 (2005): 98–111.

Schallert, D. L. "The Significance of Knowledge: A Synthesis of Research Related to Schema Theory." In *Reading Expository Material*, edited by W. Otto and S. White, 13–48. New York: Academic, 1982.

Schneider, W., and R. M. Shiffrin. "Controlled and Automatic Information Processing: I: Detection, Search and Attention." *Psychological Review* 88 (1977): 1–66.

Schon, D. A. *Beyond the Stable State*. San Francisco: Jossey-Bass, 1971.

Schory, M. E. "Whole Language and the Speech Language Pathologists." *Language, Speech and Hearing Services in Schools* 21 (1990): 206–11.

Schuster, D. H. "A Critical Review of American Foreign Language Studies Using Suggestopaedia." Paper delivered at the Aimav Linguistic Conference, University of Nijmegen, Netherlands, 1985.

Schwartz, J. M., and S. Begley. *The Mind and the Brain: Neuroplasticity and the Power of Mental Force*. New York: Regan Books/HarperCollins, 2002.

Scruggs, E., and J. Brigham. "The Challenges of Metacognitive Instruction." *RASE* 11, no. 6 (1987): 16–18.

Seaward, B. L. *Health and Wellness Journal Workbook*. Sudbury, MA: Jones and Bartlett, 1996.

Segerstrom, S. C., and G. E. Miller. "Psychological Stress and the Human Immune System: A Meta-Analytic Study of 30 Years of Inquiry." *Psychological Bulletin* 130, no. 4 (2004): 601–30.

Shapiro, K. H., V. Li, Champagne, and D. De Costa. "The Speech-Language Pathologist: Consultant to the Classroom Educator." *Reading Improvement* 25, no. 1 (1988): 2–9.

Sheth, B. R. "Practice Makes Imperfect: Restorative Effects of Sleep on Motor Learning." *Society for*

Neuroscience. Program 14-14 (2006).

Simon, C. S. "Out of the Broom Closet and into the Classroom: The Emerging SLP." *Journal of Childhood Communication Disorders* 11 nos. 1–2 (1987): 81–90.

Sizer, T. R. *Horacel's Compromise: The Dilemma of the American High School.* Boston: Houghton Mifflin, 1984.

Slabbert, J. "Metalearning as the Most Essential Aim in Education for All." Paper presented to faculty of education. University of Pretoria, South Africa, 1989.

Slife, B. D., J. Weiss, and T. Bell. "Separability of Metacognition and Cognition: Problem Solving in Learning Disabled and Regular Students." *Journal of Educational Psychology* 77, no. 4 (1985): 437–45.

Smith, A. *Accelerated Learning in Practice.* Stafford, UK: Network Educational Press, 1999.

Solms, M. "Forebrain Mechanisms of Dreaming Are Activated from a Variety of Sources." *Behavioral and Brain Sciences* 23, no. 6 (2000): 1035–40, 1083–121.

Springer, S. P., and G. Deutsch. *Left Brain, Right Brain.* New York: W. H. Freeman & Company, 1998.

Stengel, R., ed. *TIME Your Brain: A User's Guide.* Des Moines, IA: TIME Books, 2009.

Stephan, K. M., et al. "Functional Anatomy of Mental Representation of Upper Extremity Movements in Healthy Subjects." *Journal of Neurophysiology* 73, no. 1 (1995): 373–86.

Sternberg, R. "The Nature of Mental Abilities." *American Psychologist* 34 (1979): 214–30.

Stickgold, R., et al. "Sleep, Learning, and Dreams: Offline Memory Reprocessing." *Science* 294, no. 554 (2001): 1052–57.

Stickgold, R., and P. Wehrwein. "Health for Life: The Link between Sleep and Memory." *Newsweek*, April 17, 2009. http:/www.newsweek.com/id/194650.

"Stress," *Harvard Health Publications* (accessed December 15, 2016). https://www.health.harvard.edu/topic/stress.

Sylwester, R. "Research on Memory: Major Discoveries, Major Educational Challenges." *Educational Leadership* 42, no. 7 (1985): 69–75.

Tattershall, S. "Mission Impossible: Learning How a Classroom Works Before It's Too Late!" *Journal of Childhood Communication Disorders* 11, no. 1 (1987): 181–84.

Taub, E., et al. "Use of CI Therapy for Plegic Hands after Chronic Stroke." Presentation at the Society for Neuroscience. Washington, DC, 2005.

Taubes, G. *Good Calories, Bad Calories: Fats, Carbs and the Controversial Science of Diet and Health.* New York: Anchor Books, 2008.

Thembela, A. "Education for Blacks in South Africa: Issues, Problems and Perspectives." *Journal of the Society for Accelerative Learning and Teaching* 15, no. 12 (1990): 45–57.

Thurman, S. K., and A. H. Widerstrom. *Infants and Young Children with Special Needs: A Developmental and Ecological Approach.* 2nd ed. Baltimore: Paul H. Brookes, 1990.

Uys, I. C. "Single Case Experimental Designs: An Essential Service in Communicatively Disabled Care." *The South African Journal of Communication Disorders* 36 (1989): 53–59.

Van derVyver, D. W. "SALT in South Africa: Needs and Parameters." *Journal of the Society for Accelerative Learning and Teaching* 10, no. 3 (1985): 187–200.

Van derVyver, D. W., and B. de Capdeville. "Towards the Mountain: Characteristics and Implications of the South African UPPTRAIL Pilot Project." *Journal of the Society for Accelerative Learning and Teaching* 15, nos. 1–2 (1990): 59–74.

Vaughan, S. C. *The Talking Cure: The Science behind Psychotherapy.* New York: Grosset/Putnam, 1997.

Von Bertalanaffy, L. *General Systems Theory.* New York: Braziller, 1968.

Vythilingam, M., and C. Heim. "Childhood Trauma Associated with Smaller Hippocampal Volume in Women with Major Depression." *American Journal of Psychiatry* 159, no. 12 (1968): 2072–80.

Walker, M. P., and R. Stickgold. "Sleep, Memory and Plasticity." *Annual Review of Psychology* 57 (2006): 139–66.

Wark, D. M. "Using Imagery to Teach Study Skills." *Journal of the Society for Accelerative Learning and Teaching* 11, no. 3 (1986): 203–20.

Waterland, R. A., and R. L. Jirtle. "Transposable Elements: Targets for Early Nutritional Effects on Epigenetic Gene Regulation." *Molecular and Cellular Biology* 23, no. 15 (2003): 5293–5300.

Watters, E. "DNA Is Not Destiny: The New Science of Epigenetics." *Discover*, November, 2006. http://discovermagazine.com/2006/nov/cover.

Wenger, W. "An Example of Limbic Learning." *Journal of the Society for Accelerative Learning and Teaching* 10, no. 1 (1985): 51–68.

Wertsch, J. V. *Culture, Communication and Cognitions: Vygotskian Perspectives.* Cambridge, UK: Cambridge University Press, 1985.

Wilson, R. S., et al. "Participation in Cognitively Stimulating Activities and Risk of Incident in Alzheimer's Disease." *Journal of the American Medical Association* 287, no. 6 (2002): 742–48.

Witelson, S. "The Brain Connection: The Corpus Callosum Is Larger in Left-Handers." *Science* 229 (1985): 665–68.

Witelson, S. F., D. L. Kigar, and T. Harvey. "The Exceptional Brain of Albert Einstein." *Lancet* 353 (1999): 2149–53.

Wright, N. H. *Finding Freedom from Your Fears*. Grand Rapids: Revell, 2005.

Wurtman, J. *Managing Your Mind-Mood through Food*. New York: HarperCollins, 1986.

Young, Larry J. "Being Human: Love: Neuroscience Tells All." *Nature* 457 (January 2009). http://www.nature.com/nature/journal/v457/n7226/full/457148a.html.

Zaborszky, L. "The Modular Organization of Brain Systems: Basal Forebrain, the Last Frontier, Changing Views of Cajal's

Neuron." *Progressing Brain Research* 136 (2002): 359–72.

Zaidel, E. "Roger Sperry: An Appreciation." *The Dual Brain*. Edited by D. F. Benson and E. Zaidel. New York: The Guilford Press, 1985.

Zakaluk, B. L., and M. Klassen. "Case Study: Enhancing the Performance of a High School Student Labelled Learning Disabled." *Journal of Reading* 36, no. 1 (1992): 4–9.

Zdenek, M. *The Right Brain Experience*. New York: McGraw-Hill, 1983.

Zimmerman, B. J., and D. H. Schunk. *Self-Regulated Learning and Academic Achievement: Theory, Research and Practice*. New York: Springer-Verlag, 1989.

Connect with

DR. CAROLINE LEAF

For more information, visit

DRLEAF.COM

f @DrLeaf

🐦 @DrCarolineLeaf

📷 @DrCarolineLeaf

ALSO AVAILABLE *from*
DR. CAROLINE LEAF

I n this revolutionary book, Dr. Caroline Leaf packs an incredible amount of information that will change your eating and thinking habits for the better. Rather than getting caught up in fads, Leaf reveals that every individual has unique nutritional needs. You'll find that this book is the key to discovering how you can begin developing a healthier body, brain, and spirit—for life!